PRAISE FOR *"YOU'RE NOT DOING IT RIGHT"*

"The vulnerability that Ellen displays throughout *"You're Not Doing It Right,"* creates an incredibly authentic view into the most difficult experience someone can go through. I went through a spectrum of intense emotions while on the journey of Ellen and her family. I learned so much about dementia, what to look for, and what to expect during different stages, specifically Lewy body dementia. This book is a must-read for anyone who has gone through the loss of a parent or loved one, anyone who is struggling with intergenerational relationships, and anyone who will likely be faced with difficult decisions for aging loved ones, so basically *everyone*. Ellen has a gift for telling stories in a way that makes them so relatable. Several times while reading the book, I thought, *That's me too! The same thing happened to me!* I am so grateful to have read this book."

~Denette Suddeth
Former Caregiver
Bank Executive

"In Ellen Patnaude's groundbreaking book *"You're Not Doing It Right,"* readers are offered a raw, real, vulnerable look at caregiving for an ailing parent. Unlike the typical (and often unhelpful) dementia books that preach unending patience, acceptance, and understanding, Patnaude gives an unfiltered account of the struggles she faces when her already strained relationship with her mother undergoes an impossibly difficult change. This book will resonate with caregivers who are just looking for someone to say, 'Yes, this absolutely sucks. All your feelings are legit. And most importantly, you aren't alone.' She provides hope in the darkness, offering her own hard-won wisdom by sharing what she wishes she would have known when she was wrestling with her own journey. This unconventional and honest memoir is a beautifully written testament to the power of sharing your own story so that others no longer feel alone."

~Bailly Morse
Author

"I am writing this testimonial with tears in my eyes because Ellen Patnaude's memoir touched my heart. *"You're Not Doing It Right"* is raw, authentic, and powerful. My wife and I have just been through this same experience with her mom who was tormented by Lewy body dementia and recently died. I resonated with the pain, anger, helplessness, and exhaustion that Ellen bravely portrays. This is a perfect book for caregivers, physicians, healthcare providers, and families who are dealing with this horrific disease. I was deeply moved by how Ellen was able to take the worst moment in her life and extend so many lessons she learned through this experience. If we had read her memoir before my wife's mom's diagnosis, it would have helped us in so many ways."

~Midge Noble
Former Caregiver
Coach, Speaker, Podcaster
Author of *Gay with God, Reclaiming My Faith, Honoring My Story*

"Our mission at Cariloop is to relieve the stress and anxiety felt by all caregivers. We have a front-row seat to the struggles of many family caregivers. Ellen Patnaude's *"You're Not Doing It Right"* was a page-turner for me, even though I've been hearing about the struggles of caregivers for many years. Ellen gives us an intimate glimpse into her family's journey in a way that is real, helpful, honest, and heart-breaking—all while being very readable. I couldn't put it down. This is a memoir, not a self-help book, yet I came away feeling like I learned something valuable about my own feelings through Ellen sharing hers. I recommend this book to all caregivers, as so many struggle with self-doubt, and to anyone who can relate to juggling the balance of work, family, and life."

~Wendy Whittington, MD, MMM
Chief Care Officer of Cariloop

"As someone who cared for both parents as my dad's Alzheimer's got worse, I found Ellen's book filled with compelling storytelling that spoke to my truth. Her telling of the emotions involved, along with all the contradictions every caregiver feels in that role, were spot-on for me and will be for many others. My mother and I had a complicated relationship, and caregiving together (me handling all the logistics while she lived with my dad) involved making a lot of compromises while swallowing my rage, venting my frustrations, managing the overwhelm, and working very hard to engage and include my siblings who could not be there helping day-to-day. I, too, did all this during COVID, which added a ridiculous level of complications."

~Fern Pessin
Caregiver
Author of *I'll Be Right There: A Guidebook for Adults Caring for their Aging Parents* and *When Can We Talk? A Caregiver Guidebook for Holding Discussions Around Difficult Topics*

"I'm not religious, but I found myself saying 'Amen!' during my reading of this book. Ellen's experience resonates with me on so many levels. Her thoughts, the realizations she had about her mother in each moment, and even some of the harsh doctor-speak remind me of my own experiences. The emotional, mental, and physical roller coaster of caregiving is real. Every caregiver needs to read this book. Many themes within caregiving are similar. There will be unknowns, there is always denial, and of course, the person you care for will be less like themselves at the end of the journey. This is life, but if we talk more about this reality, we'll know some of the things to look for and have a few ways to care for ourselves and our loved ones. Thank you, Ellen, for letting your thoughts, feelings, and very clear tips pour out of you."

~Erna Alfred Liousas
Caregiver, Strategist, Changemaker
Host of the podcast *The Whole Caregiver*

"I feel validated. *"You're Not Doing It Right"* hits so many marks I went through as an only child caring for my mom, who I am the spitting image of. Instead of over-romanticizing the opportunity to be there in ways never imagined, this book is a real take on the hills and valleys of tending to an aging parent with whom one has had a loving yet tension-filled relationship. The dichotomy of spending countless hours with this person you love more than anyone—this person who can pluck your ever-loving last nerve in two seconds flat while they're just trying to be 'helpful' with their suggestion or observation—was mind-numbing. Ellen's experience is one that will resonate widely as she takes us on that roller coaster with her."

~Clinton Crow
Former Caregiver
COO of LEAD

"As a daughter-turned-caregiver in a similar situation, I resonated deeply with Ellen's story. Her honest, often raw recount of events along the journey was both riveting and unsettling, and anyone who has been in this situation can relate. While we all know how the story will end, this is no fairytale. The beauty of Ellen's uncut version is just that: it's real life. We see her struggle with 'all the feels' that this responsibility brings: her love for her parents mingled with realistic resentment, the uncertainty and unpleasantness of the surprises along the way, the remorse and relief, and the seasons of grief.

Ellen's transparent story is a must-read for anyone who is, has been, or anticipates being a caregiver for a loved one. It is a reminder to embrace the moments we have with those we love, to forgive our own (and their) imperfections, and to make space for self-compassion sans guilt."

~Lisa Madden
Caregiver
Yoga Therapist (C-IAYT) at Sattva Yoga Therapy

"You're Not Doing It Right" is a vital guide for anyone who has experienced or will experience the roller coaster of being a caregiver to a loved one. As someone who has been the primary caregiver to two family members, I deeply felt Ellen's commitment to caregivers receiving support, practical advice, and most of all, love. A unique and excellent read."

~Chris McNeany
Former Caregiver
Leadership Development Facilitator

"In sharing her stories and experience, Ellen offers readers a raw, honest look at the journey of a caregiver. She does not shy away from the dark side of relationships that most are unwilling to discuss but rather invites us to look at ourselves and our loved ones and to know deeply that we are not alone. This book is a gift of love to caregivers, to mothers, to daughters, and to all those who wonder, 'Am I the only one feeling this way?'"

~Grace VanDenBrink
Former Caregiver
Cofounder of Know Honesty

"The stories in *"You're Not Doing It Right"* resonate at a frequency that reverberates throughout your soul. I have been taking care of my extended family in one way or another for 20 years, but my most recent stint has left me with many of the same feelings Ellen so clearly details, including anger, guilt, grief, exhaustion, and inadequacy. Knowing in your head that you are doing all that you can does not often translate to your heart and your feelings. Whether brought on by a harsh or uncaring comment from a friend or your own insecurities, dealing with those feelings is complicated and will be exacerbated as you travel this winding road of caregiving. Ellen's experience is our combined experience in a world where more and more family members are caring for others. Put on your own oxygen mask first, then you can help others, even if you don't have all the answers in the beginning."

~Cindy Underwood
Caregiver and Mother
Senior Director of Solera

" *"You're Not Doing It Right"* is so honest and intimate that it's almost painful to read. Ellen Patnaude's difficult relationship with her mother, Charlotte, does not get less acerbic as Charlotte falls into Lewy body dementia. Until Charlotte can no longer use her voice and body language to insist on her own way, criticize, and disagree, daughter and mother continue to spar verbally.

I wish I had known Charlotte before the dementia took over. She was charming in the early stages of the disease, and I could almost see the woman described at her memorial service: involved, determined, community-minded, and loving."

~Missy Malcolm
Former Caregiver
Library Executive Director (retired), a.k.a. "The nice little library lady"

"You're Not Doing It Right"

Loving My Mother Through an Unpredictable Caregiving Journey

ELLEN PATNAUDE

For permission requests, write to the publisher, addressed "Attention: Permissions Coordinator" at the address below.

Publish Your Purpose
141 Weston Street, #155
Hartford, CT, 06141

The opinions expressed by the author are not necessarily those held by Publish Your Purpose.

Ordering Information: Quantity sales and special discounts are available on quantity purchases by corporations, associations, and others. For details, contact the publisher at hello@publishyourpurpose.com.

Edited by: Nancy Graham-Tillman
Cover design by: Nelly Murariu
Typeset by: Jetlaunch

ISBN: 979-8-88797-100-1 (hardcover)
ISBN: 979-8-88797-101-8 (paperback)
ISBN: 979-8-88797-102-5 (ebook)

Library of Congress Control Number: 2024930212

First Edition, May 2024

The information contained within this book is strictly for informational purposes. The material may include information, products, or services by third parties. As such, the Author and Publisher do not assume responsibility or liability for any third-party material or opinions. The publisher is not responsible for websites (or their content) that are not owned by the publisher. Readers are advised to do their own due diligence when it comes to making decisions.

Publish Your Purpose is a hybrid publisher of nonfiction books. Our mission is to elevate the voices often excluded from traditional publishing. We intentionally seek out authors and storytellers with diverse backgrounds, life experiences, and unique perspectives to publish books that will make an impact in the world. Do you have a book idea you would like us to consider publishing? Please visit PublishYourPurpose.com for more information.

DISCLAIMER

This book is a memoir. It reflects the author's present recollections of experiences over time. Some names and characteristics have been changed, some events have been compressed, and some dialogue has been recreated.

TRIGGER WARNING

This book contains profane language and stories of intergenerational clashes, mother–daughter struggles, detailed accounts of hallucinations and other dementia-induced mental health episodes, and death. Please take care of yourself as you read.

DEDICATION

This book is a labor of love dedicated to my mother, Charlotte Patnaude. I know you always loved me fiercely in the best way you knew how, and I know that you know I loved you just as fiercely back. I hope your spirt has found peace. Don't be mad at me for sharing our story.

Charlotte and Ellen, August 2016,
six months before initial diagnosis

CONTENTS

PART 3: FALLING OFF THE CLIFF

HOW IT BEGAN

"Is this Robin's mom?" came the voice at the other end of the phone line. My stomach instantly dropped.

"Yes, it is. Is everything okay?" I asked, trying to keep the panic out of my voice. "Is Robin okay?"

"Robin is fine," the reassuring voice answered smoothly. "It's just that it's past pickup time and no one has come to pick him up."

I looked at my watch. Robin, my 10-year-old, was at summer day camp, which had ended 30 minutes ago. "His grandparents were supposed to pick him up today," I answered, mild irritation setting in along with the panic. "I'm in a meeting twenty minutes away, but I'll leave right now to get him. I'm so sorry about this. We must've gotten our wires crossed."

I shoved my notebook and papers into my bag while glancing up at my graphic designer, who I'd been in a meeting with when the call came through. "Hey, I gotta go," I said, worry now evident in my voice. "My parents were supposed to pick up Robin from day camp today but haven't shown up. I've got to make a mad dash over to Dearborn to get him."

He indicated he totally understood and encouraged me to go. I waved my thanks and ran out the door to my car, pulling my mom's cell phone number up as I did.

The phone rang several times before going to voicemail. I hung up, cursing under my breath as I got into my car and threw my bag onto the seat next to me. I sped out of the parking lot and headed for the highway while I waited for my car to pick up the Bluetooth before dialing my parents' home number. My mom answered on the third ring.

"Ellen?" she said, already sounding alarmed, typical of her anxious mind. "What's the matter?"

"Robin is waiting to be picked up at day camp. That's what's the matter!" I spat, already angry. "What the hell, Mom? You guys were supposed to pick him up today! We just talked about it last night!" I was speeding down the highway now.

"What?" she retorted, immediately defensive and indignant. "No, we weren't. Today is Tuesday. You said you would pick him up."

I hesitated, thinking for a second. I was sure that wasn't right. "No, I had a meeting scheduled for this afternoon. Today was one of the days you were picking him up. We just talked about this last night," I said again, this time gritting my teeth. "Well, it doesn't matter now. I'm on my way already." I'm sure she could hear the anger and disgust in my voice.

"Well, we're closer," she opined. "Ron!" she hollered to my dad. "You need to go get your grandson!"

"No," I nearly shouted back. "You're not listening! I said I'm already on my way. I'll be there in another fifteen minutes."

"We're only ten minutes away, so your father will go," my mother said defiantly.

I hung up, fuming. This was typical of my mother, who had to have it her way, even when we were talking about my child.

I pulled into the parking lot and barely turned off the car before I ran for the front entrance of the building. I yanked open the door and saw Robin sitting at a table, looking very small and alone. A young woman was standing a few feet away and looked up from her phone as I walked in.

"I'm so sorry," I exhaled, looking at her and then at Robin. "I think me and my parents got our wires crossed today. I was in a meeting thinking they were coming." Robin was already by my side looking betrayed. "Sorry, honey," I said to him softly, hugging him to me.

As we walked back out to the parking lot, my dad pulled in. My mom wasn't with him, which was unusual. He looked upset. Robin was his favorite grandchild, and my dad was mortified that he'd been forgotten. I told Robin to climb into the car while I talked to Papa.

"What the hell?" I whispered angrily to my dad. "I just talked to her last night! You guys were supposed to pick him up today. I was in a meeting!" He looked so worried that I took a breath and tried to make myself calm down. "It's fine," I relented.

Continuing to look worried, he said, "Well Robin may be fine, but I'm not sure about your mother." I waited, still feeling annoyed. "She's forgetting things more and more. She's been confused about the schedule all week. When I tell her what I remember, she insists that you've called and changed the schedule."

"I didn't," I said, my tone still flat. "You were supposed to pick him up today and take him back to your house to spend the night, then bring him back tomorrow morning. I was planning to pick him up tomorrow." I glared at him, trying to get my anger at my mother under control. "I reiterated all of that last night when I talked to her."

He shook his head, still looking worried. "She can't keep track of it," he said softly.

Looking back, I see that this was the first moment I realized something was going on with my mom. She'd always been the master of logistics, organizing complicated sequences of events, trips, and schedules throughout my life. There were two incidents with Robin getting left at day camp that week, something previously absolutely unheard of with my mom.

Learning that my mom struggled with those logistical details was a big red flag, but one that I chose to ignore at the time. Instead, I stayed stuck in the pattern of interaction we'd had for all my 43 years. I was used to being annoyed with her. I was used to getting angry when she didn't do what she said she was going to do. It was the narrative of our relationship.

What followed over the next four years was nothing short of a nightmare, which ended with my mother's death in December 2020. My grandmother had Alzheimer's disease, and in the beginning, we assumed my mother was suffering from Alzheimer's as well. Since my grandmother had lived with the disease for more than 20 years, we also assumed that my mother's journey would be similarly long. Neither turned out to be the case. My mom had a much more aggressive and unpredictable form of dementia called Lewy body dementia, or LBD.

Throughout that time, I searched for ways to help all of us cope. We connected with the Alzheimer's Association of Michigan and their wealth of resources, from a social worker in a neurologist's office to a caregiver's support group and educational seminars. I looked for books to read and attended any workshop I could find that would help me figure out how to face the challenges. But I never found quite what I was looking for. I felt like most of the stories that were shared were told by people who were either unwilling to talk about the ugly side of things or who were simply living a very different experience than we were. Either way, I didn't see my experience, nor my struggles reflected anywhere.

I was often the person sitting in support meetings feeling like there must be something wrong with me. I listened to other people talk about the sadness, the slipping away, the fading of their loved one's very being, yet I wasn't feeling those feelings of sadness. I was furious, filled with rage and frustration, and their stories compounded my feeling that I was doing it all wrong. But I had no idea how to do things differently. Even with all my years of professional experience working with teams to communicate more effectively with one another, I was too close to this experience to think through how to handle it differently. Until it was too late.

I know my journey isn't unique. I often talk to people whose stories sound familiar to mine. But a daughter caring for her mother with dementia faces a particular kind of challenge. I'm sure the challenges of caring for any close family member with dementia will resonate broadly, but mother–daughter dynamics carry a special kind of emotional weight. It was this specific relationship that I found most complicated.

I needed to know the ugly and honest truth about what this journey can look like. I needed to know that I wasn't the only one experiencing that ugly truth. I needed to know that I wasn't alone and that the fact that I couldn't "just figure it out" didn't mean there was something wrong with me. So I'm writing the book I needed to read when I was going through this journey with my mom.

If you've picked up this book, chances are you're going through some shit yourself. Or maybe you suspect someone close to you has dementia and you're being proactive. Whatever your circumstances may be, I hope you find solace in these pages.

I share my story with brutal honesty. I share every strategy I tried and a few I wish I had tried because they work so well in other emotionally charged relationships. I share lessons I learned and insights along the way.

Before we get started, there are two things I want you to know:

There's nothing wrong with you if you're struggling.

You're not alone.

Fall 2016 at the farm
Back row, left to right: Ellen, Ron, Charlotte, David
Middle row, left to right: Dani, Mary (David's daughter), Robin
Front row, left to right: Sam, Jean (David's daughter)

PART 1

THE TANGLING OF CHARLOTTE'S WEB

My mother's name was Charlotte. One of her favorite books from her childhood and then ours was *Charlotte's Web*. My mother loved the crafty spider and her character, even while being terrified of spiders in real life. When her dementia began, we learned about plaques and tangles in the brain that are primarily associated with Alzheimer's disease. Since we thought that's what she had in those early days, I often pictured her lapses of memory as Charlotte's web getting tangled up.

Sometimes Alzheimer's disease is referred to as "the long goodbye." That did not apply to our situation at all. The reasons for that are complicated and were a significant part of our journey, which had three parts. The first part was noticing something was wrong and taking steps to try to address it. The second part was learning to live on the roller coaster that my mother's dementia took all of us on. And the final part was the bitter end.

Welcome to part 1 of the story.

My father had been telling us for a year or so that he was noticing small changes in my mother, but neither my brother nor I could see them. We just saw the same argumentative, controlling mother we'd always had. Any slips she made, she covered quickly with anger, impatience, or accusations. In those early days, because my mother's nature had always been one of volatility, we'd become desensitized to such displays and lacked the empathy and compassion to clearly see what was causing them.

It wasn't until the summer of 2016 that I began to see the changes in my mother's behavior for myself. My mom was known for being an excellent navigator, for instance. When I moved back to Michigan in 2005 after living out of state for eight years, I'd often get turned around. In those days, I didn't have a GPS unit, nor a phone smart enough to give me directions. Always running late, I didn't have time to figure directions out on my own, so I'd call my mom from wherever I was in the Metro Detroit area. She'd pull out a map for that area, find where I was and where I needed to go, and guide me there. Even though she'd tease me for forgetting my way around the area where I'd grown up, those are some of my fondest memories with her. Despite our many differences, fights, and arguments over the years, she was always there for me when I needed her. Navigation was one concrete example of that. It was a point of pride for her. So it was quite noticeable when she began getting lost while giving my dad directions to places they'd been going for years.

My mom had a strong voice. When she was sure she was right, which was most of the time, she got loud quickly. On the rare occasion I got to talk to my dad alone, he shared the stories of these episodes, which often ended with him pulling into a side street or parking lot because my mother was screaming in frustration. She'd get turned around and yell at him that he was going the wrong way. He'd turn the car around to appease her, unable to think clearly for himself through all the yelling and panic in her voice. She'd realize the new direction was also not correct and start yelling even louder.

These episodes left my dad shaken and upset. He saw them as the clearest signs possible that something was wrong with my mom's brain. He also realized that driving with her in that state was getting dangerous because his own nerves would get jangled from her outbursts.

What follows in part 1 are stories of what we noticed in the early days, how we tried to address it with my mom, and the struggles that ensued.

I don't get a do-over with my mom. My greatest hope is that the lessons I learned and my reflections from hindsight might help someone else.

CHAPTER 1

MOTHER KNOWS BEST

I met my wife, Dani, in early 2008 while we were playing soccer in a Women Over 30 league. A few months later, we began dating, and eventually we moved in together. She came into my life when my boys were five and two years old. Her daughter was between them in age, turning four shortly after we became a couple, but she didn't live with us. We were a blended family of four most of the time, and occasionally, five.

We moved around a bit in Michigan trying to figure out where we belonged, and we settled in Ann Arbor in 2013, just 30 minutes away from my childhood home in Detroit where my parents still lived. We'd barely unpacked in our new home when my mother began imposing her ideas on us about everything, from where to do our grocery shopping to how we should be spending our weekends. This was nothing unusual, as the constant push–pull of who got to be in charge of decisions about my everyday life was not only infuriating and exasperating but familiar. So the fights between us continued as they always had. I was relieved to live just far enough away that we could tolerate each other only in small doses. We didn't do well in each other's space for more than a couple of hours at a time. Sometimes even that was too long.

After nearly three years in Ann Arbor, Dani and I began to miss rural life, where we'd lived before. We missed the peace and quiet and having more land, no traffic, and clean air. We missed the simple beauty of crops in large fields, horses and cows grazing, and open space. We'd go up north to see Dani's family for the occasional birthday party and leave feeling nostalgic. We wanted to have property and horses again, so we started looking around in the areas just outside of Ann Arbor.

Two of Dani's siblings started sending us links to properties for sale in their area, an hour and a half north of Ann Arbor. We'd find a house on 10 acres with no barn in the Ann Arbor area going for $289,000, and they'd send a listing for a much bigger house on 20 acres with a barn and pastures for $229,000. The affordability of that area was hard to ignore. And their eagerness to show us places to live near them was flattering. Finally, Dani's brother found a beautiful farm in North Branch that was for sale privately, and we decided to buy it.

When I told my parents we were moving back to North Branch in the summer of 2016, my mother was not happy, to say the least. She liked having me close by. The move meant we'd not only be an hour and a half away from them again but also be more involved with Dani's family functions. My mother was possessive. She didn't like anyone else spending more time with me and my family than she got to.

I thought if I brought my parents up to North Branch to see our soon-to-be new home, it might help change my mother's mind and help her be more supportive, so I drove them up to see the property. As we pulled into the circular driveway that ran behind the house, they murmured their approval, which made me smile. I parked the car and we all got out, stretching from the drive, breathing deeply, and taking it all in. It felt like home.

The house was at the front of the 22-acre property, with stunning views of a large pond at the back and plenty of fields and woods around three sides. There was a large, old, two-story red barn with some fenced pasture. Across the driveway off to the right of the main house was a small carriage house with a shed, sitting on almost an acre and a half of its own. The previous owners had rented that house and land to their kids as they became adults, then to other renters for income. We were planning to buy it on a land contract to keep the whole farm together.

The owner, Pam, met us there to show us around. The inside of the house had as much to love as the property outside. The house was built in the early 1860s, and Pam and her family had added onto it. They renovated it a couple of times over the years, leaving an original brick wall in the living room, two separate second stories at either end of the sprawling house, and large windows along the back of the house overlooking the pastures and barn. It was over three thousand square feet, with four bedrooms, a library, an office, four full baths, and tons of character.

I'd fallen in love with this house the first time we'd seen it and was eager for my parents to approve of it. Though they made appreciative comments throughout the tour with Pam, I could tell from my mom's face that she was having a hard time getting past her sadness that we'd be so far away again. But I didn't recognize it as sadness at the time. I just felt like she was once again taking the spotlight off something I was excited about in an attempt to bring the attention back to her and how she was feeling. I felt a pang of guilt, which turned to disappointment and a little bit of anger. I wanted her to be happy for us, not ruin it by focusing on her own emotions.

My dad wanted to see the furnace and other "house guts" in the basement. My mother didn't care about that stuff, nor did she like steep stairs, so we left her admiring the view out of the large bay windows in the dining room at the center of the house and went with Pam to check things out in the basement. We were down there for about 15 minutes before I lost interest in the explanations Pam was giving, as

I'd heard them before. So I wandered out of that area and back toward the stairs to go up.

Suddenly, I heard a heavy thud and my mother cried out. My blood ran cold. I shouted back at my dad and Pam that something was wrong and took off up the stairs, two at a time. I got to the top of the steps, yelling, "Mom? What happened? Where are you?" I looked around but couldn't see her, so I stopped to listen again, my heart racing more from panic than from running up the stairs. I heard muffled, jagged breathing and soft whimpers coming from out the back door, so I hurried out that way. My dad and Pam were right behind me.

We found my mother lying stunned on the deck, just outside the back door. My heart dropped into my stomach when I saw her. Her head was bloody, her glasses were sitting askew on her face, and she was holding her left wrist protectively. She looked up at us, dazed, as though she didn't recognize us for a second. She was panting in pain, trying to sit up but not able to. Running to her side, I instantly went into task mode, trying to figure out what to do to help her.

Pam was a nurse and quickly joined me, kneeling and speaking soothingly, asking my mother what had happened. My mother couldn't tell us. Her left wrist was swelling quickly, her normally loose watch band now looking as if it might be cutting off her circulation. Pam carefully helped my mom sit up, with me trying to support her from behind. She said she had a first aid kit in her car and ran to get it while I sat with my mom. I was scared, worried about her injuries, and terrified that she was so out of it. I just kept repeating soothing words, telling her not to try to move too quickly, for fear she might pass out. She looked vulnerable, hurt, and confused. I wrapped my arm around her shoulder to keep her sitting up and tried to comfort her. She didn't seem to notice.

Pam got out her supplies and began cleaning my mother's head to see how bad the cut was. She had a pretty good bump starting to show, which was what concerned Pam the most. My mother was clearly disoriented, so Pam was pretty sure there was a mild concussion. I gently took my mother's glasses off her face to clean them and inspect the damage. One stem was broken and they were dirty, but the lenses seemed okay. I handed them to my dad, who was standing near us, shifting his weight from one foot to the other, unsure of how to help. Worry was radiating from him in waves. By giving him the glasses, I was giving him something to do to help, and he gave me a quick half-smile as he took them from me.

A few minutes later, we were able to put the story of what had happened together. It seemed my mother had wandered out the back door to breathe in the fresh air and admire the gorgeous view while she waited for us to come back upstairs. While walking out the door, she hadn't noticed that there was a step down onto the deck. She'd missed it and gone right down, hitting her head and landing on her wrist.

After a while, my mother seemed to come out of her daze and was acting more like herself, so we got back in the car. She didn't think it was necessary to seek medical treatment, nor did she trust rural medical facilities, so we decided to head back down to Ann Arbor where my parents had left their car at our house. We were to meet Dani for dinner, but I wasn't sure that was a good idea.

Confirming that she was back to feeling more like herself, my mom responded with her usual exaggerated show of "Mother knows best." She clucked her tongue at me, telling me what "nonsense" I was displaying by even raising the question of whether she should come to dinner. My dad shrugged at me, unwilling to challenge her.

During dinner, I watched my mom carefully, not sure whether she'd hit her head hard enough to have a concussion. She noticed me watching her and became irritated that I "kept staring" at her. That set my blood to simmer, causing me to snap back at her that I was simply worried about her. She then became even more annoyed when I noticed that the bandage Pam had put over her cut was bleeding through and pointed it out.

Dani gave me a worried look. She and my dad both felt my mom should go to urgent care as well, but my mother refused. So we parted ways and they headed for home.

Fifteen minutes later, as we were still driving home, my mom called me. Sounding highly annoyed, she practically spat, "Your father has made a big deal out of this fall and is insisting that I go to urgent care."

I responded to her irritation by becoming instantly angry at her. "Well, I've been telling you all afternoon that you should go, but you've stubbornly refused. I think he's right," I spat back.

She huffed out a breath and said flatly, "I called our urgent care in Dearborn, and they closed ten minutes ago."

I looked over at Dani, who was listening on the car speaker. She took out her phone and quickly looked up our nearest urgent care in Ann Arbor. "The one at Domino Farms is open until ten p.m.," she said, loud enough for my mom to hear. "We could meet you there if you like."

Another huffed breath, another show of being annoyed. "Fine," she said dramatically. "We'll turn around and meet you there."

There was no one else waiting at the clinic, so we were ushered back quickly. After the examination, the doctor confirmed she had a mild concussion and wanted to x-ray her wrist. The technician asked the rest of us to step out into the hallway. We did, and I looked at my dad. He was fidgeting around, and I could see he was fighting back tears.

"Hey, what's wrong, Dad? She's going to be fine," I said, stepping forward to put my hand on his arm and try to soothe him. "Are you just worried about her?"

He nodded, unable to speak at first. After a minute, he said tearfully, "I can't do this by myself."

"What do you mean?" I asked, furrowing my brow in concern.

He gestured to the room where my mother was. "This," he said. "I can't do this alone. I need your help. She's been getting more and more confused about things."

I sighed, taking a step away from him. Despite the day camp incidents a few weeks prior, I wasn't seeing as many signs as he was. I was still just irritated with her.

"She's forgetting more and more," he continued. "She can't remember how to get to different places we've been going to for years, and she gets really angry when I try to argue with her about any of it. Something is wrong. I think she's got Alzheimer's."

I stared at him, momentarily shocked to hear him say out loud what we'd all been worrying about silently. He was still fighting the tears but losing. His emotion jarring me back to reality, I stepped forward to hug him. "Okay, Dad," I soothed, my stomach sinking. "It's okay. We'll figure it out."

Later that night, Dani and I talked. She pointed out that the carriage house was right there next to our new farmhouse and suggested that my parents could live there, just across the driveway from us.

My rejection of that idea was instant, forceful, and angry. I'd spent my entire life locked in some sort of battle with my mom. We'd been butting heads, arguing (sometimes quite aggressively), and picking at each other for years. We'd sometimes go months without speaking to each other due to a particularly harsh disagreement, and she'd often make comments intended to make me feel bad if I didn't call at least every couple of days. She was the queen of guilt trips. At the same time, she was my biggest fan. She sang my praises to others, bragged about me, my family, and my work, and constantly wanted to spend time with me. Normal life with her was an emotional roller coaster.

So I had zero interest in living across the driveway from my mother. Especially not with my wife and two adolescent boys in the mix. I didn't need daily instruction on how I should be doing everything, along with a running critique when I didn't. That would be my worst nightmare.

And yet, that's what my dad was asking of me. He saw that carriage house as an opportunity to get help with caring for my mom.

To refuse him and reject the idea when we had this perfectly good, totally available carriage house sitting there made me feel ashamed, guilty, and awful.

It was this combination of resentment and obligation that defined my relationship with my parents. I felt trapped. Since guilt, shame, and feeling not "enough" in every sense had been the narrative of my relationship with them, I didn't think I had permission to *not* invite them to live in the carriage house. So, with trepidation and all kinds of red flags waving in front of me, Dani and I decided to extend the invitation.

When we broached the idea of them buying the carriage house and moving into it, my mother flatly refused. She said there was "absolutely no way in hell" she could imagine leaving their Detroit home and neighborhood where they'd lived for the past 42 years. They were very active and involved with every community group possible and had a wide circle of friends. They'd also helped start the local farmers market and community garden. She said, "Maybe in two or three years" they would reconsider, but for now, it was completely out of the question.

Summer turned to fall, and Dani and I moved with the boys up to the farm. My parents came to visit often, sometimes staying four or five days at a time. The newness of the farm, having horses, and settling into the huge house seemed to distract my mom from picking at me constantly, so those visits weren't too bad, just some minor squabbles. Yet they were almost always about how I wasn't "doing things right," a common theme between me and my mother.

As we began noticing that there might be something wrong with her brain, my mom remained adamant that there was nothing wrong and refused to acknowledge anything unusual any of us noticed or pointed out. She'd shut down conversations by yelling at us, arguing that whoever was calling her out on a memory issue was the one who was really slipping, and generally refusing to accept that there could be something wrong with her. Her approach with us was aggressive, which wasn't out of character for her, but it was more forceful than normal. I could tell that she feared being evaluated and being told by a doctor that she was indeed showing early signs of Alzheimer's.

During one of their visits, Dani and I were making dinner while my parents sat at our kitchen island. When I brought up the subject of having her evaluated, my mom started down the same path of resistance, and the fight began. Inspiration struck, and I decided to try something else. I met her challenge with a challenge of my own.

"Okay, Mom," I said. "If you're convinced that nothing's wrong, let's prove it. Let's make an appointment with a neurologist and have the baseline tests done. Since Grandma had Alzheimer's, you already know you're at a higher risk, so this way they'll have your baseline results to compare to over time. I mean, you're about to turn seventy-four. It's probably not a bad idea to have that baseline."

As I looked up at my mom, I saw that she was struggling, not only to make an argument against mine but also with feeling extremely vulnerable, defensive, and terrified. My compassion kicked in. "Mom," I said gently, reaching across the counter to touch her hand, "none of us wants the results to show anything other than normal. You know that, right? No one wants you to be anything other than just fine."

She was fighting tears then but lashed out anyway. Anger was always her go-to shield against anything she didn't like. "Are you sure about that?" she spat angrily. "It sounds to me like you're all just on a witch hunt looking for reasons to lock me up in a loony bin somewhere!"

I pulled my hand back, familiar anger rising up in me too. "Well you're wrong," I said flatly, going back to chopping. "I'm sorry you have such a low opinion of all of us. That must be pretty hard to go through your life feeling like your husband and your kids have it out for you. What a way to live."

She sat silently then. After a few minutes, Dani changed the subject and we all moved on.

A couple of weeks later, just before I was about to hang up the phone after talking with my mom, she said, "Oh, by the way, you'll be happy to know you won." She sounded haughty, which I now recognized was a cover for her fear.

"Oh?" I asked innocently. "What did I win? I hope there's a prize involved," I jested, trying to keep things light. We had made it through a phone conversation without fighting for a change, and I was eager to do my part to keep it that way.

She laughed, but it sounded forced. "I decided to prove you all wrong. I set up an appointment to have baseline testing done for dementia. I'm sure it will come out completely normal and then you'll all owe me a big apology."

I was truly surprised. "That's great, Mom!" I said, my enthusiasm genuine. "And I am fully prepared to eat crow and take you out for a nice dinner to celebrate being wrong." I paused, taking a more serious tone. "Mom, I hope you know, we all want to be wrong. I would love nothing more."

"I know," she said softly. "The appointment is in February." It was October.

"Wait, what?" I said, more sharply than I meant. "What the hell? Why are you waiting nearly five months?"

Her self-righteous indignation was immediate. "Because there's too much going on to deal with this right now. Your aunt and uncle are coming to visit in a few weeks, then there's the holidays. It's too much. When I called to make the appointment, they said there was no reason it couldn't wait until February if that's what I wanted."

I was furious. "You're defeating the whole purpose of baseline testing, you know that, right? What if things are worse by then?" I couldn't hide my anger.

She responded in kind.

We exchanged a few more unpleasant words and ended the call, the previous 20 minutes of pleasant conversation forgotten.

In the months that followed, Dani and I started noticing more memory issues with my mother. While visiting us at the farm, she'd suggest running out to a store that was in her neighborhood. When I'd point out that that store was an hour and a half away, she'd get defensive and snap at me, saying, "I know that. I was just telling you that they also carry [random item] there too." It was a weak cover, and I think she knew it. Unable to quite accept that her memory was actually slipping, I would belabor it, pointing out when she said something different from what she'd been trying to say.

The normal terms of my relationship with my mother meant a lot of squabbling, so instead of constantly confronting my mom, I tried to talk to my dad whenever I could. It was difficult for us to speak privately because my mom didn't want us talking about her, nor did she like being left out of any conversation. So I took to calling him on the rare occasion when I knew she was out at a function they didn't attend together. We talked about the things we were both noticing and compared notes. We worried together, convinced more than ever that something really was wrong, and we lamented many times her defiance about moving up the testing.

My mom must've also started noticing changes in herself that were scaring her because she'd go from being adamant about *not* moving up to the carriage house to being unbending about moving there. One week she'd say it wouldn't be for "at least two to three years," and the next she'd say it would be "maybe within a year." Then it was to be the spring of 2017, when a home tour in their historic neighborhood came through in early May. My mother came up with the idea of getting their house on that tour and putting it up for sale then. She figured the home tour would bring a lot of traffic through and they might find a buyer more quickly. Making the move over the summer seemed like the right timeline to her.

We agreed with the plan, figuring it was the best we'd get. The previous owners of our farm still owned the carriage house and parcel, so we entered negotiations with them for how things would move forward.

In early February, before my mom's evaluation, I discussed with my parents the preparations of their home for the tour. My dad is a retired cabinet maker and renovated their kitchen a few years earlier, but there were other parts of the house that needed updating. It felt overwhelming. They had accumulated so much stuff over the years that I didn't know where to start. And they were looking to me for guidance.

We decided to call a realtor who lived in the neighborhood and was very successful selling homes there. We had only three months to get things ready before the home tour and thought she could guide us on what was needed and how to prioritize. She came and evaluated the house, then advised a listing price that pleased my parents. She even thought she might already have an interested buyer.

A couple who'd been renting a home at the other end of the block were looking to buy. We agreed they could see my parents' house "as-is" later that afternoon. They did, and they put in a full offer three days later. Though they didn't want any renovations done, the caveat was that because their lease was ending, they needed to be able to move in by June 1. That meant my parents would have to be completely out by the closing, which was projected to be in early May. Based on how much there was to sort through and move, we'd need to start moving them out in the coming weeks.

We made a plan to get started on that huge process while waiting for my mother's baseline testing day to arrive, and the tangling of the web began.

Looking Back Now

Neither my mother nor I did a good job of acknowledging what was happening to her. Each of us, in our own ways, was trying to fight against dementia by clinging to our fights with each other. We both were strong-willed, not only preferring our own ideas best but needing a lot of autonomy to figure things out for ourselves. Since I was the daughter, there was an expectation communicated—often and loudly—that I submit to my mother's will, ideas, and ways of doing things in my own life, including the way I was raising my children, handling my marriage, and generally moving through the world. The older I got, the more I rejected that expectation, which caused even more kerfuffles between us.

My mother and I also loved each other deeply. She would've walked over hot coals for me, and I always knew she was my biggest supporter. It's just that that didn't make it any easier to accept how controlling she was on a daily basis. Instead, it created a ton of friction between us. At the same time, I absolutely wanted and felt I needed her approval. I just wanted her to be proud of me, which she was great about saying to her friends but not great at demonstrating to me. If I had thought she didn't love me fiercely, it would've been much easier for me to disengage. I just wanted room to figure things out for myself, and she was terrified that I wouldn't "do it right" (fill in the blank on what "it" was at any given moment). This led her to try harder to impose her will and me to dig my heels in harder in response.

So, life was pretty normal in those early days. If we hadn't been fighting about her going to get tested, it would've been about something else. It always seemed like just another day. There was no looming feeling of foreboding, no sign that we were entering into something life-changing and profound, just annoyance at the disruptions it was causing in our lives. As terrible as that might sound, it's the truth. By being brutally honest about all my feelings along the way, I'm sincerely hoping you'll feel less alone if you're feeling the same way.

The gift of hindsight has allowed me to see that I simply did not know what I did not know. The pervasive feeling of annoyance I felt during the earliest days of recognizing that something might be wrong with my mom was exacerbated by my being "unconsciously incompetent" at everything about the situation. I didn't know how to get my mom in for testing, how to work with her in a rational and logical capacity to plan what would be best for her, what the road would look like, nor how short that road would be. At the time, these things felt like inconveniences more than anything else, mostly because I was overwhelmed by the old narratives in my head telling me that my feelings were shameful, that I was a bad person, and that I'd never figure out how to help my mom "correctly." Looking back now, I wish I'd been able to understand a few things then:

➢ Your emotions are legit, no matter what they are.

➢ You probably aren't sure what's happening at this stage, and that's okay. The most important thing you can do when you begin noticing changes in a loved one is to get them to their primary care doctor for some baseline testing. They may refer you to a neurologist to do further testing, which is appropriate and helpful, no matter what the results show.

➢ Start keeping track of what you notice, when, and how often. This is especially true for any behaviors you notice that seem out of character for your loved one. Either with a notes app on your phone or a small notebook or journal, you will not regret writing things down. One regret I have (and I have many) is not doing a better job of tracking things as they were happening. At all stages of any disease, but especially in the beginning, it can be extremely helpful for doctors to know specifics about what you're noticing as well as factual timelines. Those details can be hard to remember on the fly. It's so easy to get flustered when you're in a doctor's office, and if there are months between appointments it's impossible to remember everything correctly. Keeping a log will help you recount things with accuracy, which allows doctors a greater chance of treating your loved one effectively.

CHAPTER 2

HURRY UP AND WAIT

Amid the preparations at my parents' house came my mom's appointment. My brother, David, and I decided we should attend along with my dad. We were all worried about what the results would show.

As we sat in the waiting room, we each were reacting and displaying emotions in line with our personalities. My mom acted angry, picking at my dad and scolding him for dumb little things. My dad stayed silent in response, occasionally clicking his tongue and rolling his eyes in annoyance but otherwise saying nothing. David remained stonily silent. I was reactive to everything my mom picked at. I could tell she was scared, but I didn't have any patience for how she was choosing to show it by picking on my dad. She was also quietly criticizing the doctor's office for every little thing, from the types of magazines they had in the waiting room to the slight delay in being called back for her appointment. The hushed, clipped tone of her running commentary grated on my nerves.

Eventually, a nurse called my mom to follow her and have the initial tests done. A moment later, a woman came out and invited the rest of us to go into a conference room to talk with her. She introduced herself as a social worker from the Alzheimer's Association of Michigan. Her job was to talk with families about what they'd been noticing about their loved ones, talk to the patients about what they'd been experiencing, and then talk with us all together about ways we could support each other.

With a calm and professional demeanor, the social worker began asking us questions about what had caused us to set up the appointment in the first place. She seemed almost too calm. Like my family members, I was scared of what we would learn that day, and her serenity made me tense. I wanted to scream, but I managed to keep myself under control.

As I described to the social worker what I'd been noticing, my trepidation surged. I told her about the two incidents of Robin being forgotten at summer day camp seven months earlier. My dad shared some of his observations, fear, and nervousness, which caused him to stumble over some of his words as he spoke softly. I could tell he was uncomfortable talking about my mother's confusion and felt like he was betraying her. David chimed in at the end, sharing that he hadn't really noticed as much as we had because he wasn't around her that often, but he supported what we were saying.

The social worker calmly took notes, thoughtfully listening and watching us as we spoke. I wanted to be reassured by her demeanor, but I just wasn't. After a while, my impatience got the best of me and I blurted out, "So when will we know what's going on with her?"

She smiled at me, nodding her head with understanding. "We'll have some preliminary results today from the initial memory tests the doctor is performing now. Then, based on what she finds, she may recommend some additional routine screening tests to make sure your mom's overall brain health isn't being compromised by something else." She paused, having been looking around at all of us but now returning her thoughtful gaze to me. "Does that help?"

I nodded mutely, suddenly feeling overcome with emotion. I didn't trust myself to speak. I glanced over at David, who must've recognized what was going on because he took over asking questions.

"What are some of the other tests they might order?" he asked.

She gave a half-smile. "I don't want to speak for the doctor. I'm not a neurologist. What I can tell you is that there are lots of things that contribute to or can harm our overall brain health. Dr. Nartes will share her recommendations with you when she's done evaluating your mom."

As if on cue, the door opened. My mom had finished her tests and came into the room to join us. She immediately looked suspicious and defensive. "I see you've all been in here talking about me," she snapped angrily as she sat down next to my dad. We were all a little taken aback, but none of us were surprised. I barked out a short laugh, rising to her bait.

"Yes, because we were asked to," I said, not hiding my irritation. "How will anyone be able to help you if you don't want us to talk about what we've noticed?"

Pursing her lips in a telltale expression of disapproval, she said indifferently, "Well, there's nothing to tell. I'm perfectly fine."

As she sat there glaring at me, I spread my hands wide in a gesture of surrender. Though I was really thinking *What's the fucking point?*, what I said was, "Great! Is that what the neurologist said?"

Before she could answer, the neurologist walked into the room and joined us. "Hello, my name is Dr. Nartes. I ran some initial tests on your mom's memory, and I'd like to share what I found."

We all nodded, except for my mom who just sat looking very uncomfortable, scared, and defensive. There was a tiny part of me that saw through her and wanted to comfort her. But in that moment, my anger at her insistence on keeping her head in the sand about what was happening to her won out. I sat glaring at her, fuming.

"Mrs. Patnaude has what we call mild cognitive impairment, or MCI, which is the term we use to describe the earliest stage of dementia," she began as she opened her leather-bound portfolio to look at her notes. "When the brain ages or is compromised in health from some other cause, we begin to see this effect of MCI." She then went into a description of changes to brain structure and function that are common with dementia and a plan for initial treatment. "Brain health is complex and can be influenced by a number of factors. In order to rule out possible causes of this impairment other than dementia, I'd like to have you complete a couple of other tests, Mrs. Patnaude."

She paused, looking at my mother who was sitting with her arms crossed tightly, her lips pursed, and a frown on her face. She looked miserable. Still irritated with her, I suppressed a sigh.

"First," Dr. Nartes went on, "I'd like you to have an MRI so we can see if there is any initial shrinkage to your brain. I'd also like you to have a sleep study done."

My mother clicked her tongue disapprovingly, a look of horror on her face so dramatic that I had to stifle a giggle.

Dr. Nartes frowned slightly at her before continuing. "A leading cause of compromised brain health is sleep apnea. We stop breathing during our sleep cycle, which deprives the brain of oxygen. When this happens too frequently or for too long, it can cause brain fog, memory loss, and other health problems over time. If you have sleep apnea, we can at least stabilize that part of what could be contributing to the diminishment of your brain health by having you use a CPAP machine while you sleep."

"I'm not the one who needs a sleep study," my mother snapped haughtily, her gaze now directed toward my father. "My husband snores so loudly he can wake up the whole house!" She looked quite pleased with herself. Smug. Back in control.

Dr. Nartes looked a little surprised but quickly recovered and smiled. "Well, that might be the case, but your husband isn't my patient, Mrs. Patnaude, you are. I'd like to check *you* out, if that's alright, so we can help minimize as many negative effects on your brain health as possible."

My mom looked uncomfortable again and was pursing her lips. "I won't be using a CPAP machine at night," she said defiantly. "I'll never be able to sleep with that thing on my face."

As my mother began rearranging the papers the social worker had put in front of her and studiously avoiding everyone's eyes, my father and I exchanged a look of resignation, knowing we wouldn't be able to change her mind. I looked apologetically at the social worker and neurologist who were watching this exchange quietly. Their faces gave nothing away.

"I'd also like to wean you off the two medications you're taking," Dr. Nartes continued, referencing her notes. "You reported that you've been taking Premarin for hot flashes, is that right?" For confirmation she looked up at my mom, who nodded. "And when did you begin taking that medication?"

My mom looked at my dad, as if the answer would be with him. He shrugged and made a face indicating that he had no idea.

"I had terrible hot flashes when I began menopause, so my primary care doctor prescribed it then."

"About what age were you at that time, Mrs. Patnaude?"

My mom thought for a minute. "I think I was in my late forties maybe?"

Dr. Nartes stared at her for a moment. "And you're"—she referenced her notes—"you're seventy-four now?"

My mom nodded.

"We need to get you off that medication immediately. You've been taking it for nearly twenty-five years, and it's only meant to be taken for two to three years, to help alleviate the worst of menopause symptoms." Her expression was hard to read as she referenced her notes again, but something in her tone caused me alarm.

"You're also taking Paxil for depression and anxiety, is that right?"

Another confirming nod from my mom.

"And how long have you been taking that medication?"

My mom looked at her, her brow furrowed with concern. "For about the same amount of time, maybe a little less. I started taking it when both of my children went off to college," she said, turning an accusing look at us and matching that with her tone. "I had trouble coping with my depression and anxiety."

My eyebrows shot up and my mouth dropped. Was she blaming us for her depression because we went to college?

"Well, that medication is less harmful long term, but I'm not sure if you still need it. I'd feel better if we could wean you off both medications as soon as possible. Let's see what happens when you're medication-free." She smiled at my mom, who pursed her lips and wouldn't meet the doctor's eyes. "I'll put in the order for the sleep study and MRI, Mrs. Patnaude," she confirmed while moving to the door of the conference room. "I'll let you finish up here and will see you back after your tests in about six weeks. It was nice to meet you all today." She nodded to all of us and left the room.

The social worker looked around at us, the thoughtful expression back on her face. "Mrs. Patnaude, we were talking a little bit about the best ways you can support your brain health without a sleep machine or medications. I'd like to share some more information with you and your family if that's alright?" She looked at my mom, waiting patiently for her to give her consent to proceed.

My mother nodded, lips still pursed. I could see she was fighting back tears.

The social worker then went over the three pillars of prevention: eating a Mediterranean diet, walking or exercising 30 minutes every day, and staying socially engaged and active. My mom bragged about how she'd been playing brain games on her iPad and computer for years, was an avid reader and very socially engaged, and that she loved to walk. My dad gave her a side look when she made that last comment, not wanting to reveal that they hadn't done any consistent walking in several years. My mother ignored his look.

Wanting to be honest about the realities so we could understand where she could make the most improvement, I started to speak up. My motivation was to have the best picture of reality possible, not to make my mother look or feel bad but to be armed with information that could help her. She didn't see it that way at all. As soon as I started revealing how much their diet and exercise habits could improve in the ways the social worker was suggesting, my mother shushed me. She raised her voice and scolded me for discussing things I didn't know about. It lit me the fuck on fire.

That was how it was between us. She was far more interested in upholding appearances of perfection, and I was more interested in what was real. She got angry with me for spoiling her facade, and I became furious with her for being unwilling to operate in reality. Round and round we went, just as it had been throughout my life.

The meeting ended shortly after that. The social worker gave us some brochures on the brain health recommendations and guidelines she'd shared, along with pamphlets on how to communicate with people affected by Alzheimer's and dementia. We all thanked her for her time and left the office.

Once we got into the elevator, my mother lit into me, hissing through clenched teeth. "You had no business telling them those things," she whisper-yelled. "You're just trying to make me look bad and make them think there's something wrong with me! If that's how you're going to behave, you don't need to come to any more of these appointments."

My blood started boiling the second she started in on me, and I lashed right back, doing some hissing of my own. "For the life of me, I can't understand why you wouldn't want to tell them everything that's going on! And be honest about what you're already doing and what you're not, so you can find things to do to help! What a waste of time to go to a doctor if all you're going to do is lie about that stuff and expect us to do the same! How the hell are you going to get the help you need if you're not honest with them?"

The elevator doors opened, and we all got out. My mother smiled and said a very polite hello to the people getting onto the elevator, trying to make it look like we were a happy family. I was scowling angrily, not giving a rat's ass what they thought. I felt like a petulant child trailing behind the rest of my family as we all walked out.

After that initial appointment, my mother really started digging in her heels about further testing. "I don't need to be tested; *you* need to be tested!" was her mantra. She was in total denial that anything was wrong with her.

Convincing her to have the MRI was relatively easy, but she really fought us on doing the sleep study. She kept saying that she didn't snore and always slept like a log, so she didn't need to have a sleep study. My father would laugh obnoxiously to hide his annoyance, then point out that she snored terribly, which she vehemently denied. She tried turning our focus to my dad, who was well-known as a snorer and a light sleeper.

Neither my parents nor I knew much about sleep apnea, but David had been diagnosed with it the previous year and was using a CPAP machine at night. He tried explaining to our parents what it was and why Mom should just get the sleep study, saying the use of the machine had helped him immensely. He was sleeping much better, and the brain fog he'd had prior to using the machine was completely gone. David was her golden child, so I was surprised by how dismissively she waved her hand at his comments, as though she were trying to bat away the words themselves. She relented to the sleep study only after my father agreed to have his doctor recommend he do one too.

When the day of her appointment came, we took my mom to the sleep clinic. Outwardly, she appeared angry, defensive, and irritable. She also was confused. We had to remind her several times what she was having done and why and reassure her that my dad's test was the following week. The cyclical conversation was on a repeat loop, one of the first times I remember that happening. It would become more common later on.

Though my mom had convinced herself that she'd never be able to sleep in an unfamiliar place with monitoring devices attached to her and people watching, she came back from the sleep study declaring it hadn't been nearly as bad as she'd imagined. She'd slept "like a rock" and saved face by turning her attention to my dad's upcoming test. She was eager to compare their numbers, sure that his would be much worse than hers.

While sitting at my dad's appointment with them a week later, I noticed my mom kept saying that she just knew his numbers would be way worse than hers and scolding him over nothing. Always one to defend my silent father, I hissed back at her to leave him alone and quit picking at him. As was his way, he sat silent, staring at the posters on the wall, arms folded, not responding to either of us.

By the time the doctor came in, you could cut the tension between me and my mom with a knife. As he reviewed my dad's sleep study results, my mom became very smug. My dad did in fact have quite serious sleep apnea, and the doctor recommended that he be fitted for a CPAP machine and mask. My dad didn't say much but made embarrassed sounds and sighed a lot as my mother crowed about how she'd known for years that he had it. I'm not sure how he just sat and took it from her. She was being so mean that I finally called her out—while the doctor was still in the room. I told her to just stop, that we needed to listen to the doctor, and that her comments weren't helping. She pursed her lips in the tight way she did when she was feeling scolded and wanted to keep arguing, but she stopped.

When it was my mom's turn to review her results a few weeks later, she was certain she wouldn't have sleep apnea. In fact, her numbers were even worse than my dad's. No one dared say the kinds of things to her that she'd said to him about it though. She silenced all of us with an angry warning look, scowling at us and daring one of us to point out how wrong she'd been. No one did, but I couldn't help smiling at the absurdity of it all. I felt a laugh bubbling up but did my best to suppress it.

Dr. Nartes wrote the order for my mom's CPAP machine, explaining how imperative it was that she use it. She said my mom's sleep apnea was bad enough that it could cause heart failure. She also said it's a contributing factor to dementia when untreated; it creates brain fog, forgetfulness, and other symptoms that are also seen with dementia. The doctor wanted to treat all causes of my mom's diminished brain health, and using a CPAP machine was one of the ways she was trying to do so. She told my mom to start using the machine as soon as she could get it, then said she'd see us again in six months.

Six months? And after already waiting for five?

When my dad had cancer in 1996, there was a clear urgency to get treatment underway. When David had cancer in 2000, there was a clear urgency to get treatment underway. When I had skin lesions that were precancerous over the years, there was a clear urgency to get treatment underway.

You get the idea.

We're used to fixing problems. When someone is sick, we want to find the right medicine, treatment, exercises, or breathing techniques to fix it. With dementia, there's nothing to fix. Sure, you can make adjustments that might slow down the progression of the disease, but really you just go back to living your life. And wait.

Intellectually, this made sense. Emotionally, it sucked. It felt like someone should *do* something. I wanted there to be more urgency from the doctors to address the problem. But there wasn't anything to address. All we could do was get my mom to use the CPAP machine, convince her she really didn't need Premarin or Paxil anymore, and keep her social calendar going at its robust level.

As the web continued to tangle, I began to realize that no one gets out of dementia alive. It may not be the thing that ends your life, but once you have it, you won't recover. Yet that realization was on an intellectual level. Emotionally I was in turmoil. Not because of the diagnosis, but because I thought it meant we'd travel the same road we'd been down with my grandmother, a journey that lasted for more than 20 years. All I could think about was how the hell I was going to survive 20+ years of this with my mother living across the driveway.

Looking Back Now

I now understand that regardless of what she was presenting outwardly, my mother was absolutely terrified. But at the time, all I could see was her defensiveness and misplaced anger, which she seemed so eager to take out on all of us. When I tried to reassure her that the test was really no big deal and that everything was going to be fine, she attacked me. It was a familiar tactic she'd used in our interactions throughout my life, so instead of realizing that she was probably using her anger to protect herself and keep from falling apart, I just got mad too. And when I got mad, we argued and exchanged harsh words. That pattern was well-worn between us.

I wonder now if perpetuating that pattern was comforting to her at a time when everything else was starting to feel less familiar. Looking back now, I also wish I'd known a few other things:

> ➤ To date, there are over 70 identified variations of dementia. The only way to definitively diagnose it is through autopsy. That means it's a guessing game from the word go.

➤ Dementia-like symptoms can be caused by other medical conditions, so it's critical to get your loved one checked out when you start noticing them. A urinary tract infection (UTI) can cause dementia-like symptoms in elderly people, even those unaffected by actual dementia. Sleep apnea can too.

➤ Do some research to gain a better understanding of the diagnosis you receive. If it's a form of dementia, the Alzheimer's Association, or ALZ, is a national organization with a robust website, a 24/7 hotline, and loads of resources in local communities all over the United States. Help is available for learning about the warning signs, what to expect, ideas on how to navigate changes, and so much more.

➤ The early stage is the best time to start planning for the future. My mother was so busy fighting her diagnosis that she refused to discuss much. The time when you can have conversations about your loved one's wishes, their assets, and what they want these last chapters of their life to look like is now. At the back of this book, I've listed some resources that could be particularly helpful.

➤ Fighting a dementia diagnosis is pretty common. Refusing to accept the diagnosis is equally common. As of now, there's no cure for any form of dementia. The best that can be done is slowing its progression, and the drugs that are used for that either aren't available to or don't work for everyone. Sometimes a patient doesn't qualify for one reason or another.

➤ Keep a journal of how you're feeling. It's way too easy as caregivers to keep our focus on everyone else around us who needs our attention. Pour a little of that attention on yourself. Reflect on your feelings. Slow down, even just for 10 minutes, to feel those feelings and sort through them. If you don't care for yourself, who will?

CHAPTER 3

BLINDSIDED

While we waited for my mom's next appointment, we were in full swing helping my parents pack up their house in preparation for their move to the carriage house on our farm. They'd lived in their house for 42 years, raising both me and David there. As children of the Great Depression era, they had a tendency to "save" a lot of things. I wouldn't call their house a hoarding situation, but there was a definite accumulation of way too much stuff. It had just been the two of them for many years at this point, so our old bedrooms had been used to store extra things that my mom bought and my dad salvaged.

Though it was a huge relief that the buyers didn't want any of the renovations we thought we'd need to do, my parents were moving from a 2,000 square-foot home with a full basement to a 1,200 square-foot carriage house with no basement. So there was considerable downsizing that needed to happen. I started going down to their house once a week or so to try to help out. Owning my own business gave me greater flexibility than David had. Plus, my mother in particular relied on me for guidance in moving, as I had moved a number of times in my adult life. It never occurred to me to wonder why she didn't ask my brother for help like that, nor did I feel any resentment toward him about it. But I did absorb the stress of feeling obligated to help even when I had a full plate myself. My mom didn't shy away from using guilt to get me to come, and I gave in to it even though I felt resentment toward her for using it.

"I thought we could work on the den today," my mother said on one trip.

The den had a wall of bookcases built in that were chock-full of photo albums, photo envelopes from the picture processing kiosk at local drugstores, empty albums never used, framed pictures of family and close friends, and knickknacks accumulated over the years that had no other logical homes. I assumed the task would be fairly straightforward.

"Why don't you let me pack up the den," I countered, "and you focus on another room where you need to be the one making decisions about what you're taking and what you can get rid of. Time's going by quickly, and the moving date will be here before we know it. I think we should divide and conquer, don't you?" My tone was reasonable, I thought, and the suggestion seemed very logical. I also knew with certainty that if we worked on something together, fights along the way would be almost guaranteed.

"Well, there are things that need to be sorted in the den as well, and you can't make those decisions without my input," my mother retorted, making an effort to keep her tone from becoming confrontational but not fully succeeding. My visceral response was immediate.

"Seriously?" I said, not hiding my incredulity. "You can't trust me to pack a few boxes of old pictures?"

My mother shook her head, ramping up her anger as well. "It's not just 'a few boxes of old pictures,'" she sputtered. "There are a lot of things in those cabinets. There are projects I plan to do. You won't know what to save and you'll just"—she waved her arms in a grandiose gesture—"throw everything away!"

I stared at her for a moment, simmering, then said, "If all I'm here to do is hold your hand while you sort through everything, making every decision about every item in this house, you'll never move." I was fighting to keep my tone even and controlled, trying to get her to see reason, but she wasn't having it.

She shook her head again, pressing her lips firmly together, like a child refusing a bite of food. "No," she said again, her tone calmer now too. "I don't make any progress when I'm on my own. I need you here to help me." I noticed her bottom lip starting to quiver. "I can't do this by myself. I just sit and look at all the stuff and I don't know where to start." Her eyes were shining now. "You're just so good at all this stuff," she said with another vague arm gesture aimed around the house. She paused, then said again in a smaller voice, "I can't do this by myself."

My anger and frustration slowly drained away. I could see that she was struggling and overwhelmed. Empathy kicked in. I took a few short steps to where she was standing and hugged her. She hugged me back, letting the tears come now. "It's okay," I said softly. "It's all going to be fine. This move will be over before you know it, and you'll be settled into the new little house across the driveway from me, waking up in the morning to the peace and quiet of the farm. Well, except for the rooster."

She chuckled and pulled away, heading for a box of tissues on the side table. "I hate birds," she said, blowing her nose.

I laughed, glad that the tension had eased for the moment, and said, "Yeah, I know. But he's harmless and won't fly up at you, so you're safe." I smiled at her sympathetically. "I'll get some boxes and we can get started."

Everything went smoothly while packing the first few boxes, which contained pictures that had been on display and photo albums that were full. The trouble started when we got to the empty albums and duplicate pictures in the envelopes from the film processing labs.

"Hey, these envelopes have the duplicates in them for what's already in these albums," I said. "I don't think we need to save them."

Looking at the closed envelopes she replied with certainty, "No they don't. Those are the originals. I need to save those."

I frowned, confused. "What do you mean, 'the originals'?" I asked, pointing to the album where I had just matched up what was in the envelope to what was in the album. "All of those pictures are in that album already."

My mom shook her head. "No, those are the originals," she said again, more urgently. "I need to save them." She reached over and took the envelope from my hand, placing it into the next box and turning back to the open cabinet door.

"But Mom," I tried again, "why do you need that set of prints? They're the same as what's already in the album. Look." I took the envelope out of the box and removed the prints. I opened the album where I'd seen them and showed her that they were the same. When I looked back up at her face, she had a strange look. It was troubled but also confused, almost like she didn't understand what she was looking at.

After staring for a moment, moving her head slightly to change angles and looking from the album pages to the prints in my hand, she shook her head again and repeated, "No, those are the originals. I need to save them."

My patience evaporated, and irritability and some fear at the weird look on her face took over. "Mom," I said more loudly, "you're not making any sense. This is ridiculous! Can't you see that it's the same picture in both spots? Why the hell would you save the ones in the envelope? You have very limited storage space at this new house. You have to get rid of a lot of stuff! Saving duplicate prints of the same damn photos makes zero sense!" I was trying not to shout, but I was unnerved. My mom just shook her head again and turned back to the cabinet, reaching for the next envelope. Exasperated, I stood up. "I'm going to see what dad is doing. I'll be back," I said flatly, then stepped over the piles and boxes and left the room.

This encounter is indicative of how the packing experience went over the course of several weeks. My mother repeatedly told me she wanted and needed my help to keep her focused and on track, as well as to help her make decisions about what to pack, what to donate, and what to leave behind. When I followed her wishes and tried to help, we ended up fighting, every time. I had no patience for her resistance to change, which became stronger and stronger as we went along. I tried to argue logic with her, which had always worked in the past for us to be able to move forward without killing each other. That tactic was now completely failing.

The look I'd seen on my mother's face that unnerved me appeared at random times, accompanied by not making sense, being completely confused, or getting things totally wrong. Even though she had a diagnosis, I wasn't aware of how or when her cognitive impairment would show up. She still looked like my mom, still got angry with any one of us at the drop of a hat, still bossed everyone around, and still declared what she believed to be fact with confidence and defiance. The difference was in how often she'd be wrong or say things that made absolutely no sense in the context of what we were doing or what object was in her hands.

I started calling that look "dementia face," meaning that my mom's eyes seemed unable to focus properly on what was in front of her. She'd turn her head slightly, as if trying to adjust her view, her lips would pout forward in concentration, and her brow would furrow slightly. Alarmed and unsettled by it, I talked to my dad and David about it privately. My dad had noticed it a few times as well. David hadn't, but he didn't dispute what I described and my dad confirmed. He was just frustrated and irritated by both our parents' unwillingness to downsize their possessions.

Despite being unnerved by that look, not to mention the weight of running my own business and maintaining my responsibilities at home, I kept showing up. I was afraid that if I didn't, moving day would come and they wouldn't be ready. Some days it felt like we were rearranging deck chairs on the Titanic, but the alternative didn't feel like an option. So we soldiered on.

The day before we were set to move my parents' "bare necessities" up to the carriage house, we were blindsided by a "friend." I was at my parents' house helping to finish gathering what would go with them in this first phase of the move. My mom and I were upstairs sorting through their clothes, arguing as usual, when we heard the doorbell. When my dad answered the door, my mom and I stopped working and listened to see who was there. We heard him invite someone in.

"Charlotte, Karen is here," he called up the stairs.

As soon as my mom heard who was there, she smiled with delight and perked right up. I figured it would be a nice break from the packing. With the moving truck coming the next day, tensions were quite high, and David and I had been arguing on and off with my parents for weeks about what would fit and what they'd really need there. We'd hoped this first move would make the downsizing process a little easier.

Grateful for the reprieve, we both went down to greet Karen. We'd known her and her family for close to 30 years at that point. She'd always been a lovely person to be around, with a gentle nature and extremely soft-spoken voice. She was one of those people who could hide any troubles, stresses, and imperfections about her own life and family while showing genuine and attentive interest in others. My parents made her family cookies and holiday table centerpieces at Christmastime, and she baked cookies and wrote beautiful cards for each of us on special occasions. The bonds between us were strong.

"Karen!" my mother exclaimed in delight, hugging her friend. "So good of you to stop by."

I was right behind her and smiled at Karen as well, hugging her too. "Good to see you," I said, the irritation at my mother still receding from our interaction just moments before.

Karen accepted my mother's invitation to sit down in the living room. "I can only stay for a few minutes," she said, hands held up in a gesture of warding off the possibility of being pulled into helping. *Good*, I thought. *We still have a fuck ton to do before tomorrow.*

After some preliminary questions about how everything was going with the moving process, Karen seemed to gather her courage for a moment, then blurted out, "I don't think this move is a good idea."

My mom just stared at her for a moment. I frowned, quicker to speak. "Uh, well, it's a little late now," I said with a forced chuckle. "Why don't you think it's a good idea?"

Karen folded then refolded her hands in her lap, keeping her attention directed at my parents, not looking at me. "I think you'd be better off staying here, Charlotte," she said in her soft voice. "There are so many support services available here in Detroit. Plus you've got all your friends and neighbors around you who've known you for years and who all want to help." Giving me a quick side glance, she then added, "You shouldn't feel compelled to leave your home of forty-two years."

I was flabbergasted. Was she really saying that friends, neighbors, and city services would do a better job of supporting my parents than Dani and I could from across the driveway? Realizing my mouth was hanging open, I quickly shut it. I looked at my mom, then my dad. They seemed equally surprised.

I was the first to speak again. "Wait, what?" I said, trying to keep my tone from getting hostile. I'm not sure I succeeded. "Are you serious? You think my parents would really be better off staying here?"

My mom shot me a look that meant "stop talking," so I did. She looked at Karen and smiled at her, but with concern. "Karen, we've already sold our house. Closing will happen in another month or so. We're getting ready to move our necessities up there tomorrow."

"I know, but it's not too late," Karen cut in, with more passion than I'd seen in her before in all my years of knowing her. "You can undo agreements. Stay here, friend." She sounded like she was almost pleading with my mom.

My mom smiled at her, a little sadly now. "I don't think we can, Karen," she said softly. "Ellen and Dani have found such an idyllic, beautiful spot. They bought that farm with the carriage house before realizing we would want to move closer to them. It's like it was meant to be."

I stayed quiet, recognizing that this was my mom's fight. But I was fuming. How dare Karen? She hadn't been there in urgent care when my dad begged me to step in and help. Where was she when my dad had to pull the car over because my mother's screams that he was going the wrong way made it unsafe for him to drive?

And yet, another part of me wondered if she was right. Were we making a mistake in moving my mom? Would it make her condition worse? Would she find happiness in the tiny town where we lived, away from her friends of many years and familiar surroundings? I resented Karen for calling it all into question and speaking my fears aloud. I clenched my teeth and swallowed hard to keep from yelling at her.

After a few more minutes of listening to both my parents talk about how beautiful the farm was and how much they were looking forward to living so close to me and my family, Karen seemed to realize it was time to leave. She patted her hands on her lap with an air of finality and stood. "Well," she said, a bright smile once again on her face, "I think it's time for me to go and leave you to your packing. I'm sure there's a lot to do yet." She hugged both of my parents and wished them luck with the move, then turned to me, looking at me for the first time since launching into her crusade to get my parents to stay. "Walk me out, Ellen?"

I nodded numbly, following her to the door. She reached to hug me, which I automatically reciprocated even though I was still upset. As we embraced, she whispered, "Please think about what you're doing. This is a big mistake. This move is not in your mom's best interest. Don't be selfish."

I pulled back, my mouth hanging open again. I couldn't believe what I was hearing from this woman I'd known for so long. "I'm not the one who asked for this, Karen," I whispered back more forcefully. "My dad begged us to help and has been the one pushing for this from the beginning."

She smiled at me in what now felt like a condescending way. In a louder voice, she said, "Well, best of luck tomorrow with everything. I hope this works out the way you hope." And with that, she turned and walked out the door, closing it gently behind her.

The initial move of my parents' essential items up to the carriage house went fine from a logistical standpoint. We had a lot of help from family and friends (not Karen). My mother directed the show, of course, but she often got confused about which things were going and which things were staying behind. My primary job became helping manage and oversee what she was directing to be loaded. We bickered back and forth a lot, but I managed to keep most of what was supposed to stay behind out of the truck.

Once all that was done, Dani and I helped with the unpacking. David and his then-girlfriend, Lauren, also came up a couple of times to help. My parents came over to our house for dinner every night. In those early days, I was feeding them three times a day, as they hadn't settled enough to go grocery shopping and buy their own food.

My mom was clearly rattled and unsettled, but also clearly happy to be with us. She was agitated a lot of the time. Nothing in the house was familiar nor where she thought it ought to be. She couldn't find anything that had been packed and struggled to find things that had been unpacked. When I'd take a break from working and try to go over to help, it would often get ugly.

One evening, my mom was clearly in a foul mood at dinner, snapping at my dad every time he spoke. "I don't know why you took so much food, Ronald," she scolded as though he were a child. "Your gut is getting quite large."

My dad chuckled nervously, one of his tells that he was uncomfortable or embarrassed. He glanced over at her robust figure but said nothing.

No one would've dared comment on my mother's weight, but she somehow always thought it perfectly acceptable to make comments like this to my dad in front of other people. I was used to this behavior from her, but my family wasn't. Trying not to laugh out of her own shock and discomfort, Dani avoided my eyes and concentrated on her plate. Both my boys looked at me wide-eyed, knowing enough not to say anything but clearly also shocked and uncomfortable. I shook my head at them slightly, trying to silently reinforce their instincts to stay quiet, then frowned across the table at my parents. They both avoided my eyes.

After a few minutes of quiet eating with no one talking, my mother looked out the large bay windows of the dining room and pointed suddenly. "Oh look!" she said in a delighted tone. "The horses have decided to explore a new area!"

Dani and I immediately snapped our heads around to look and see what was happening outside. The horses had just one enclosed pasture at that point, so if they were "exploring," it meant they'd gotten out. We saw the horses grazing in their pasture, where they were supposed to be. Dani stood up quickly, craning her neck and scanning to see what was going on, immediately on alert, ready to run out the door to go catch them. "Where?" she asked urgently. "Where do you see the horses exploring?"

My mom pointed to the pasture. "Right there," she said, matching Dani's urgent tone. "They're right there!"

We were confused. "Wait, that's their regular pasture, Mom," I said, watching Dani head for the back door to go out and double-check. Catching unsecured horses can be arduous, and we had seven of them out there. Dani had grown up chasing animals that got out of their fences, so she wasn't taking any chances.

My mom frowned. "No it's not," she said defiantly. "They were over there yesterday." She pointed to the open field next to their pasture that wasn't fenced in.

I stared at my mother, not understanding. "That's not possible," I said, the first chilled fingers of concern walking up my back. "They don't go out of that pasture unless someone's riding them." I glanced at my dad. He was staring at me like he was trying to tell me something, but he didn't speak. I didn't know what he was trying to communicate with his eyes. "What?" I asked him, feeling mildly alarmed now. He shook his head and looked back out the window.

Dani came back in, a little breathless, and said quietly to me, "The horses are fine. Nobody got out." She sat down heavily in the chair, clearly relieved. "Oh, good," I said distractedly. I was more worried about what my mother had just said.

"Tell us again what you saw, Mom," I said. "You said the horses were over in that field?" I pointed straight out the window to the barren field.

My mother nodded eagerly, like a child trying to please a parent. "Right there!" she exclaimed, now pointing to the barren field. "They were running around and playing." She looked at us expectantly. I saw her expression. She had dementia face.

I was now thoroughly confused and even more alarmed because of that look. She seemed unfazed and went back to eating. My dad looked at me, again like he was trying to communicate something. I was going to need to get him alone for a minute and find out what was going on.

"Okay," I said, trying to lighten my tone. "Well, they seem to be where they're supposed to be now." I paused, watching her. She appeared to be unaware of the concern she was causing.

"Well, good," she said, her tone indicating the matter was closed. She turned her head and looked at my older son, Sam, who was sitting next to her. "How was school today, Sam?" she asked.

Old enough to realize something strange and significant had just happened that no one was talking about, Sam looked at me and Dani. I nodded at him slightly, indicating that he should just answer his grandmother's question.

"It was good," he said, then started chatting about friends and things he'd done.

As Sam continued, I looked at my dad again, trying to figure out how to get him on his own so I could find out what the hell had just happened. His looks back at me seemed to indicate that he knew.

I finally got my chance when my parents were leaving to head back to their house. As I was walking them to the door, my mom realized she'd forgotten her purse. She started to head back to the short flight of three steps that led to the living room, glancing sideways at my dad, hoping he'd offer to go get it for her. He seemed to know we needed to talk privately, so he didn't budge.

"We'll wait right here," I said to her. "Dani is up there and can help you if you can't find it."

She pursed her lips but went anyway.

I turned back to my dad and whispered, "What the hell happened back there?"

"I don't know," he said, keeping his voice low too. "But it's not the first time it's happened. She sees things." He shook his head, not sure how to describe it. I pressed him.

"Like what?" I asked urgently, aware that we didn't have much time before she'd be back.

He shook his head again. "I don't know, weird things. Like thinking the barn cats are our cats who've gotten outside," he said, looking over my shoulder toward the stairs where my mom would be back any second. "Or that the chickens are in the yard when they're not."

I stared at him, not fully understanding. "Like she's hallucinating?"

He shrugged. "Yeah, I guess so. She's seeing things that aren't there," he repeated, at an apparent loss for another way to describe it.

"Well, dinner was delicious, as always," he suddenly said in a voice too loud for the space. "Thank you for feeding us again." I heard my mom coming down the stairs.

"Always our pleasure," I said, matching his casual tone and volume. I turned around and feigned surprise at seeing my mom coming back down the short hallway. "Did you find your purse?" I asked, even though I could see it over her arm.

She frowned at me, the dementia face long gone. "Don't be silly," she said in her scolding tone. "It was right where I left it on the couch." She then waggled her finger at me and my dad and said suspiciously, "What were you two conspiring about over here?"

My dad made a show of rolling his eyes and sighing. "Nothing, dear," he droned. "Can't I just talk with my daughter without you thinking we're out to get you?"

"No," she retorted with a sharp laugh. "I know you two too well."

Dani came down the stairs and we all said goodnight. As we watched my parents walk back across the driveway to their house, I turned to Dani and said, "What the actual fuck was that about?"

She shook her head, smiling nervously. "I have no idea, but that was some creepy shit."

I agreed, turning back to make sure they'd made it to their house in the dark.

Looking Back Now

So much of what we experienced on this unpredictable journey with my mom fell into the category of not knowing what we didn't know. But in some ways, the beginning was the worst. Every experience felt like we were navigating something new. It had me feeling disoriented, behind the 8-ball as they say, and off-balance much of the time.

One of the ways I was caught off guard was through believing that everyone saw what we saw with my mom. It's easy to assume that everyone in your loved one's life witnesses the same behaviors, comes to the same conclusions about what's happening, and has the same ideas about what's best for your loved one. Based on my own experience and what I've heard from countless other caregivers, that's almost never true.

When relocation becomes necessary for the safety and well-being of your loved one, whether to a new home closer to or with family, or to a care facility, the move will likely not go as it does when someone unaffected by dementia moves. I thought it was early enough in her illness that we had time to get her moved and settled before it got worse. I didn't understand how much the moving process itself would exacerbate her symptoms.

There were simply so many things I wasn't even aware I didn't know at that point. Looking back now, I wish I'd realized a few things:

➢ Family and friends of your loved one may not see what you see in the early days of the disease. People with dementia can be very skilled at "masking" in the early stage, which means they're able to hide their mistakes and confusion. You may feel like family and friends are calling your judgment into question, which can lead you to feel uncertainty, anger, and other strong emotions. That's completely normal.

➢ Family members and friends of your loved one are also affected by the dementia diagnosis and may have a wide range of opinions about what's best for them. It's important to hear them out because being heard makes them feel better, in and of itself. But it's also important to make decisions based on what you believe to be in the best interest of your loved one. It's okay if not everyone agrees. If the best interests of your loved one are at the center of each decision you're making, it's okay to proceed.

➢ Ask questions of your loved one's doctors and do some research on the type of dementia diagnosis you receive and what to expect. Call the doctor for a phone or video consultation if asking questions in front of your loved one isn't feasible or too uncomfortable. My mom's diagnosis of MCI didn't tell us much about what to expect, and I didn't ask. I was afraid of her reactions in the moment if I had, and once we were back at home, it simply didn't occur to me that I might need more information until we started seeing confusing and alarming behavior. Forewarned is forearmed, as they say.

➢ A good therapist can be a critically important partner to support you throughout this journey. I didn't realize I needed one until about a year into my parents living on the farm. I wish I'd gotten one sooner to help me process what was happening and my emotions in response. It might've helped me lessen the effects of Karen's comments, which caused tremendous shame and uncertainty to rise within me.

➢ Every feeling you have is valid and allowed. No one gets to tell you what's "normal" to feel during this time, or at any time. You're going to get through this. Trust yourself, take care of yourself (for real), and just keep doing your best. That's all you can do.

CHAPTER 4

"I'M NOT CRAZY!"

In the short time between starting the move and finishing it, we noticed many small changes in my mom. My dad reported her becoming more forgetful about activities they'd planned, especially noticing that she'd get frustrated very easily when she couldn't keep everything straight in her mind. They'd be heading down to Detroit for a social function with friends, and she'd forget how to get where they were going even though they'd both lived in Detroit their entire lives. She'd argue with my dad the whole time that they were "going the wrong way" or that the person they were visiting "doesn't live there." When he'd ask her which way she wanted him to go, not wanting to fight with her and for her to just be fine, they'd end up lost for hours, missing the activity or appointment altogether.

My parents had unpacked what they could fit and were now starting to fill the shed with boxes of things they wanted to keep but had no room for in the carriage house. My mom had a tendency to get frustrated easily and quickly when she couldn't find something. She'd be convinced that something had been in the initial load they'd moved from their house, only to realize it wasn't. These small incidents and others like them began to add up, and I started having a bad feeling in the pit of my stomach that would never fully go away.

My mother regularly asked me in an exasperated voice to come and help them "get organized." Her bluster, frustration, defensiveness, and anger quickly had me rising to the bait, and those visits ended with a fight more often than not. I'd storm out and stomp back past the barn to my house, muttering under my breath about what a mistake we'd made in moving them up here.

We had a particularly disturbing exchange one day when I came to help. Determined to maintain my cool (as I always was starting out), I'd cleared my desk of work responsibilities for the day and was convinced I'd be successful in keeping the peace since my stress level was relatively low. As I walked into my parents' house, singing out a hello to them, I heard them arguing upstairs. The little house had a half-second floor, meaning it had only half the square footage as the main floor. It's where the primary bedroom was, along with a large landing area and the only full bath at the time. The stairs were steep, as the building had originally been built as a pole barn and was then converted to this carriage house later on. I climbed the stairs, listening to them to try to understand what was going on.

"Don't tell me it's not here!" my mother shouted. "I've already seen it and moved it to another room! Stop acting like I'm losing my mind!" My dad was at his limit, growling at her while turning on his heel and walking out of the bedroom as I got to the landing.

"What's going on?" I asked him quietly. But she heard me and spoke first.

"Don't you two start!" she screeched.

I bristled, instantly ready to fight.

"Don't start talking about me like I'm not here!" she went on. "I'm not crazy!" Her voice cracked and she started to cry. She sat down heavily on the bed and covered her face with her hands. I could see they were trembling as I walked over to her. "Without my Paxil, I'm such an emotional mess," she whimpered through her hands. "I never used to cry at anything!"

I sat down on the bed beside her and put my arms around her in an awkward side hug, immediately compassionate at her distress. "It's okay, Mom," I said softly, laying my cheek on her heaving shoulder. My tenderness seemed to only make her cry harder. "It's okay," I said again.

After a couple of minutes, she sat up straighter, gently pushing my arms off her and reaching for a box of tissues on the nightstand. I sat and waited while she pulled herself together. My dad had gone downstairs.

"What's going on?" I asked her, still keeping my tone soft.

"Your father's trying to convince me that I'm losing my mind," she said, her voice rising again with accusation. Pounding her knee with one fist for emphasis on each word, she continued, "I know for. a. fact. that we brought that old corner table with the spindly legs that was Grandma and Papa's table." She paused, turning to look at me. "It's almost black. Do you know which one I'm talking about? It sat on the landing going upstairs at our house."

I nodded that I knew which one she meant.

"Well, there is no way I would have left that table behind. It was my parents' table and has been in my family for generations!" Her voice broke again. "And in fact, I remember moving it from up here to downstairs in the living room!" She was angry again.

I suddenly remembered watching her struggle to carry the table in question from the landing in their Detroit house down to the living room in their Detroit house on the initial moving day. I remembered arguing with her about it because she was already unsteady on stairs and I'd been worried she was going to fall. I'd rushed over to try to help her, scolding her for trying to move it alone, and we'd ended up snapping at each other for the thousandth time that day. But I remembered her taking it to the living room after getting it down the stairs. In their Detroit house. Not the carriage house.

"Mom," I started, sure that she just needed reminding of that incident, "that was in the Detroit house, remember? I saw you struggling to bring it downstairs, and I yelled at you about it? Remember that I argued with you that it shouldn't go in this first load because it wasn't an essential item?" I felt hopeful.

She turned on me. "Yes I remember," she snapped, swiping my hand off her arm and standing up. "And I remember that it was NOT down in Detroit, but at THIS house! You are all trying to convince me that I'm crazy!" She was screeching now as she walked away from me, heading for the stairs to go down and calling for my dad.

Instead of feeling angry, I felt scared. This was yet another example of things she seemed to be getting increasingly confused about. It felt like her cognitive impairment was accelerating quickly, and it terrified me. The ache in the pit of my stomach threatened to make me nauseous. Suddenly, I remembered the conversation with the social worker at the neurologist's office. She'd given us reading materials and contact information for the ALZ hotline. I remembered her saying it was a 24/7 line that could help in moments of crisis.

I went downstairs and said lamely, "I forgot something at home. I'll be right back." Too caught up in renewing their argument, neither of them noticed. I walked out and headed back to my house, pulling my phone out of my pocket as I went. I needed to find the number for the hotline. I needed answers.

"How can I help?" the woman's voice said calmly and kindly. It undid me.

"I'm not sure," I said through my tears. "Something is wrong with my mom. She's got a diagnosis of mild cognitive impairment, but this is way worse than it was just a few weeks ago. I don't know what to do." I was trying to hold it together, not sure what to ask for.

"Just a moment, ma'am," said the kind, patient voice. "Let me connect you with one of our social workers."

I waited, and after a moment another kind and patient voice was on the line. "How can I help?"

"I'm not sure, honestly," I said with a little laugh. "My mom got this diagnosis about a month ago, maybe a little more now. Up until recently, we just noticed a little forgetfulness. Now she's seeing things that aren't there, or at least aren't correct, like thinking the barn cats outside are actually her house cats that have escaped from the house." I spoke in a rush. "Now she's arguing with me and my dad about things we just know aren't true, but she's convinced they are, or at least that they happened in one place but really they happened in a different place. It just feels like a significant escalation of her dementia, like it's going super-fast, and we don't know what to do." I finally paused. "I'm sorry, I feel like I must sound like *I'm* the one losing my mind!"

"No, no, not at all," came the reassuring voice. "Have there been any significant changes in your mother's life recently?"

"Yes," I said. "We've been moving them from their house in Detroit up here to North Branch near Lapeer, where we have a farm. They're moving into the carriage house. We made the initial move a couple weeks ago."

"Okay," she said. "That helps me a lot, thank you. What your mom is experiencing is totally normal. When people with dementia go through significant changes to their living space, routines, or environment, it can cause a temporary state of much more significant symptoms." Her voice was calm and reassuring.

"Oh my god," I cried, panic coming over me. "Was Karen right? Did we make a huge mistake by moving them up here?!" I crumpled into a dining room chair, my hand to my mouth in horror. "We were trying to help!"

"No, no," she soothed. "Moves are often necessary for your loved one's own safety and well-being. These changes are most often temporary. Once she gets settled into the new house, she should return to her former level of symptoms within a few months."

I barked a short laugh through my tears. "Great," I said sarcastically. "We're not through it yet. This is going to drag on for another month at least. We have to finish cleaning out their house and getting through the actual closing."

"I understand," she said. "If at all possible, try to keep your mother away from the moving process. Try not to encourage her to be involved. Make decisions about things the best you can with your other family members. The more your mother is involved, the more her symptoms may become worse."

I felt drained, knowing there was no way in hell we could keep my mother away from the moving process. "Yeah, that's not going to be an option," I said. "She's a pretty controlling woman. She insists on being at the center of everything and won't let anyone make decisions without her."

"I understand," she said again. "You can only do your best."

I nodded, knowing she couldn't see me. "Okay," I said, not feeling very reassured. "Thank you for your help."

"Anytime," she said. "And I mean that. We're here 24/7. Anytime you need to call, you can. For reassurance, for help with whatever is happening with your mom, or for information. That's why we're here." She paused, but when I didn't say anything, she continued. "It's okay," she said softly. "What you're feeling is completely normal. And it sounds like you care about your mom very much. Don't forget to take care of yourself, too."

That brought my tears full force again. I barely managed a "goodbye and thank you" before hanging up and giving into sadness, grief, shame, helplessness, and anger.

With closing day on the sale of my parent's house fast approaching, we had a very long way to go to get the house cleared out. My brother decided to gather a few friends and his girlfriend and spend the day speeding up the process, and we'd gotten a dumpster for hauling out all the stuff that needed to be trashed. I decided to stay home that day to give myself a break from the whole ordeal and let David have a turn dealing with our mother.

Remembering the social worker's advice, I tried to talk my mom into staying up at the farm with me. But she wouldn't hear of it. She waved me away with her hand, walked away from me, and made all sorts of dismissive "you're ridiculous" noises every time I suggested it. I even tried to bribe her with an offer to get a pedicure with me, but she would not be swayed. She was going.

I'd shared with my dad and David the social worker's advice, and while we all agreed that it made sense, we felt equally powerless in doing anything to change her mind about being at the center of things. It completely went against her nature. So when I warned my brother that our parents were coming to help him and his friends, "Great" was all he said, his voice dripping with sarcasm. I smiled, in both recognition of our shared family trait to say "great" in that way and delight that I wouldn't have to be there. The farm felt more peaceful when they weren't there, and there was so much tension and anxiety radiating off my mother at any given time that I didn't realize how much it affected me until they weren't there.

Since it was rare that I was at the farm when they weren't, I sat out on our expansive deck overlooking the barn, pasture, fields, large pond, and woods stretching all across the back of our property, and I relaxed. I sipped my coffee while listening to the spring birds and watching the horses graze. They all looked across in my direction when I came out onto the deck, so I shouted a greeting to them, feeling happy as I sat down.

My parents had planned to stay overnight with one of their close friends so they could work on the house for two days in a row, which made sense since the drive from the house to the farm was long. That evening, Dani, the boys, and I enjoyed dinner in front of the TV, something we never did while my parents were there, and we watched some movies. Everyone's mood was light, and I remember feeling like I had some reprieve from a physical weight on my shoulders.

Late that evening, David called to tell me about the day. The boys had gone to bed, and Dani and I were still on the couch. I put the phone on speaker so she could hear him too.

"So," I said with a smile, "how'd it go?"

"It was a fucking nightmare," he began.

Dani and I both laughed at his tone. He's a great storyteller, always finding just the right balance of humor to offset the trauma of the situation he's describing. I knew this was going to be interesting.

"Do tell," I said. "I'm so glad to know we're not the only ones in hell."

"Definitely not," he said, then began the story. "We got there before Mom and Dad did. I'd hoped to get a bunch of shit into the dumpster that Dad said could be thrown out before they got there, so we started right away. But we didn't get as far as I'd hoped before they rolled up. So then Mom, of course, wanted to know what we'd already thrown away and started screeching at me. It just went downhill from there. There was some arguing throughout the day between her and Dad, and her and me, but the worst came when we got to the cat trees."

He paused, and Dani giggled in anticipation. "Oh boy," I said, also giggling. "What happened?"

"Do they have a cat tree up there at the new house?" he asked. "Because at this point, I'm not sure if I'm also losing my fucking mind, we went round and round so many damned times."

I looked at Dani, trying to picture their little house's living room. She nodded. "Yes, they brought the newer bigger one they had up here," she said loud enough for David to hear.

"That's what I thought," he said. "Okay, good, I'm not losing my marbles then. Well, they have like three other fucking stupid little cat trees in that den. And Mom became convinced that one of those old smaller cat trees is *the* cat tree that they need to take up there. I tried every which way to Sunday to convince her that they already had one up there and it was bigger than any of these. Dad tried to convince her. Keefer [one of my brother's closest college friends who my mom adored] tried to reassure her. Nothing worked. I finally just put the damned cat tree into the dumpster and told her that she could get it out herself if she wanted it."

I wasn't laughing now. I could picture the scene. I knew how my mom must've been feeling, as I'd come to realize how much she used bluster, anger, and attacks on others to mask her own fears.

My brother continued. "Well, that didn't work because she kept screaming at me. I couldn't take it, so finally I just plucked the fucking thing out of the dumpster and threw it across the yard."

I gasped. Dani did too, but she was having a hard time controlling her laughter. She found the whole thing unbelievable and hilarious in its unbelievability. I was horrified.

"Oh no, David," I breathed. "Did you hit her with it?"

"No," he said, "of course not. I was just pissed beyond belief. No one got hurt. Well, except the cat tree. It broke."

I wasn't sure how to feel. I knew all too well the burning rage that went along with our mother not believing me when I was telling her something she simply remembered differently in her dementia-affected brain. I could imagine our mother feeling confused and scared about everything as well as angry in her belief that her son was throwing out her cat tree. But I also saw the ridiculousness of the situation and found humor in how David told the story. His frustration reaching that boiling point was something I was living on nearly a daily basis. I was relieved that I wasn't the only one who gave into it and exploded. The mix of intense emotions left me shaken.

As summer began, things seemed to quiet down. The accelerated symptoms we'd seen with my mom during the move begin to fade somewhat. My parents closed on the house as planned, and all their trips down to the old house stopped. Or so I thought.

Since my parents had been heavily involved in their old neighborhood, my mother was not about to give up attending major community events, many of which my parents had been attending and helping put together for over 30 years. Nor was she ready to stop attending the Tuesday morning coffee club that met at a neighborhood coffee shop in Detroit. They'd leave early Tuesday morning, by 7:30 a.m. when they could manage it, and stay all day, working in the community garden and visiting various friends. But they always made sure to be back in time to eat dinner with us. It felt like it was more about the free meal and a chance to point out all the ways in which my mom was still fully functioning than it was about enjoying our company.

One morning, after one of their visits down to the old neighborhood, my dad stopped by our house without my mom. Though she didn't "allow" him to come over to our house to chat without her, stopping by for a tool or to do some small task was okay with her. So he came under the pretense of borrowing something from our garage.

"So, it sounds like everything went great down in Detroit yesterday," I said. "Did it really?"

He'd come prepared to talk, so he didn't hesitate. "No. Your mother can't keep anything straight anymore. She tells stories about things and gets all mixed up. She'll start talking about one thing from the farm, and then pretty soon she's throwing in pieces from stories of things that happened when we lived in Detroit."

"Oh boy," I said. "Does she get tripped up? Like, hesitate or get frustrated?"

"No. That's the worst part. She just keeps talking like she has no idea that she's mixing things up. And if she does realize it, or like on the one occasion that I pointed it out to her, she gets really defensive."

I shook my head.

"Well, that's actually not the worst part," he continued. "The worst part is the number of people who've asked me privately if I'm sure something is wrong with her. They don't see it. They think she's acting like she always has. They sound like Karen, questioning whether we did the right thing by leaving the neighborhood."

"Oh no," I said. "What do you tell them?"

"I tell them that if they lived with her, they wouldn't be saying that."

Always a man of few words but a good storyteller, I waited to see if he'd say more. He didn't. "I'm sure that must be frustrating for you," I finally said.

"Yeah. It's annoying. But it also makes me feel bad because they don't see it. I don't want to say mean things about your mother behind her back, so I don't want to tell them what I see, but I also don't like them thinking we overreacted."

"I can understand that," I said. "But you don't live there anymore, so you don't have to deal with it any more than you want to. You guys don't have to keep going down there. You could try the seniors' group that's here in North Branch or the one down in Lapeer. You could look for things to do here instead of keeping one foot in the old neighborhood."

He shrugged. "Try telling your mother that," he said. "Oh, and then when we drive past the old house, she gets upset about the changes they're making to it. They've ripped out all of our old landscaping in the front. It looks terrible."

I stared. "Why would they do that? You guys had so many beautiful plants that came back every year."

"Not only the plants," he said quietly with tears in his eyes, "they took out the tree we planted."

"The one we planted with Liz's ashes?" I was heartbroken. Liz had been my parents' cat. They'd gotten her just after they'd gotten married, and she lived nearly 22 years.

He nodded sadly, wiping his eyes.

"Why would they do that?" I said again, incredulous. "That was a great little tree!"

He shrugged again.

"But wait, why do you keep going to the old house?" I asked, finally realizing that that probably wasn't helping my mom. "You need to just move on."

"Your mother insists," he said.

"So tell her no."

He looked away, out the window, saying nothing.

A minute later, he said he needed to get back before my mother started getting suspicious. I walked him out to the garage, and he grabbed a tool to take back with him.

Looking Back Now

The entire moving process felt like trying to strike a balance between not wanting to take my mom's autonomy from her (or at the very least to make sure that's not how she felt) and wanting to protect her from events that would serve only to exacerbate and accelerate her symptoms. Most people fight against the effects of getting older. We hear stories about it all the time. But my mom was 74, active, mobile, and independent. Her mind was the only thing we could point to as a limitation, and she wasn't ready to hear that.

My mother's dementia progressed in definitive ways during the whole process of the move, which lasted three full months from the time we began packing up until closing. Her usual need for control made it impossible to convince her not to participate in every single trip back and forth and every detail of every decision that needed to be made. I tried a few times to get my dad to just leave without her to go down to Detroit, offering to accept the blowback from her realizing she'd been left, but he couldn't bring himself to do it. He knew she'd rain holy hell down on him for it after the fact.

Had we known the move would exacerbate things so dramatically, we might've tried to keep her away from at least some of the process, like all the trips back and forth. But that very well could've had adverse consequences too. My mother was someone who derived her value and self-worth from being needed at the center of things. She hated being kept in the dark about anything, but she was especially intolerant of it when it was connected to her.

I also dramatically underestimated the effects stress would have on me during this journey. I wish I'd started with just breathing more in those early days. Looking back now, I wish I would've realized a few things at this point in the journey:

- ➢ When planning a move, which is often necessary for a loved one affected by dementia, consider ahead of time all the ways you can minimize the loved one's involvement. If possible, hire out some of the work to keep your own involvement to a manageable level, especially if you're also actively caregiving. Ask friends and family to help.
- ➢ If a move is in the best interest of your loved one, prepare yourself for an acceleration of symptoms. In most cases, according to the ALZ, it's temporary. After they've settled into the new place, you very well may see them return to the same level of dementia they showed prior to the move. Sometimes just knowing what to expect helps us handle it a little better.
- ➢ When dealing with someone who has a strong need for control and is fighting you on everything, try to remember that

it's happening because they're scared. People with dementia sometimes have a sense that they're being affected by the disease, and that causes fear, sadness, anger, and defiance. Reframing the reasons behind those emotions may help you keep some perspective and tap into your empathy. And if that doesn't work, it's okay to walk away for short periods of time. Go outside. Take deep breaths. Give yourself a minute. Or 10.

➢ Self-care is critical. Many of us, especially women, wave it off. We're so busy caring for others and taking care of our never-ending lists of tasks that we don't feel we have time to care for ourselves. I'm calling bullshit for you right now. Make the time. Start simple. There are many apps, books, YouTube videos, and local yoga studios where you can learn simple yet powerful breathing techniques to help you reduce stress, sleep better, and get back to your center when you get pushed off balance. Like they say, when your bucket is empty, you have nothing left to pour out to others.

CHAPTER 5

THE NEW NORMAL

O nce the move was over, we all tried in our own ways to settle into our "new normal," long before that phrase became popular. My parents were still unpacking, and my mom was endlessly rearranging papers, sure that she'd misplaced something critical. I'd taken a lot of time away from work, so I put my focus back on that. School would be out for the summer soon, and I knew I'd be distracted by the boys as much as I was distracted by my parents.

One of the mundane but important questions that arose was about what doctors my parents would see for their care now that they lived on the farm. For 30 years, my dad had worked in the carpenter shop of Henry Ford Hospital in downtown Detroit, so my parents had always used that hospital's doctors and facilities. Though they were abundant in that area, the closest one to the farm was nearly two hours away. There was an unaffiliated one about five minutes from the farm, but that didn't matter to my mother. She was insistent that they keep seeing their old doctors.

Before her diagnosis, my mother always managed all their healthcare appointments. While she never allowed my dad to go into the exam room with her, she always insisted on going in with him. Her justification was a continuation of her tendency to infantilize my father. She felt he couldn't be trusted to give full and accurate information to the doctor, nor to remember everything the doctor said and convey the information fully to her. At the same time, she insisted her superior communication skills meant that she'd always tell the doctor everything and never forget what she was told. She didn't always tell my dad everything the doctors said to her, but she justified that as well by claiming it was no one's business but her own. She was a very controlling woman, and this was just one more way she exercised that control.

With the MCI diagnosis, all of that changed. I was appointed my parents' primary power of attorney with my brother as secondary, and I started going to many of their doctor's appointments with them. I could tell that my mother fought an inner battle about this. On the one hand, she relished having all that extra time with me. On the other, she didn't like me asking too many questions or disclosing information she was omitting or had forgotten.

In the beginning, I traveled to these appointments with my dad driving their small SUV while my mom sat in the front seat and I sat in the back. I'd usually use the time to work from my phone, answering emails and trying to keep my business running. I sat behind my mom because they relied on me to give them directions, and my dad could hear me better if I wasn't directly behind him.

"Dad, you're going to be turning left onto a road coming up in two miles," I said on one of these early trips.

Trying to see me, my mom whipped her head to the side, but she couldn't turn far enough without moving her whole upper body. She fought to do that for a moment, which looked quite comical. I laughed as I leaned to one side to help her see me more easily.

"Don't you laugh at me," she snapped.

I laughed again, this time with incredulity. "Oh, come on. That was funny from where I'm sitting," I said, trying to keep things light.

She sat facing forward again. I could see her shoulders indicating her unhappiness and almost feel her lips pursing. I didn't understand why she was so enraged all of a sudden.

"What's the problem, Mom?" I asked, trying to sound concerned rather than annoyed.

She shook her head and said nothing at first, then blurted out, "It's not your job to give directions! It's mine!" She was tearful, which still caught me off guard. For more than 20 years, it had taken a lot to move my mom to tears. But the way she said it lit me the fuck on fire.

"Seriously?" I raised my voice. "Are you joking right now? You are the one who literally asked me to pull up directions on my phone and 'direct my father.'" I added that last part in a mocking voice, making fun of the way she talked, which was often through barking orders. "And now you want to be pissed off because I'm doing exactly what you asked? I can't." I was fuming and turned to look out the window. My dad just kept driving in silence.

When my phone indicated his turn was coming up quickly, I said in an exaggerated tone, "Mom, Dad needs to turn left at the next road. Can you please give him that direction?" I sounded like a snot even to my own ears, but I was so angry that I didn't care. My mother didn't respond.

There was no talking in the car for about five minutes. Since my dad would be following the road we were on for many miles, I went back to my email. One of my mother's new favorite CDs was playing quietly, one I'd given to her. It was by a band that did covers of a wide variety of songs in a folk music style. She loved it. Suddenly, she reached over and turned it up, turning to smile at my dad and humming. The side profile of her face showed no trace of the pouting and angry exchange we'd just had. I stared in silence.

"Ron, why aren't you singing?" she asked him, sounding genuinely surprised. I saw him glance at her with a slight frown on his face and knew he was also still thinking about the nasty exchange just a few minutes before.

My mom twisted her body around so she could see me. "You're not singing either!" She sounded just as genuinely surprised and turned back around. "You both have such beautiful voices. You should be singing."

I didn't feel like singing. I felt like screaming.

She started singing quietly, always very self-conscious of her voice and inability to sing on key. My dad cleared his throat and began to hum. By contrast, he had a beautiful voice, but it sounded forced. I remained quiet, feeling annoyed and confused about the sudden change in my mother's behavior.

A lively song came on a moment later and my mother sang louder, tapping out the beat on her legs. She looked over at my dad with a smile, no hint of anything from the previous conversation on her face. "That's more like it!" she said loudly over the music, then twisted around again to look at me. "Ellen, you're still not singing! Sing!" It was like she was manic.

"I'm not in the mood to sing," I retorted.

She twisted again, that surprised look back on her face, this time with a hint of concern. "But why not?" She looked and sounded completely innocent, and I knew she fully felt that way. I was perplexed, and it immediately gave way to fury.

"Are you fucking kidding me?" I screeched, startling my dad, who stopped singing. "You're like a crazy person right now! One minute you're super aggressive about me doing what you asked me to do, which was to give Dad directions. Then you get all weepy about it. Now you're acting like none of that just happened and being super surprised that I don't want to have a fucking family sing-along!? I just can't!" I was so mad, breathing hard. As she continued to quietly tap on her legs and hum, I felt like I was in an alternate universe.

"You know I do not like that word," she said curtly, enunciating each word through gritted teeth. "If you must use foul language, you will not be coming with us on these trips anymore."

I stared, mouth agape. It was like she thought we were on a field trip that was a privilege for me to attend rather than a doctor's appointment I'd been informed I now *had* to attend. I shook my head and went back to my phone.

While my mother sat looking out the window, tapping her legs and humming tunelessly along, I finished guiding my dad to the doctor's office. After their appointments and grabbing some lunch, we were heading back to the car for the long drive home when my mom said, "Ellen, why don't you drive since you know where you're going?" Her question sounded innocent enough, so my hackles stayed down.

"Sure," I said, holding out my hand for the keys from my dad. He dropped them into my hand. "Is that alright with you, Dad?"

He nodded. "Whatever makes your mother happy," he said, sounding resigned but not annoyed.

I headed for the driver's seat, and my mom went to the front passenger seat. My dad watched her for a second, then headed for the back seat. He has poor circulation in his legs, so it was really difficult for him to sit in the back seat of their car, being that it was a compact SUV and didn't have a lot of room. He couldn't move his legs back there. If he were to ride back there for over an hour, he wouldn't be able to walk by the time we got home.

"Wait, should you be sitting in the back?" I directed my question to my dad on purpose, wanting him to speak up for himself. "Wouldn't you be better off in the front seat?"

He shrugged, not looking at either of us. I could feel his aversion to more conflict rolling off him in waves. "It's fine," he said, opening the car door.

My mom seemed oblivious and opened her door. I frowned.

"Wait," I said again. "Dad, you won't be able to walk by the time we get home."

My mom paused and looked at me. "He said he'll be fine. I don't like riding in the back seat. I can't hear what's going on." She sounded incredibly entitled and self-absorbed.

I laughed without any humor. "Are you kidding?" I said. "Then he can just drive." I left the driver's side door open and headed around the car to get into the backseat. "I'm not having him sit in the back and then not be able to walk. That's absolutely ridiculous. Your need to be in the center of every conversation does not supersede his need to walk." My tone got increasingly angry with each sentence.

My mom threw up her hands in exasperation. "Fine!" she shouted. "Have it your way! I'll sit in the back like a child and you two can talk about me all you like!" She sounded like a child, for sure. A paranoid one.

My dad hadn't gotten in, knowing it would be difficult to get in and then have to get back out. He stood watching us both, waiting for us to make the decision so he could just follow directions and try to keep out of the line of fire. We all stood still for a moment, my mom and me locked in a battle of wills.

I raised my eyebrows at her. "It's up to you," I said, crossing my arms. "Either you sit in the back or I do. I'm not getting in the car if Dad has to sit in the back."

She glared at me full of hostility, then pushed my dad out of her way so she could climb into the back seat. She wasn't strong so he didn't even stumble, just took a step back and softly chuckled his nervous laugh. Once she had climbed in, he closed her door for her, shot me a quick smile over the roof of the car, and we both got into the front seats.

With my parents getting restless at the farm pretty quickly, we looked for ways to help keep them both socially active. Dani's brother told us there was a seniors' group that met twice a week in the school administration building, and we encouraged my parents to check it out. My mother resisted at first. She wasn't sure she wanted to meet new people. Even though she'd agreed to the move and was happy about it in some respects, it was clear that she was struggling to adjust to the dramatic change of location and lifestyle between urban Detroit and rural small-town farm life. We finally convinced them to just go check it out.

They'd been living at the farm for nearly six months by the time they went to their first group meeting. I kept watching out of my office window for their car to come back down the road because I was half-convinced they'd leave partway through. When they finally got back, I hurried to finish what I was doing so I could go hear how it had gone.

I walked across the driveway to their house as they were still gathering their things from the car. "So? How was it?" I asked hopefully.

My mom was half in the front seat, collecting her water bottle and purse, and my dad was standing next to the car waiting for her. "Great!" he said with enthusiasm. "They have two adjoining rooms. They play cards and other games in one room and do puzzles and knitting and crafts in the other. I learned to play Euchre!" He sounded like a little kid. I was glad to see he was so happy.

My mother finally pulled herself out of the car. I noticed she was frowning, and my shoulders slumped. "How did you like it, Mom?" I asked with trepidation. It would be just like her to decide something my dad had enjoyed so much was not someplace she wanted to go back to.

"It was fine, I guess," she said with a shrug. "The people seem nice enough." She frowned at my dad. "But your father left me alone with the puzzle group while he played cards," she said with disgust. She hated cards.

My dad clicked his tongue and rolled his eyes playfully. "You seemed to enjoy yourself just fine, Charlotte," he said gently.

That night at dinner, I brought up another group I'd been wanting to try out with my dad: an ALZ caregiver support group. There was one that met once a month in Lapeer, about 30 minutes away, and they had a meeting scheduled for the next evening. I'd read about it in the literature we'd gotten from the social worker at the initial neurologist appointments.

"I was thinking about trying out the support group tomorrow," I started. "Anyone want to go with me? Dad? Dani?" I looked hopefully at both of them. My dad tensed across the table and gave my mom a quick side glance. *Oh boy*, I thought. *There's been a conversation about this already.*

"I'd like to go," my mom said, a hint of defiance in her tone. "I'm not so far around the bend that I can't follow a conversation, for crying out loud."

I stopped eating and stared at her. "Mom, it's for caregivers, not for people affected by dementia," I said, keeping my tone soft. My heart went out to her, as I could clearly see her struggling to accept that our participation in this group was one more sign that she really did have dementia. That empathy was short-lived.

"Well too bad!" she nearly shouted while slamming down her fork, startling Sam who was sitting next to her.

I immediately met his big eyes and said quietly, "It's okay, son." To my mom, I said, "Mom, maybe they have support groups for people in the early stages like you." I was trying to keep my tone reasonable as my temper flared. "Let's look into that, okay?"

She was sulking now. Sam half-turned away from her, nibbling at his food. "May I be excused please?" he asked in a small voice.

I nodded and smiled reassuringly at him. As he got up, my mother glared, first at him and then at me.

"We've not finished our meal and he has not cleaned his plate," she snapped. "He shouldn't be allowed to leave the table!" That had been a hard and fast rule in their house when I was growing up. Everyone sat at the table to eat together. No one was allowed to begin eating until everyone was seated, and no one was allowed to leave the table until everyone was finished, which meant cleaning our plates. While we nearly always sat together to eat with our kids, Dani and I didn't feel it was healthy to make them clean their plates or important to stay until everyone else was done. As long as they excused themselves, it was fine with us for them to move along.

I noticed Robin on the other side of Dani watching the scene with huge eyes. Nearly three years younger than Sam, Robin is much quieter and more introverted than his brother. He saw me look over and turned his face to me, the same question in his eyes. I smiled at him. "Yes, you may be excused too, honey," I said softly.

My mother was clucking her tongue and shaking her head, clearly disapproving. "You're not raising them right," she said, stabbing at her food.

I glared at her, taking a breath to calm myself. "I'm sorry you feel that way," I said evenly, then paused for a second. "Well, I'll be going to that meeting tomorrow, Dad. I'd be delighted if you came with me." No one spoke for the rest of the meal.

The next morning, my dad found a reason to stop at our house alone. I gave him the details on the meeting and told him what time Dani and I planned to leave. My mom was fine to be left alone at that point, and the boys were old enough that they were also fine alone for a couple of hours, especially with my mom next door. He agreed to go with us and said he'd figure out how to tell my mom.

Dani and I were in our pickup truck waiting for him when he finally came dashing out the door of their carriage house like he was running away. He opened the door and climbed in as fast as his arthritis would allow, grunting from the effort. "Quick! Let's go before she changes her mind!" He chuckled his nervous laugh.

"I'm guessing you're only half-joking," I said as Dani pulled out of the driveway. I turned and looked at him in the back seat, which was more spacious than the front seat of his car. He chuckled again nervously and shrugged. "Wait, are you serious?" I asked. "She wasn't going to let you come with us?"

He shrugged again, finding his words. "Let's just say she's not excited about it. She thinks we're going to go there to talk about her and she hates that idea."

"Well we are," I said flatly. "She's got dementia and she's a fucking handful. We need help. At least I do, before I take her head off."

We drove to the Lapeer Library, all of us nervous. The group had about 10 people in attendance who welcomed us warmly. Each member went around the table introducing themselves and giving updates on the status of their loved one. I was struck by how calm and slightly sad everyone seemed to be. Most of the people there were caregiving for spouses like my dad was. There were a couple of people caregiving for a parent, but they were at a different stage of life than I was, many with grown children or even grandchildren. I was 44 at the time, and my mom was 74. Most of the people in the group were caring for loved ones at least 10 years older than my mom.

My dad didn't want to talk and looked at me imploringly when it was his turn. "Would you like me to talk about Mom?" I asked him quietly, trying not to laugh at his obvious discomfort. It was endearing, but it also made me sad. He nodded, and I began.

I introduced the three of us and gave a summary of where we'd started, the move, and the diagnosis. I talked about the challenges we were facing not only because of the dementia but because of my mother's nature. Just dealing with her regular personality was challenging enough, and the addition of dementia was adding layers of challenge I didn't know how to navigate. I got emotional, much to my horror, as no one else had shed a tear, even while describing some pretty sad situations. Everyone was very kind and understanding. A few shared tips about things they'd tried when facing the earliest stages like we were.

By the time we left, I felt like a weight had been lifted and knew I'd go back. I asked Dani and my dad how they felt about it.

"Everyone seemed nice," my dad said. "But I'm not a talker. I enjoyed listening, but at the same time it's scary to hear some of what we might go through," he said, his voice catching.

I glanced at him, giving him an empathetic smile. "I know," I said softly. "But at the same time, it feels reassuring to me to know that we're not alone."

"I agree," Dani said. "I think this group will be a great resource for us as we go down this road. I think it will be especially important for the two of you to keep going."

I looked at her. "You don't want to go too?" I wanted her to go with us. She was my lifeline, and having her there gave me strength and comfort.

She smiled at me, glancing over as she drove us home. "I'll go whenever I can, babes," she said reassuringly. "But we do have kids and a farm, and your mom isn't going to be fine on her own forever. I'm just saying that if someone needs to stay home, it should be me."

I felt a little better. "Well, if my grandma's progress is any sort of gauge, we've got literally years in front of us before she can't be left alone. Like, at least ten."

I looked out the window as we drove, remembering my grandmother's slow, steady decline into Alzheimer's. Little did I know that my mom would be gone long before then. And her decline would be anything but slow or steady.

One afternoon a couple of weeks later, I was at the carriage house helping my mom sort through some clothes. She hadn't had time to sort through them all before the move, so she'd brought them with her. It had always been difficult for her to decide what she liked wearing and what she didn't. She was very self-conscious about her body and had very strong opinions about what she thought was flattering and what wasn't. At the same time, she didn't trust her own opinion about what looked good on her. For that, she often turned to me.

We managed to get through the process without fighting. She trusted my opinion, and I was comfortable giving it, so the afternoon was pleasant. She was having a pretty lucid day, so there weren't any squabbles about remembering things incorrectly either.

After we went back downstairs to the kitchen, I started getting ready to head back to my house to start dinner. "Before you go," my mom said, "there's something I want to talk to you about."

My stomach did a flip-flop. Something about her tone put me on my guard. "O-kay," I said slowly.

She busied herself straightening little things on the counter while avoiding looking at me. "I can't end up like my mother," she said quietly, still avoiding my eyes. "You can't let that happen."

I stared at her, waiting for her to say more. When she didn't, I said, "What exactly do you mean?"

"I watched my mother live her own worst nightmare," she said, looking at me now, her eyes shiny with tears. "She was a highly educated woman who wrote books and guided tours for people to learn about history. I watched her be reduced to wearing a diaper, drooling, unable to feed herself or do anything else for herself, mute, and miserable." She was crying now. "That can't happen to me," she whispered. "You can't let it."

I was fighting my own tears now, remembering how hard the final visits with my grandma had been and trying to imagine watching my mom live through a similar hell. Then I frowned, thinking of the fact that assisted suicide is illegal in Michigan, and I sobered. "Wait, what are you asking me to do?" I said warily.

"Whatever you have to," she said. "Crush pills and feed them to me in yogurt or applesauce. I don't do pain, so don't do something that will hurt. You just do it once you know I don't understand what's happening anymore. There was a point in time with Grandma when I knew she didn't know what was going on anymore. That's when I wish I had helped her. And that's when I want you to help me."

I stared at her in disbelief. "You've obviously given this some thought," I said, frowning. My dad walked into the kitchen then. "Do you know about this?" I asked him.

He looked defiant but said nothing. My mother answered instead. "Yes, and he's already told me what a sin suicide is in his Catholic church, so he won't help me." She sounded irritated but looked genuinely scared when she looked back at me. "So I'm counting on you."

"Mom," I said, continuing to stare, "I have kids. I'll go to jail." I couldn't believe she was asking this of me.

She shook her head. "Only if someone asks for an autopsy. Just you and your father and Dani will know about it. If none of you requests an autopsy, they won't do one. And no one will know." She looked determined now, tears gone. She was serious.

I shook my head, trying to clear the whole conversation away. "Mom, I have to think about this," I said, turning to the door. "This is a lot. This is asking a lot." I turned back, not wanting to tell her no and cause her to sink into despair, but also not wanting to commit murder in the eyes of the state. "I'll tell you what," I said while walking back to her and taking her hands in mine, "I promise you that I will be with you every step of this journey, no matter what." I locked eyes with her. She was tearing up again, causing me to do the same. "I will not leave you. And I will do everything in my power to make sure you don't suffer. I promise you that."

She nodded, then lost her fight to hold back her tears. I hugged her, looking at my dad who was also crying. He shook his head to indicate he didn't agree, then walked out of the room. I pulled away from my mom.

"Now, I'm going to go home and make some dinner," I said, wiping my eyes. "That day is a long, long way away. But we're all going to be hungry soon, so let's focus on what's in front of us and we'll worry about the other thing when the time comes."

She blew her nose and wiped her eyes. "Just promise me you'll think about it," she whispered.

I looked at her, my heart in my throat. "I promise," I whispered back. And I walked out the door.

As we endured the new daily life routines on the farm, my mom did return to a similar level of dementia she'd had prior to the move, just as the staff from the ALZ hotline said was likely. But that didn't mean everything was rainbows and unicorns. It meant that this was the normal reality of the relationship between me and my mother, which put everyone else on edge.

As combative as my mother and I were, my parents wanted me at the carriage house quite a bit to help with various things. Much of the time, it felt like my mom was just making something up to have an excuse for me to go over there. I can't count the number of times I walked back spitting fire, shaking and muttering with fury about something she did or said. Just as often in that first year, she'd storm away from my house, shouting to my father—loud enough to make sure I could hear her—that they were going to have to move someplace else because she couldn't live there any longer.

But my mother wasn't just becoming a little forgetful like my grandma had. She had plenty of moments when she was perfectly lucid, and others when she had dementia face and made no sense. She also started hallucinating more and more. It was jarring for me, to say the least. I was never quite sure which mother I'd encounter, and she'd slip in and out of lucidity in one conversation. I said to Dani often during that time, "If this wasn't so personal with it being my mom, it would be absolutely fascinating to watch."

Since I'd been fighting with my mother literally my whole life, I was used to it. My hard-wired nature is not averse to conflict, and neither was hers. My dad was also used to it, even though he hated how much we argued and would say something sharply to one or both of us when he reached his limit. When that happened, my mom and I both felt chastened, as though we were two fighting kids who'd been scolded by a parent. It always caused us to either abruptly end the argument or resort to arguing through gritted teeth in hushed, hissing tones. (Thinking back on it now makes me chuckle. It was ridiculous.)

But Dani and the boys had never lived with me and my mom in proximity like this, with daily interactions and my parents at our dinner table nearly every night. The stress levels became high for all of us. Dani was more tense than normal and would often excuse herself to go outside to work on random things in the barn or one of the pastures. When I'd ask her about it, she'd share that she couldn't handle the amount of arguing my mom and I were doing. It was totally foreign to how she'd been raised. Her own parents fought viciously at times, but it wasn't part of the daily undercurrent of how they communicated. It made her very uncomfortable to witness the arguments between me and my mom. Given her own hard-wired natural tendencies to avoid conflict, she dealt with it by leaving the scene whenever possible.

This period of time is when we really started living the tangling of the web and riding the roller coaster. Unbeknownst to us all, we'd just been sitting at the edges, waiting in line.

Looking Back Now

Adjusting to living in very close proximity to my parents for the first time since college was, well, an adjustment. Waiting for my mother to scold me, criticize me, or pick a fight with me, I felt constantly on edge. I now imagine she was feeling much the same way. Without the benefit of distance at that time, and with the intense stress of not only our "normal" relationship but also her increasing symptoms of dementia, neither of us benefited from the gift of insight. We weren't able to change the script in the moment.

Given how well-worn the pathways of communication were between us, I'm not sure anything anyone could've said at the time would've changed them. However, looking back now, I realize it might've helped me feel less alone, less angry, and less inadequate had I known a few things:

➢ The nature of your relationship with your loved one prior to dementia is likely to be the nature of your relationship with them during dementia. If you've always had tension and argued, you're still going to do that, maybe even more than before. If you were best friends, you're probably going to experience a lot more sadness and have more patience for the changes. Dementia happens in stages. It didn't fundamentally change my relationship with my mom. It won't likely change yours in a dramatic way either.

➢ Support groups for caregivers exist all over the country. In more densely populated areas, there are sometimes support groups for people in the early stages of dementia. Find one for yourself as a caregiver. If you need to find someone to stay with your loved one while you attend, do whatever you have to do to make it happen. It's the only group of people I've met with whom you can laugh at things that happen. In other settings, laughing would seem cruel. Strong bonds are formed in these groups, and their members genuinely support one another.

➤ The stress of living with someone who has dementia will take a toll on everyone in the house. If you've got multiple generations living together as we did, carve out time to talk with the kids to help them understand what's happening and why, and prepare them as much as possible for "weird" things your loved one might do or say. Everyone handles it differently, so make sure everyone gets support regardless of age and relationship to the person affected.

➤ I've said it before, and I'll probably say it again because it's so incredibly critical: keep a journal. Whether you write, voice record, type on a computer, or use some other form of keeping a log of events and feelings, do it. Make sure to include dates, your observations or descriptions of events, and your feelings about all of it. It's not only hugely cathartic to get it out of your system but also serves you later when you need to reflect over a three- to six-month period at a doctor's visit and want to remember accurately what has changed.

PART 2

STUMBLING MY WAY THROUGH

About a year into my parents living at the farm in the carriage house, it became clear that my mom did not have Alzheimer's but something very different. It was nothing like what we'd gone through with my grandmother. There were certainly phases when my grandma became very paranoid and lashed out, and there were times when we were visiting when it became obvious that she wasn't living in the present, nor did she recognize us. But my grandma never described seeing things that weren't there nor hallucinating like my mom did regularly. She also never seemed completely lucid for more than a moment here and there once the disease set in.

We stumbled our way through the experience, with me at the helm but my mother still fighting to be at the helm while chastising me for not doing enough at the helm. The hallmarks of this part of the journey were the takeovers. It was no longer safe for my mom to handle my parents' finances. She couldn't settle herself. She wasn't able to tell the doctors everything that was happening with her. And yet, she still had plenty of moments of lucidity when she'd lash out at me, at my dad, and occasionally at other people because we were trying to help.

My mom had always been a robustly built woman, standing 5'10" and weighing pretty close to two hundred pounds. The move to the carriage house in early 2017 coincided with losing much of her sense of smell, which is common with dementia. Smell is connected to taste, and she started eating less and not feeling as hungry as she always had before. By the beginning of 2018, she'd lost 50 pounds without trying.

This part of our journey was complicated and messy. I was desperately trying to get my hands on any and every resource to help us while trying to hold my family together, run a business, and support my dad in caring for my mom. It was exhausting on every level, and there were many days when I wasn't sure I could keep going.

This is the stage when shame set in. The messages in many books I read, classes we attended, and social media we saw were painting a picture of a very different experience than we were having. I started to believe that I must, in fact, be doing it all wrong. No matter what I did, it wasn't enough. My mom would still be upset, angry, or hostile.

We came to understand that the only thing we could expect was the unexpected. We all felt like we were on a roller coaster and couldn't get off. At the same time, we were so consumed by navigating everything that we couldn't stop and think about what to do next, how to cope better, or just regroup.

If you're in this middle stage with your loved one, my heart goes out to you. This was the toughest part of the journey for me. There's no way to pretty it up.

Whatever you have to do, you can't do it if you don't take care of yourself. The thing I regret most about this period is how poorly I did with self-care. I know you're thinking that you don't have time, you can't, you have too much to do, and/or that everyone else's needs must come first. I'm here to tell you that's a dangerous road that can lead to serious consequences on your health. If you go downhill, you won't be able to support anyone.

Just remember this: it's fine until it's not.

CHAPTER 6

THE FARM AND THE CIRCUS

By 2018, we'd become a real hobby farm. We had a herd of seven horses and donkeys, over 30 chickens, many goats, and a lot of barn cats. We'd raised meat chickens and turkeys and put up fencing ourselves (with some help from family and friends), enclosing roughly 10 acres for two large pasture areas. It was a lot of work, and Dani and I loved it.

My dad loved it too. He'd spent summers growing up with his best friend on their family's farm down in Alabama. Every time he talked about it, he'd use a ridiculous southern accent. He loved helping us with anything we'd let him. When we were going to get home late or had to leave early in the morning, he was always happy to have an excuse to be the one to feed all the animals and lock up the chickens at night.

My mom was less excited about some of the animals, as they were sometimes noisy and smelly. She also didn't like the chickens and wasn't happy that the coop was behind their house down a little hill. She'd always been a little afraid of birds and their flapping wings. She didn't like it when the chickens pecked at each other and was terrified when they'd flock toward her patio to clean up the birdseed.

But she loved the peaceful, quiet, beautiful space. The farm was the last on a dead-end road. From our driveway, you could walk a mile down a dirt road past fields and woods until you came to a river where the road ended. My parents took daily walks down that road. I'd sometimes go with them when my work schedule allowed.

One such day, we'd returned from a nice walk and were chatting in my parents' driveway. I was standing facing them and their house, my back to the barn and my house. Suddenly, my mom frowned and pointed, exclaiming, "Ron, what is that?!"

Immediately alarmed, I turned around quickly and looked in the direction of the barn where she was pointing. "What?" I asked urgently. "What is it?"

"Right there!" she shouted, pointing wildly at the opening between the barn doors. "It's a man! He just went into the barn!" She was whisper-yelling now.

My blood went cold and my heart stopped. "Fuck," I muttered. "Dad, did you see him?" I started walking toward the barn, my mind racing, trying to think who could be there. There was no other car in the driveway besides ours, but I couldn't see around to the front of our house. We had a long circular driveway, and sometimes people who didn't know us parked there. I was looking around wildly, trying not to panic.

"No, I didn't see anyone," my dad said, keeping his voice low while walking toward the barn with me.

We walked up the ramp to the barn doors, cautiously looking around. I didn't see anyone. I pushed one of the doors open wide to let the light in. There was no one there. My dad and I looked at each other.

"This has been happening more and more," my dad said in a low voice so my mom couldn't hear. "She's seeing things. It's creepy."

"Who is it, Ron?" My mom's voice sounded like she was getting a little hysterical. "Who's there?!" Whatever she'd seen, it had clearly scared her.

"No one, dear," my dad said calmly as I walked further into the barn, looking around to be sure. "It must've been a trick of the light."

My heart began to slow down, and the adrenaline rush hit me. I sat down hard on a bale of hay to gather my wits. "That scared the shit out of me," I said quietly to my dad, who was still in the doorway, keeping an eye on both of us. He chuckled his nervous laugh.

I got up and walked back outside. "No one there, Mom," I confirmed. "Did you see what he looked like or what he was wearing?" I was still mildly concerned.

"No," she said. "I just saw the movement of him going inside." She was calming down now, seeing that I was calm. She seemed to mirror my emotions a lot.

"Okay, well, Dad might be right. It might've just been a trick of the light," I said reassuringly. "I'm going to head back to the house now. I've got some work to do today. I'll see you guys at dinner." I waved and walked back to the house. When I got to our back door and looked back at them, they were slowly walking back to their house, my mom holding onto my dad's arm.

A couple of days later, Dani and I were finishing making dinner while my parents chatted with us in the kitchen. My mom was looking out the window to the pastures and barn. She was facing the window, hands on her hips, swaying slightly. Suddenly she jumped, like something had startled her.

I frowned. "You okay, Mom?"

We all stopped what we were doing and watched her. She was still facing the window but pointing out to the big pasture.

"The acrobats did a trick and one of them fell to the ground!" She sounded excited more than worried.

We all looked at each other, confused and alarmed. To get a better view, my dad went to look out the window of the dining room, which was adjacent to the kitchen. The pasture was empty.

"Sorry, what did you say?" I asked, sure I'd misheard her.

"The acrobats!" She sounded impatient now. "They were doing a trick, and one dropped the other one. I think they were supposed to catch her, but she fell right to the ground." She paused. We were all speechless. "Oh, look at the clowns!" She clapped her hands in delight, then turned toward me suddenly. "El, do you remember when you were a clown?"

I was totally confused. "Ye-es," I said slowly. I'd been about nine years old when our neighbor across the street was in a clowning group and invited me to join them in a parade. I'd had fun but didn't really feel like it was my thing. "There are clowns out there now?"

"Yes, right there!" She sounded impatient, as though we were all stupid for not being able to see what she was seeing. "Don't you see the giant orange tent they have?" she asked with snark.

Dani and I walked into the dining room and stood next to my dad. I gave him a side glance. He had a faint smile, which confused me more. "Umm, can't say that I do . . ." I said slowly, not sure how to handle this. "What else do you see?"

She sighed impatiently, then said sarcastically, "I suppose you don't see all the animals either? The horses, the tigers?"

Dani stepped in. "Do you think it's a circus or a carnival?" she asked without a trace of sarcasm.

"Oh, I think it's a circus," my mom said, sounding confident. "Carnivals usually have rides, and I don't see any of those, do you?"

"Nope," said Dani. "I don't." She looked at me and smiled, raising her eyebrows in a way that indicated she thought my mom was losing it.

We all drifted back to the kitchen and resumed dinner prep. I was disturbed, not understanding what was happening. It was alarming to hear her describe things we couldn't see with exasperation that we weren't seeing them too. Hallucinations are a hallmark of LBD, we later found out. And seeing circuses in the pasture and a man in the barn were the most harmless of them.

My parents had spent years traveling the world. When my brother and I were small, my maternal grandparents spent a year traveling in Europe. My grandfather was from Germany and had two sisters there, as well as other family. My parents went to Europe for a few weeks while my grandparents were there, leaving us with a nanny. We traveled as a family when we got a little older, taking cross-country trips to Arizona, Colorado, New Mexico, Wyoming, and many other places in between. When I was in college, my parents discovered cruises and were hooked. They had close friends they traveled with, and they took a lot of great trips. They invested in a time-share and used it extensively for many years.

When my mom started experiencing symptoms of dementia, my parents didn't stop traveling. In the two years before they moved to the farm, they took a trip to Hawaii and went on an Alaskan cruise for two weeks. About a year into living on the farm, they got the travel bug again. My mom made random comments about how nice it would be to take another trip. I scoffed but didn't respond because they were just vague "wouldn't it be nice" comments. Then, one night at dinner, it became more concrete.

"We got a lovely new catalog from Princess Cruises today," my mom said, sounding like a kid getting Christmas catalogs in the mail. "We're thinking of going on another trip." She was beaming, clearly excited about the idea.

I looked at my dad for any signs of concern. He was putting on his best innocent face, but I could see sadness too. I think he knew it was risky for them to travel alone. My mom had always organized the entire trips herself, from booking the cruises online to buying the plane tickets, coordinating transportation to and from the boat, planning their excursions, getting all their documents together, and arranging every other little detail of the trip. I'm not exaggerating. Every. Little. Detail. She even told my dad which outfits to pack.

With all of that in mind, I said carefully, "Is that really a good idea at this point?"

My mom appeared to be having a pretty lucid day, so she reacted as if I'd said something highly offensive. "What's that supposed to mean?" she said with a frown.

I shrugged, looking back and forth between her and my dad. "I think it's a fair question, given that you have dementia and sometimes details are hard, and navigating pretty much anything is hard. I'm a little worried about your well-being and safety, to be honest." She was shaking her head and going back to eating her dinner, dismissing my concerns. "Not to mention your ability to really enjoy the trip at this point with all the stress and anxiety it's bound to cause you," I finished, ignoring her reaction as she was ignoring mine.

She ate angrily, stabbing at her food, not looking at me. A minute later she said, "Don't be ridiculous," in that sharp tone she had. "I'm not that far around the bend yet, missy." She shot me a warning look, like I was being a disrespectful child.

My own anger flared, and I threw my hands up. "Fine!" I practically shouted. "But don't call me when you get stranded somewhere and can't find your way back."

We all ate in silence for a few minutes. I tried to get my temper to calm down. Dani put a hand on my leg under the table to try to soothe me, but it served only to make me madder. "So where do you think you might go? Just so I know where to send the emergency crews," I said.

My mother scoffed but didn't answer. My dad spoke instead. "We're thinking of taking a seven-day trip, just down to the Bahamas and Virgin Islands." His tone held a forced cheeriness, like he was trying to dispel the tension just by sounding happy.

I shook my head again, looking at my plate and avoiding their eyes. "Whatever," I muttered. I wanted badly to leave the table, but I was aware, even in my fury, that that would mean leaving Dani and the boys to deal with the aftermath, which didn't seem fair. So I just kept pushing food around on my plate, my appetite gone.

"And when is this?" I asked.

"When is what?" my mother asked, frowning. I stared at her.

"Umm, the trip you just talked about taking?" I couldn't believe she'd asked that, and I was confused.

"Oh, that," she said, as though we'd long moved on and I was bringing up some old conversation. "I don't remember. When was that trip, Ron?"

I raised an eyebrow at my dad. "I'm not sure of the exact dates," he said, "but it's in April." That was two months away.

I suddenly felt like a switch had flipped and I no longer cared what happened. I felt like I *couldn't* care anymore. I shrugged again, then said, "Well, it's up to you. For the record, I don't think it's a great idea, but maybe you should go while you still can."

With my help, they began making arrangements. My godparents, Tom and Jean, friends of my parents for nearly 50 years by then, lived in Bradenton, Florida, and helped on their end with some information for transportation to the cruise ship. The cruise was leaving out of Fort Lauderdale, more than three hours by car from Bradenton, and Jean found a shuttle that would take them to and from the port. My parents would fly to Bradenton from Bishop International Airport in Flint and stay with my godparents for a couple of days at either end of the trip.

My mom was still having lucid days at that point. Since she'd always done all the planning for their trips, she struggled to let me help with this one. True to form, she insisted on doing everything herself but wanted me sitting with her while she made all the arrangements. Using her old laptop, we booked the cruise and their stateroom, and she seemed quite happy to have my help for that. The real challenge started when we went to buy plane tickets.

"We need to get there in time for the ship to leave," my mom said, looking at me expectantly.

I waited, as the comment by itself didn't really tell me anything. Finally, I said, "Uh-huh . . . and you're flying into Bradenton to see Tom and Jean for a couple days first, so we should find tickets that go a few days early." I waited again.

She continued to stare at me, her expression clouding over a little, then frowned. "The ship doesn't leave from Bradenton," she said.

"I know," I replied patiently. I could tell this was going to be tricky. Keeping details straight was the earliest and most persistent way dementia affected her. "It leaves from Fort Lauderdale on the eighteenth. If you'd like to spend a couple days with Tom and Jean first, you should go down on the fourteenth or fifteenth."

"But how will we get there?" she asked, still frowning.

"Get where?"

"To the ship!" she exclaimed, now getting agitated.

I took a deep breath to try to stay calm. "You'll fly down to Bradenton on the fourteenth or fifteenth. Tom will pick you up from the airport and you'll spend a couple days with them. On the eighteenth, early in the morning, you'll take a shuttle bus to Fort Lauderdale and board the ship."

My mom was looking back at her computer screen, shaking her head. "No, that won't work," she said flatly.

I waited once again. She was scrolling up and down the page with flights on it. "What part won't work?" I finally asked.

"We've never taken a shuttle before. We won't know where to go. Your father can't find his way around. He relies on me for that. How will we get to the ship?"

"The shuttle takes you right to the port so you can board the ship," I answered.

"We need to board in the first group," she said insistently. "We need extra time with the wheelchairs."

I stared at her, then gently asked, "What wheelchairs?"

"For Bonnie and Carol!" she shouted at me, looking at me like I was stupid.

Bonnie and Carol were close friends of my parents for many, many years. They'd both been neighbors in Detroit and traveled many times on cruises with my parents over the years. Bonnie had been diagnosed with Alzheimer's back in 2012 or 2013 and had been in an assisted living facility since 2014. Carol was in her 90s and wasn't well. Neither of them had traveled with my parents in seven or eight years.

I looked at my mom, my emotions jumbling together. I had a visceral reaction to her shouting at me like I was dumb, along with a surge of compassion and sadness at the realization that she thought they were all still traveling together. I took a breath, prepared to let compassion win out, when she clucked her tongue and shook her head like she really did think I was stupid. I reacted immediately, as if her clucking tongue had lit a match.

"Seriously?" I sneered at her. "They haven't traveled with you in years."

My mom seemed to realize her mistake and tried to cover it. "Well, you never know, they might decide to come," she said defensively.

I barked out a sharp laugh. "Nope, pretty sure they won't, Mom," I said. "Neither of them is in any shape to travel anymore."

My comment cut through her mental fog, and I saw her eyes well up with tears. I immediately felt like a piece of shit. "I'm sorry, Mom," I said softly.

She brushed me off and went back to scrolling through the flights.

Once we settled on and purchased the tickets, I made sure she forwarded me the confirmation email so I could print it out for her. Without a document to reference, I knew she'd be asking me several times a day what the plans were. Not being able to retain new, short-term information is one of the most common symptoms of early dementia, and it was absolutely affecting my mom.

That night at dinner, it started. My mom had the printouts I'd just given her of the cruise details and airline reservations.

"Ellen, I don't think you did this right," she said with her usual frown. "We're flying into Bradenton, but the cruise leaves from Fort Lauderdale. How are we going to get there?"

I nodded and told myself to remain calm. "Yup, and you're taking a shuttle to get from one to the other."

"No, that can't be right," she said. "I don't have tickets for that."

"Jean made those reservations and has the tickets for you when you get to Bradenton. It's all taken care of." I was working hard at keeping my tone even and my voice assuaged.

"Don't talk down to me!" she shouted suddenly, hitting the table and making everyone jump.

"Geezus, Mom!" I shouted right back. "I'm not talking down to you! But I am getting frustrated! You asked me to help make all the reservations, so I did! Jean very kindly took care of getting your shuttle trip back and forth booked. All the reservations are made, and they are all correct. I don't know what your problem is!" I was seething with anger. Not only were her comments about not having all the information incorrect, but she was so aggressive and condescending in how she communicated her confusion and concern that I was stripped of all my empathy.

She sat quietly then, lips pursed, looking at the printouts and shuffling the pages. I was trying to get my anger under control as I watched her. I glanced at my dad. He was eating and pretending nothing was happening right next to him. He looked tired and my heart went out to him. That calmed me down.

"Why don't we just try to enjoy dinner, and I'll be happy to go over it all with you again when we're done," I said more quietly. "I can type out a schedule in chronological order so you can see what's going to happen step-by-step in one document. How about that?" I looked at my mom, my voice under control but my gaze cool.

She nodded somewhat haughtily and said, "That would be very helpful, thank you. More helpful than you yelling at me."

I stared. Dani's hand went to my leg. This time I let it calm me, and we all went back to eating.

When it came time to get my parents packed and ready for the trip, it was difficult. My mom couldn't keep anything straight and kept getting confused about the steps between getting to the airport in Flint and getting on the cruise ship a few days later. She clutched like a lifeline the one-page document I'd created and printed out that walked her through it. Though she was insistent on carrying all their travel documents as she always had, I didn't trust that she wouldn't lose them. So I made sure my dad had copies of everything, and he tucked them away in his carry-on bag.

I drove them to the airport and dropped them off at the entrance with all their bags. My dad brushed off my offer to park and come in to help them get to security, but I did it anyway. By the time I got back inside, they were handing over their checked bags to an agent. My mom was patting her bag, her purse, and her pockets, looking for something.

"What do you need?" I asked her as I walked up to them.

She looked at me like she didn't recognize me for a second, as if I were a stranger approaching her. "Mom?" I said, concerned. "Are you okay? Did you lose something?"

She relaxed as a look of recognition came over her face. "No," she said, mildly agitated. "I'm just making sure I haven't forgotten anything."

She suddenly seemed frail. She reached for my dad, who offered her his arm, and they started toward the escalator. I walked behind them, watching her. She'd never liked escalators and was even more uncertain of her step now. I was poised to grab her if she missed one.

My dad successfully coaxed her onto the first step, looking over his shoulder at me with a reassuring smile. I stepped on behind them.

Something about the picture of the two of them going up, my mom looking around in wonder, made my throat catch. I swallowed hard.

Bishop International Airport is a lovely, small regional airport, and security is right around the corner when you get to the second floor. I continued to follow behind my parents, fighting with my emotions. I'd come around to being happy they were taking the trip and glad for the two-week break it would give me and my family, but I was deeply saddened by the idea that this might be the last trip they took. I took a deep breath to calm myself. I didn't want anything to upset my mom, as she got confused and combative easily when she was upset.

When they reached the edge of security, both turned around to face me. My mom registered a moment of surprise, like she'd forgotten I was there, but it quickly passed. I smiled at them both. "Have a wonderful time," I said, trying to push the sadness away and smiling. I reached to hug my mom first, then my dad. "Be careful. Give Tom and Jean my love. I'll be here waiting for you when you get back."

I stood watching as my dad guided my mom up to security and into the checkpoint. My mom looked to him every step of the way to tell her what to do next. I could see him getting a little impatient and silently sent him encouragement.

They got through the checkpoint and my dad turned around to wave. My mom seemed confused about what he was doing, so he pointed to where I was standing and waving back. She frowned in my direction and said something to him, then he pointed again. I could see impatience in his gestures and expression. My mother finally waved back, but I'm not sure she knew it was me. I'm not sure whether it was because I was too far away and her eyesight was beginning to fail or because she didn't quite recognize me. Either way, sadness overwhelmed me, and I choked back a sob as I watched them gather their things and slowly make their way toward their gate.

I watched them until I couldn't see them anymore, fighting a strong urge to run after them, tell them not to go, and hug them again.

Instead, I hugged my arms to myself, took a deep breath, and headed back to my car.

The trip went surprisingly well, for the most part. My dad reported that in the few days beforehand, while visiting their friends, my mom fretted and worried a bit about "getting to the ship on time." The cruise itself went well, which I was relieved to hear, as they'd both loved cruising so much over the years that I was happy they'd been able to enjoy it again.

Once they returned to Tom and Jean's house, things got a little rough. A couple of days before they were to return home, my mom became fixated on their bank account, which she wasn't able to access online. She'd forgotten the password and locked herself out. As her anxiety grew, she became more and more agitated, lashing out aggressively against my dad. Jean frantically texted me, asking whether I needed to intervene because she was worried that my dad wouldn't be able to keep her calm enough to make the trip home.

I spoke to my mom, which seemed to help some, and they made the trip home safely a couple of days later. I was there at the airport to meet them and felt tremendous relief when I saw them walking through airport security to meet me. My mom seemed surprised to see me there, even though I'd told her several times I'd be there to pick them up, but she looked happy. I exhaled the breath I'd been holding the whole time they were gone.

Despite my father being the first one to raise the alarm that something was wrong with my mom, despite his asking for help, to move closer, and for intervention, he was still in denial on a daily basis. But I didn't realize that at first. He didn't talk about it. He simply lived it.

My parents' marriage worked because my mom liked to be in charge and my dad was mild-mannered and accommodating enough to allow it. My mom not only said jump but directed how high, when, and how to land. My dad always obliged. He loathed conflict and confrontation and went to great lengths to avoid it.

So, even after a year into living on the farm, my parents were still making frequent trips down to their old neighborhood in Detroit to attend social gatherings and visit friends. They were also watching the progress (or destruction) of their years of landscaping efforts at their old house. Early on, they'd make the round trip in a day, but as time went on, they'd use it as an excuse to stay with friends.

Even though my mom was having increasingly more difficulty keeping things straight, and though she was struggling with trusting my dad to drive "the right way" and find wherever they were going, my dad acted like everything was fine. Sure, he noticed when she got things confused and commented on it often, but he didn't seem to think it was a permanent state. He seemed to think that if he just reminded her what was what, she would remember. The morning they were preparing to leave for one of their visits to Detroit, I saw this "reminding" in action.

I was at their house chatting with them before they left, getting the details of where they'd be staying and when they'd be back. They had three house cats, and Robin and Sam looked in on them when my parents weren't there.

"We'll be staying with Nancy," my mom said while my dad was gathering water bottles and snacks into a cooler.

"No," he said, straightening up and looking at her with a patient expression on his face. "We stayed with Nancy last time, remember? We're staying with someone else this time." My mom and I both looked at him expectantly. He continued to look at her expectantly. "Remember?" he said again.

She looked troubled, like she was in school guessing incorrectly at what the teacher wanted to hear. "It's . . . um . . . you know," she gestured around vaguely, trying to come up with a name, then more to herself said, "Oh, come on." She looked at my dad hard, still gesturing. "You know, the ones with the dog."

My dad was smiling patiently. I was uncomfortable. Making my mom guess didn't seem very kind.

"The McLeod's?" I guessed, trying to come to my mom's rescue and frowning at my dad.

He didn't take the hint and was still looking at my mom. "Nooooo . . ." he said as if they were playing a game. "Another couple though."

"Not cool, Dad," I said quietly, still frowning at him. "Don't make her guess. Who are you staying with?"

"They live on Glastonbury . . ." He was still prompting my mom.

Suddenly her face lit up. "Oh! The um . . . oh, come on now . . . they have a daughter you were friends with, El," she said, turning to me as though we were game show contestants trying to win a big prize.

"The Washburns?" I said, looking back and forth between my parents.

"Yes!" my mom said excitedly, snapping her fingers in delight. Turning to my dad, she said, "Right?" Her face was eager.

"Yes!" my dad said gleefully to her. Looking at me, he said, "See? She just needs some help sometimes, that's all."

I stared at him, a sinking feeling in my belly. He went back to packing their cooler while my mom gathered up things in her tote bag. I didn't want to start a fight right before they left, so I just said, "Okay, well, if you don't need anything, I'm going to head back home and do some work. You'll be back tomorrow?"

My dad looked at my mom expectantly again. *Not again*, I thought.

"Well, we're going to play it by ear," she said, then smiled at me.

I stared. My mom didn't play anything by ear. She planned everything. Like, everything. "Oh, yeah?" I said. "Well, alrighty then. Have a great time, and keep us posted on when you're coming back so we know how long the boys need to be on cat duty." I turned to go.

We said our goodbyes and I crossed the driveway, heading back to my own house, shaking my head.

Whenever my parents would visit Detroit, my mom seemed to spend most of her mental energy masking. The result was that she didn't notice anything about anyone else—including when my dad started having chest pains while staying with the Washburns. He'd been having them for a few days, we later found out, but true to form, he never said a word to anyone.

Before dementia, my mom would've been on him, noticing quickly that something was wrong. Now she didn't. But the Washburns did. My dad kept rubbing his chest, wincing, and giving other subtle signs that he was in pain. Finally, Mr. Washburn told my dad he needed to get checked out because he was worried my dad was having a heart attack. This must've frightened my mom because she resisted having my dad go to the hospital. But Mr. Washburn insisted and offered to drive them. My dad was worried enough himself that he agreed to go.

I got a call from Mr. Washburn telling me what was going on and that they wanted to keep my dad overnight for observation. Mr. Washburn was taking my mom back to their house overnight so my dad could rest. My mom still had her cell phone and was usually able to remember how to use it at this point, so I decided I should call them both and check in. I started with my dad.

"What's going on, old man?" I began when he answered, trying to keep my tone light to hide my worry. "You weren't getting enough attention or something?"

He chuckled softly. "Yeah, that's it." His voice sounded tired. "You caught me."

"Tell me what happened," I said, still keeping my voice light.

"Well, Ben said he was tired of watching me clutch my chest, so he was taking me to the emergency room," my dad answered. "I told him I was fine, but he wouldn't listen."

"How long has this been going on? How long were you feeling pain?"

"Oh, a few days now."

"What?" I snapped. "A few days? Like, as in before you guys even went down to Detroit?" I was incredulous and angry, and I knew I sounded like it.

He stayed quiet, accepting my tirade, then simply said, "Yep."

"For crying out loud, Dad! Why didn't you say anything?"

I could almost hear him shrugging. "I don't know," he muttered. "I was too busy wrangling your mother, I guess." He sounded defeated. I softened.

"Dad," I sighed, "if you don't take care of yourself, you won't be here to wrangle Mom." I paused, then added, "Don't do that to me. You know one of us will kill the other. Think of the trauma you'll cause your grandchildren." My attempt at humor was weak, but he welcomed it and chuckled softly again.

"She was really confused," he continued. "I could hardly hear what the doctors were trying to say because she kept interrupting and asking weird questions. She didn't make much sense. She kept getting agitated and I'd have to try and calm her down." He paused.

I could imagine the scene, as I'd seen it before at other doctor's appointments. "Well, I'm betting that's part of why they're keeping you," I said. "They probably wanted to give you a break and a chance to rest without having to manage her from your hospital bed."

"I had to keep reminding her that I was the one they were admitting, not her. She kept acting like she thought she was the patient. But I reminded her enough times that she finally got it." He sounded relieved, like he'd finally gotten through to her.

I was immediately saddened. "Dad, she's got dementia," I said, softly. "Reminding her isn't going to work. When she's confused about something, you can't just explain logic to her and expect that she'll get it. That's not how dementia works."

He was quiet for a minute, and I could tell he didn't agree. "Hmm," he finally said. "Well, it must've worked this time because she finally stopped asking the same questions over and over again." He sounded a little defiant, which was unusual for him, so I let it go and moved on.

I asked more questions about what tests the doctors were running, what they suspected was going on, and when he'd have results. He said his heart seemed to be just fine but that they wanted to keep him for observation because of the severity of the pain. They suspected it was pulled muscles from over exertion. My dad had a habit of overdoing things and behaving like he still had a 40-year-old body rather than his actual 77-year-old one.

"They don't want me to do much the next few days," he said. "They've got me on pretty strong muscle relaxers and painkillers."

"Mm-hmm," I replied, waiting to see what he was really trying to say. "And?" I prompted.

"Well, it's probably fine for me to drive all the way back up north, right? I think it will be fine."

This is how my dad "asks" for help. His tendency is to make statements about a problem but stop short of asking for some help with it.

"Umm, I'm gonna say that's a no," I said slowly. "Pretty sure you're not supposed to drive under the influence of those drugs. I'll talk to David. We'll figure something out to get you both home."

As though he were channeling my mother, he clucked his tongue and sighed in annoyance, barely concealing his relief that we'd come get them. "That seems ridiculous for you both to drive all this way when I can just get us home."

I laughed. "Dad, there are a lot of ridiculous things about this situation, but your adult children coming to drive you home so you don't get in an accident while under the influence of prescribed drugs is not one of them." I waited to see if he'd say anything else, but he didn't. "Okay then," I finally said. "I guess I should call Mom now and make sure she's doing okay."

"Be nice to her," he said softly. "She's pretty confused and upset, and you don't need to make it worse."

My cheeks flushed on the other end of the phone. His opinion of me was important, and I didn't like that he thought I was too hard on her. I didn't like that he'd always thought our clashes and fights were way more my fault than hers. "I won't," I mumbled, feeling like a scolded child.

After we said goodbye and hung up, I sat staring at the phone for a minute. I didn't want to call my mom but knew I needed to. I took a deep breath and called her cell.

When she answered the phone, she sounded shrill, anxious, and like she didn't know who it was, even though my name would've popped up on the screen.

"Hi, Mom, it's me," I said. "How are you doing?"

"I know it's you," she snapped. "I'm fine, but I don't know where your father has gone," she continued, sounding irritated. "He's been gone for hours!"

I heard Mrs. Washburn in the background gently remind her that he was in the hospital. "Oh, that's right," my mom said with a little forced laugh. "Your father is in the hospital."

"I know," I said, keeping my tone friendly and calm. "I just talked to him. He seems to be resting, which is what he needs. They expect he'll be released tomorrow."

"I know," my mom said defensively. "I was there with him and talked to the doctors."

"Yeah?" I said, annoyed now and feeling defiant about how she was masking. "So what did they say?" I knew she wouldn't be able to answer, and in my angry state I wanted to prove it.

She stuttered a little, looking for the right words and correct answers, but they weren't there. Finally, she said, "Well I don't know! I'm not a doctor! How should I know what's wrong with him?!" She was doing her whisper-yell at me now, not wanting her friends to hear us fighting.

I bit back my retort about how she'd literally just said she'd talked to the doctors. Some small part of me recognized through my anger that she couldn't answer and to push the issue would've been doing the same thing I'd just gotten after my dad for doing. So instead, I took a deep breath to calm down before speaking.

"Okay," I said more calmly. "It sounds like you're going to stay there with the Washburns, and Dad will be monitored at the hospital. I'm going to call David so we can make arrangements to come get you both tomorrow."

Before dementia, my mom would've scoffed at that and just driven them back herself. But she'd voluntarily stopped driving a couple of years prior when she'd scared herself getting lost in downtown Detroit on her way home from ushering at a local theater late at night. So thankfully, this was one battle we didn't have to fight. She happily handed over her car keys and embraced being driven everywhere. A little too much sometimes. On top of that, there wasn't much she enjoyed more than the attention of her children, so the idea that we were *both* coming delighted her.

We said our goodbyes and ended the call. I sat shaking my head for a minute and called my brother.

Looking Back Now

Many people living in the circle of dementia experience denial, including the person affected by dementia, caregivers, spouses, siblings, children, any and all other family members of the person with dementia, friends, acquaintances, and even random passersby. That's just to say that denial is super common and isn't confined to specific people. And it's not confined to the beginning of the process either. In some cases, it can last right up until the end.

At this stage of my mother's illness, I was quick to anger at both her unwillingness to accept what was changing and her masking, defiance, and defensiveness when called out on it. I wish with my whole soul that I could've recognized her fear, anxiety, and attempts to hold onto her dignity. But I didn't. Instead, I continued to engage with her just as I always had. Much to my surprise, I was displaying some denial of my own. Even while I scolded my father for his denial, the ways I interacted with my mother were no better.

The roller coaster of emotions combined with (and caused by) the unpredictability of her disease left me feeling like I couldn't keep up. My uncertainty about what I was doing as a caregiver fed my shame and conviction that I was doing it all wrong. Looking back now, I see some things I wish I'd realized then:

> Denial is normal. You may experience it, your loved one affected by dementia may experience it, and literally everyone around you may experience it. No one wants this horrible diagnosis to be true. And when there are good days, lucid moments, and the person still looks the same as they always have, it can be damn hard to accept the diagnosis.

> Quizzing a loved one who has dementia doesn't work. In fact, it can be damaging to them. Don't quiz your loved one about things that just happened or ask them to remember someone's name. It doesn't help them or you. Though it's instinct and a part of denial, it does far more harm than good.

> If remembering details is hard for your loved one, having things written down to serve as reminders can work well. At

some point, many people suffering with dementia lose the ability to read or comprehend what they're reading. While they still can, it can be helpful to make lists, write down the names of things on cards, and use other visual cues.

➤ Caregivers really will get sick from exhaustion, overexertion, worry, stress, anxiety, survivor's guilt, and grief. There are scary statistics out there, some of which show that an alarming percentage of caregivers will die before their loved ones who are affected by dementia.[1] Pay attention to your body's signals. Make time for your own wellness. Sneak in breaks however you can. They don't have to be time-consuming or extravagant to be helpful. Here are some ideas of what you can do in 10 minutes that can make a big difference:

  ✓ take a brisk walk
  ✓ meditate and focus on your breathing
  ✓ stretch
  ✓ scream into a pillow
  ✓ power nap
  ✓ drink some water
  ✓ throw a solo dance party
  ✓ write in your journal
  ✓ sit with whatever emotion strikes you and give yourself 10 minutes to just feel it
  ✓ pet an animal
  ✓ call a friend

There are plenty of other ways you can engage in effective and efficient self-care as well. Whatever you decide to try, the important thing is that you do it.

CHAPTER 7

"YOU KNOW YOU'RE NEXT, RIGHT?"

More and more, I ended up driving places with my parents, especially when there was a medical appointment. But I didn't want to spend my *life* driving. Coupled with the fact that the drives down to see Dr. Nartes were so long, she didn't seem to be doing anything other than monitoring my mother's progress, so they just didn't seem worth it. In the ALZ support group, we'd asked for recommendations of who other people took their loved ones to see for care that might be closer to home. Several people mentioned Dr. Wendell, a gerontologist who specialized in memory care patients. His office was in Grand Blanc, which was about 45 minutes from us. That felt much more realistic. We set our first appointment for him to see my mom.

Getting out of the house to get places on time was always a rushed affair for my mom. She was one of those people who are chronically late. There was usually a lot of yelling, frantic searches for various items, and last-minute rushing around involved with any exit from the house. With dementia, it only got worse. This day was no exception.

My dad had started just handing me the car keys anytime we were all going to an appointment together. It wasn't that he couldn't or didn't want to drive, but he was deeply affected by my mother's running commentary, criticism, and occasional outbursts while he drove. It stressed him out, so he was more comfortable letting me drive.

I was waiting outside of their house by the car that morning when it was time to go. I could hear my mother yelling at my dad, screeching that she couldn't find her purse, as though it were his fault. Determined not to go inside, I shook my head and took a deep breath, knowing that if I went in I'd start yelling at her and everything would go downhill from there. Though I suspected that she was nervous to see a new doctor, she so completely hid those emotions behind her nasty verbal jabs at everyone else that it was hard to maintain empathy for her.

Finally, they came out of the house. I looked at my watch and noticed we were leaving 15 minutes later than planned. Luckily, knowing my mother's tendencies, I'd told them we needed to be ready to go 20 minutes earlier than we really had to leave, so I was able to stay calm. My dad looked flustered. As he handed me the car keys, he clucked his tongue, rolled his eyes in a way any pouty teenager would've appreciated, and said in a low voice, "Good grief." I stifled a laugh.

My mom sat in the back seat, something she'd come to accept doing when I was accompanying them somewhere. But she was more agitated than usual. She kept taking things out of her purse like she was looking for something, then putting them back in. I kept glancing at her in the rearview mirror as I drove.

"Everything alright back there?" I asked in a voice loud enough for her to hear me. She ignored me and kept rooting. "Mom," I said, a little louder, "are you missing something?"

She looked up, frowning, and I could see she was troubled. She didn't answer me.

"Mom?" I said again, getting a little concerned. "Are you okay? Did you forget something? Tell me now if you did so we can go back before we get too far."

She shook her head and went back to rooting. I glanced at my dad with a questioning look. He shrugged and said in a low voice, "She does this. She seems to need to just rearrange everything. I ask her all the time what she's looking for, and she gets really frustrated and doesn't seem to know." He shrugged again. "I don't know what she's looking for." He looked out the window.

We got to the doctor's office without incident. As we were getting out of the car, I looked back at my mom. She was putting everything back into her purse. "All set?" I asked, trying to keep my tone light.

"Just a minute," she hissed. "I need to get all my things together." She was looking at what she was putting back in and seemed confused. She had her dementia face.

I got out and closed my door. "She's got dementia face," I said quietly to my dad. "Did you make sure she had her wallet in her purse? We're going to need her insurance cards. I should've thought to double-check that before we left." I was worried now, wondering whether the doctor would see us without having insurance info.

He nodded at me. "Yes, it was in there when we left, so if it's not now, it's somewhere in the back seat."

I felt relieved and made a mental note that we needed to check for that whenever we left the house moving forward. My mom finally got out of the back seat, looking confused and unsure.

"This way," I said, pointing to the door we needed to go in. She followed my dad reluctantly.

We walked in and were soon ushered into an exam room. There were drawings of cats decorating the room, which delighted my mother because she adored cats. Her mood immediately improved as she pointed out things she saw. I watched her, fascinated by the complete and sudden shift in her demeanor.

We sat down, three chairs in a row against a wall. My mom and I were on each end with my dad in the middle, totally symbolic of our family relationship.

The doctor came in and introduced himself. I guessed him to be in his 60s, and he had a brisk, no-nonsense air about him. He started by asking my mom her name, then my dad for his. He then pointed at me but said to my mom, "And who's that?"

My mom leaned forward and looked around at where he was pointing, seeming mildly surprised to see me there. "That's Ellen," she said in a tone that suggested he was not very smart for not knowing that.

"And who is Ellen to you?" he asked. I wondered whether he really couldn't figure it out or if this was part of how he assessed people.

My mom stared at him like she was wondering the same thing. "Well, that's my mother," she said.

I frowned at her and laughed. "Um, try again."

"Your mother?" Dr. Wendell asked. "Are you sure about that?"

She looked at me again and laughed, suddenly realizing what she'd said. "No, I'm *her* mother," she corrected. "That's my daughter." My dad and I both chuckled along with my mom. Dr. Wendell made a note.

As Dr. Wendell continued asking a short series of other questions, I noticed that my mom knew most of the answers, slipping only a couple of times. He told her she'd done just fine, and she beamed. He then started taking her history, talking directly to her the whole time. I tried not to jump in whenever my mom hesitated. When she described her own mother's Alzheimer's, Dr. Wendell suddenly looked at me.

"So, let me get this straight. Grandma had Alzheimer's, and Mom has dementia of some kind." He looked hard at me. "You know you're next, right?"

I was shocked and momentarily speechless. I hadn't really thought about it much, believe it or not. "Uh, I guess so?" I managed.

Dr. Wendell seemed unfazed by my stunned reaction. He nodded and continued in the same brisk manner. "The likelihood is high.

You're at a much higher increased risk than someone in the general population." And with that, he went on to the next question for my mother.

I sat reeling, breathing a little harder. My dad noticed my reaction and patted my leg, which reminded me of Dani. I took a deep breath and tried to pay attention to what the doctor was saying. Some of the members of the ALZ support group had mentioned that his bedside manner was lacking, but this was way more shocking than what I'd expected.

Once he finished taking my mom's history, he moved on to what had brought us in. My mom was leaving out a significant amount of detail about the changes we'd seen in her. I wasn't sure whether it was because she was unaware of them or because she was trying to downplay them. I raised my hand halfway to get the doctor's attention.

"So, I feel the need to fill in some of these gaps here . . ." I started. I looked over at my mom, who frowned and gave me a warning look. That confirmed for me that she was trying to downplay what had been going on. So I continued.

"I think it's important for you to know about some of the other things we've noticed," I said, ignoring my mom as she shifted around uncomfortably. "In the past eighteen months, since she was initially diagnosed with MCI, there's been a significant number of changes we've noticed. She sees things that aren't there. One minute she seems normal, the next minute she'll shift on a dime and either lash out at someone or completely forget what we were talking about."

"Not true," my mother said shrilly. "I don't forget what we're talking about, I just sometimes change the subject because *you*"—she stabbed at me with her bony finger—"are making things unpleasant!"

I sat looking at Dr. Wendell, waiting to see if he'd intervene. He nodded at both of us, then turned back to me. "This is all normal," he said. "It's how dementia affects the brain."

I nodded, aware that my mother was shooting daggers in my direction. My dad sat impassively, his arms crossed tightly across his chest. Dr. Wendell looked at him. "Anything to add, sir?"

My dad looked at him for a moment, but I couldn't read his expression. Finally he shook his head and just said, "Nothing to add."

Dr. Wendell nodded, looking down at his iPad where he was taking notes. "Alright," he said. "Well, there's not much we can do to control things right now other than try one of the drugs on the market designed to slow down the symptoms." He went on to explain two drugs that could help and asked my mother if she'd like to try one of them.

"My friend Bonnie takes the first one you mentioned," she said. "I'd like to try it too." She looked pleased, like she was doing something because it was fashionable or socially acceptable because a friend was doing it. I wanted to say something sarcastic, but I held my tongue. I knew it wouldn't be nice or make any difference.

Dr. Wendell wrote the prescription, then ushered us to the front desk to check out. He said he'd like to see my mother again in three months to see how the drug was working and to call sooner if we had any questions or concerns.

As we left the office and got back to the car, I was still stuck on the comment he'd made to me about how I was next.

Either oblivious to how his comment had affected me or just too self-absorbed to stop and think about it for a minute, my mother let loose once we were in the car heading home. "What's the matter with you?" she snapped at me. "You don't have the right to tell him all my private business. How dare you say all those things about me?" She sounded outraged, and I was caught off guard.

I laughed sharply. "Are you joking right now?" I said, my voice rising to match hers. "What the hell is the point of going to see a doctor if you're going to hold back on telling the truth about what's happening? Why would you waste your time going?" I was fuming.

I glanced in the rearview mirror at her. She was back to rearranging her purse. I shook my head, looked over at my dad who was looking out the window, and just drove. We didn't speak again until we were nearly home.

Around the same time we first visited Dr. Wendell, someone in the ALZ support group recommended we go through the "Creating Confident Caregivers" program. The program consisted of six weekly workshops designed to educate caregivers about the general things to expect with Alzheimer's as well as other forms of dementia. The goals of the program include helping caregivers learn better communication techniques, manage daily life with their loved ones, realize the importance of self-care, and feel more confident as caregivers.

With my travel schedule for work at the time, I couldn't commit to the program, but I encouraged my dad to go through it. Several people in our support group had gone through the course and highly recommended it. My dad agreed to sign up for the fall session.

One of the weeks was about "strengthening family resources," and the participants were encouraged to invite family members to attend the session. David and I took the day off work to go, and my dad's younger sister, my aunt Dolores, also decided to come. She lived in the Detroit area but had come to stay at our house and help out with my mom a couple of times at that point. She wanted to learn more so she could continue supporting my parents.

Based on what my dad had shared about the program thus far, I went into the session feeling optimistic. I'd done some research on my own, but not a lot. I don't learn that way. I prefer an interactive session where I can ask questions and people have the chance to share experiences and compare notes. As a facilitator by profession, I was looking forward to an interactive training session where those things would happen.

I listened as the facilitator opened things up. As people introduced themselves and their family members, it sounded like everyone was having a different experience of dementia in their loved one than we were. There was a lot of talk about "the long goodbye," which I didn't really understand. The experiences people shared seemed to indicate that their loved ones had Alzheimer's. At this point, we were skeptical that my mom had it and hadn't heard of Lewy body yet. We just knew her symptoms didn't match the descriptions of Alzheimer's.

There wasn't a lot of interaction built into the session. We watched a video about people at different stages of the disease. As it was playing, I leaned over to my dad and whispered, "Mom goes through all those stages in a single day sometimes." He nodded in agreement but said nothing.

The facilitator seemed more committed to getting through all the material and information she wanted to share than to hearing from the families in the room about their own experiences. After trying to interject a couple of times and picking up on her frustration that I was interrupting, I sat back and stewed in exasperation. I'd expected, hoped, and assumed the session would give me new insights about what was happening with my mom; that we'd have a chance to share our own experiences like we did at the support group and get some advice; that the strategies for supporting my mom more effectively would give me new insights. It did none of those things.

By the time we left, I was disgusted. The advice was this:

➢ Listen more.
➢ Don't correct your loved one when they get something wrong.
➢ Don't argue with them.
➢ Be patient.
➢ Stay calm.
➢ Learn to redirect.

I left thinking, *Umm . . . are you fucking kidding me?! Is there some switch I'm supposed to be flipping in my brain that I'm not aware of? How exactly am I supposed to go about doing any of these things given the history of the relationship with my mom and her aggression and combativeness? Not to mention all those days and moments of lucidity when she's incredibly critical and yelling. And what about these increasingly frequent and vivid hallucinations? I'm just supposed to stay calm?!* None of this seemed doable or appropriate in our situation. Something else was happening with my mom. It was nearing the time of her next appointment to see Dr. Wendell, so I decided we needed to bring it up.

As the appointment day arrived, I warned my dad that I was going to be brutally honest but promised I'd try to do it in a way that wasn't insulting to my mom. We both knew she wouldn't be happy that I was "sharing her private business" with the doctor, especially because she'd think I wouldn't be doing it right, but I knew we needed help. The drug Dr. Wendell had prescribed wasn't doing anything other than giving her diarrhea, and I was interested in getting more accurate information about what we were dealing with.

On the way to the appointment, I decided I should give my mom some warning too. I waited until we were in the car and on the way so she couldn't fight us about going to the appointment.

"Hey, Mom," I started, looking at her in the rearview mirror and making sure to get her attention before launching into what I wanted to say. She looked in my direction from the backseat, but not into the rearview mirror at first. "Mom, I think we need to ask Dr. Wendell if there's another form of dementia we're dealing with," I continued. "I don't remember Grandma experiencing a lot of the things you're going through." I kept my tone calm and gentle. "I'm worried about you," I added, feeling a sudden surge of sadness. I could see in the mirror that she was watching the back of my head and frowning, but I couldn't tell whether it was because of what I'd said or because she was confused. "Mom?" I prompted, wanting to make sure she'd at least heard me.

"What?" she responded as if I were speaking to her for the first time.

"Did you hear what I said?" I asked, trying not to let impatience creep into my voice. I was sad, frustrated, angry, in denial, and impatient all at once. I took a breath.

"Yes," she said simply, then turned away to look out the window. It looked like she didn't intend to say anything else. I glanced over at my dad, who gave a small shrug.

Once we were at the doctor's office, I shared my observations and concerns with Dr. Wendell. I told him about the hallucinations and their increasing vividness. I shared my concerns about how her eyesight seemed to be affected. I talked about the roller coaster of lucidity versus her demented state and the days when it honestly appeared as if she were totally normal.

My mother sat quietly, fidgeting slightly with the straps of her purse, lips pursed together in an expression of trying to maintain her dignity. My heart broke for her. I didn't want to be in this position any more than she did, but I was getting desperate for some answers about how to navigate this path.

My dad also sat stoically quiet. I knew he'd pay a higher price in the form of a tongue lashing from my mom if he contributed much to the conversation, so I tried not to ask him to share what he'd noticed. Dr. Wendell recognized his reluctance and seemed to pick up on the dynamics. As I was finishing what I wanted to share with him, he moved his chair closer to my mom.

"Charlotte, do you know who the actor Robin Williams was?" he asked.

My mom looked at him suspiciously and then said yes in a sarcastic tone.

"And do you know anything about his death?" he continued.

My mother stared at him for a moment. "He committed suicide, right?"

Dr. Wendell nodded. "Yes, he did. But do you know anything about what led to it?"

My mother shook her head, so he continued. "Robin Williams had struggled with depression for much of his adult life. He really battled it hard and took medication to help. But then he developed dementia. What a lot of people don't know is that he had a specific kind of dementia called Lewy body. He had hallucinations, like what your daughter has described you having. So his doctor put him on an antipsychotic drug to help control them and even out his moods a bit." He paused, looking at my mom. "Unfortunately, what the doctor didn't know then was that antipsychotic drugs cause suicidal tendencies in people who've struggled with depression."

He paused again, waiting to see whether this would sink in, looking at all three of us now. It certainly did for me.

"So—" I began, starting to understand the direction this was going in.

"I think your mom might have Lewy body dementia," Dr. Wendell interrupted.

"I don't know what that means," I said, my heart starting to beat faster.

"It means that instead of plaques and tangles in the brain, which is what we commonly see with Alzheimer's, your mom's brain is being affected by Lewy bodies instead. There's an accumulation of a protein in the brain called alpha-synuclein that builds up." Then abruptly he said, "Charlotte, hold out your arms for me, please."

She did, and we all looked at her arms. I wasn't sure what we were looking for. There was a slight tremor in her hands.

"Have you noticed this tremor in your hands getting any worse?" Dr. Wendell asked. My mom shook her head no, still frowning. I still had no idea where this was going and was getting more nervous, but I waited.

"Lewy body dementia, or LBD, is very commonly associated with Parkinson's disease," he continued. "We'll want to keep an eye on this tremor and any other difficulties with movement that develop." He was doing something on his iPad now.

My mind was reeling, questions not even forming yet. Feeling overwhelmed, I looked over at my parents. My dad looked scared. My mom was frowning. I wasn't sure if she was taking all this in.

"I'd like you to see a neurologist colleague of mine to get a second opinion and see if he can diagnose this," Dr. Wendell was saying.

"Is there some sort of test that will do that?" I asked, my brain finally engaging. "I know Alzheimer's can't be definitively diagnosed without an autopsy. Is that different for Lewy body?"

"Not really," he said. "A neurologist can assess her and give you a clinical diagnosis. There's a more definitive test called a PET scan, but you'd have to go to Ann Arbor for it, and the test itself is traumatic for the patient with dementia, so we don't encourage it. But there are some families who really want their loved one to have it." He paused what he was doing on the iPad and looked up at me over the top of his glasses. "Is that something you want?"

"No," I said quickly. "Not unless it's necessary."

He went back to the iPad. "Okay. The neurologist I'd like you to see is Dr. Bowman," he said. "I'm going to do a direct referral so that he can get you in more quickly." He looked up at us. "Have you noticed any improvement with the drug I prescribed for you before?" We all shook our heads no. He nodded, as if it had confirmed something for him. "If you have LBD, the medication I put you on last time you were here won't do anything to help, unfortunately. You can go ahead and stop taking it now."

He then looked at us and asked, "Do you have any questions for me right now?"

Still drowning in overwhelm, I didn't know what to ask or say or feel. I shook my head numbly. My parents didn't say anything either. I guessed they were feeling the same way I was.

As soon as we got home, I searched "Lewy body dementia" on Google. My mom had all the symptoms listed as the most common. I felt relieved that we were getting more clarity about what she was really suffering with, but I was scared about what could be to come. I learned that the average life expectancy for LBD is five to eight years from diagnosis. Seeing as my grandmother had lived for more than 20 years from her diagnosis, I had a hard time processing and accepting that my mom would potentially live a much shorter life.

My mom's reaction to the conversation with Dr. Wendell was more subdued. She'd stopped using her computer by then, but on good days she still used her iPad to play games and do some emailing. She was never super computer-savvy, so I'm not sure she would've known how to do research online, but in the past she definitely would've asked me to do so for her. Now, she seemed to be wrestling with the information internally and didn't talk about it out loud. To me, she seemed defeated and scared.

In the two weeks between appointments, my dad and I tried to keep things as normal as possible with my mom. We didn't bring up the suspected diagnosis to her, but she moved through those days with an air of someone who's lost a battle. I felt more compassion and empathy toward her during those two weeks than I ever had previously in our relationship. I hoped this would be a turning point in our relationship, and I had romantic notions about finally being able to engage in conversation with her without one of us losing our temper after just a few minutes.

When the day of the appointment arrived, she was agitated. I knew she didn't want to go. She'd always had something of an ostrich approach to medical issues: if she just stuck her head in the sand and pretended they weren't happening, they'd go away. She'd been so sure my father hadn't had cancer back in 1996 that she hadn't even gone with him to hear the results. I'd been working at the same hospital where he worked at that time, so I'd gone instead. After learning that he had stage four cancer, the man had fallen apart with fear and worry, and it had been me who'd been there with him because my mom didn't want to hear it.

This was no different. If there had been any chance that she could've avoided going to that neurologist, my mother would've taken it and ran. But since I didn't give her that choice, she got into the car and resorted to lashing out, picking at my dad, snapping at me, and generally being unpleasant to us both the whole way there. Only a shred of the empathy and compassion I had over the previous two weeks remained. Though I could recognize that she was acting this way out of sheer terror at what we might learn, my empathy even for that was tested by the onslaught of her insults as I drove.

As we sat in the waiting room, I watched her. I took a picture of her without her knowing. She sat rummaging through her purse, keeping her hands busy. I noticed the tremor now. Before, I hadn't really paid any attention to it, chalking it up to her diminishing physical stature. As she'd lost weight, she hadn't built any muscle and was increasingly weak, so I'd attributed the shakiness to that.

The nurse called us back and we all filed into the exam room. After the nurse asked the preliminary questions and collected my mom's health stats, Dr. Bowman came in. He moved quickly and efficiently and didn't mince words. I liked him immediately.

"Mrs. Patnaude, I'm Dr. Bowman," he said. "Can you hold your arms out in front of you, please?"

Always eager to make a good impression, she smiled and held her arms up in the air, raising them above her head. All traces of her moodiness during the car ride had vanished.

"That's very good, but can I please have you put them out in front of you?"

She brought them down, outstretched in front of her. I watched, trying to decide whether she'd initially raised them up because she hadn't understood the directions or because she was trying to be funny. The latter had never been her style, but that was easier for me to accept than the fact that she hadn't understood a clear direction.

"Thank you, you may put them down." He took a couple of steps back. "Can you please stand up for me, Mrs. Patnaude?"

She handed my dad her purse, reached for his hand to help her, and pushed herself up off the chair. It took her a moment to find her balance. I kept watching, realizing I was usually moving way too fast myself to pay close attention to how her mobility was changing. My throat tightened.

"Can you walk toward me please?" Dr. Bowman asked her. She took careful steps and reached him in just a few short strides. "Actually, let's go out into the hallway. I'd like to see you walk a little further."

"I feel like I'm on a runway!" my mother said, sounding like a giddy schoolgirl. I got up and went to the doorway to see what was happening.

"You absolutely are, Mrs. Patnaude," said Dr. Bowman. "We're all here to see you."

She giggled and walked down the hallway to him, then back toward the room away from him. I could tell from the look of concentration on her face that she was totally focused on walking as normally as possible without any missteps. He watched her legs and feet closely.

They came back into the room, and he asked her to sit down. Then he looked at his chart and recapped what Dr. Wendell had obviously shared with him. "You've been having hallucinations, a loss of smell, abrupt mood changes, and a slight tremor in your hands." He looked up at my mom. "Does that sound correct, Mrs. Patnaude?"

"So they tell me," my mom said dryly, wary now.

He smiled at her. "Tell me about your home," he said.

We all just looked at him, unsure of what he was asking. "What do you mean?" I asked.

"Are there stairs? Is your bedroom on the second floor or first? Where are the bathrooms? Things like that," he explained.

"Yes, there are stairs," my mother answered. "We have an entire second floor with two large bedrooms and a bathroom." *That's a generous way to describe the upstairs of the carriage house,* I thought. There was one bedroom, a full bath, and a large open landing area upstairs, but not technically a second bedroom, and neither space was what I'd call large. I didn't say anything, not wanting to interrupt her. "There's another bedroom on the main floor with a full bath," she continued, "along with the kitchen, dining room, living room, and den. Then there's one more bedroom with a full bath down in the basement."

My dad and I whipped our heads toward her, realization dawning in both of us simultaneously. She was describing their Detroit house.

"Um," I cut in. "That's a great description of your Detroit house, but I think he's probably more interested in the carriage house, where you live now." I looked at her encouragingly and probably a little sympathetically. She bristled but said nothing. Then her expression crumbled into fear as she realized her mistake. I patted her hand and turned back to the doctor with a lump in my throat.

"In this current house," I said, clearing my throat to gain control of my voice, "their bedroom is indeed on the second floor, as is the only full bath with a shower and tub. On the main floor, there's a smaller bedroom they're currently using for storage and a half-bath in the laundry room."

Dr. Bowman nodded. "And is that bedroom on the main floor usable?"

"You mean usable as a bedroom?" I asked. "Sure, it just needs to be cleared out. It's not very big though. Why do you ask?" I had a feeling about what he was going to say.

"Well, here's what happens to us when we're affected by dementia with Lewy bodies, as I believe your mother is," he said. My stomach clenched. That was a very casual way to drop the bomb of this diagnosis. What was it with these doctors up here?

"Wait," I cut in. "Are you saying that she has Lewy body dementia then?" I tried to keep my voice calm, but I sounded anxious even to myself. I was acutely aware of the effects of my reactions to things on my mom, and I wanted her to stay calm.

Dr. Bowman nodded again. "Yes, I'm afraid so," he said. "And that means she needs to avoid the stairs as much as possible, as soon as possible. It means her bedroom needs to be on a main floor, as does the bathroom."

I looked at my parents. My mother was shaking her head and my dad looked pensive. "That would require some renovation," I said. "How urgently does this need to happen?"

"Urgently," he said without hesitation. "Lewy body affects balance and motor function in unpredictable ways. You never know when some part of your motor function will stop working."

I stared at him, again shocked at the very direct and blunt way he was talking about these life-changing things.

My mother recovered first. "Well, that's not going to happen," she said with finality, subject closed. "Our bedroom has always been on the second floor. Ron put handrails on both sides of the staircase so I can hold on with both hands. I'm not going to fall." She started moving like she was going to get up to leave.

Dr. Bowman rolled his stool across to her quickly. He got right up to her and took her hands, looked into her eyes intently, and explained. "Charlotte, may I call you Charlotte?" He didn't wait for a response, and she didn't give one. "I don't think you understand, so I'm going to paint you a picture. You might think you're fine, and then one day your brain will try to tell your foot"—he pointed down to her feet—"to step down and the message will get disrupted. Your foot won't move. Then you'll fall. From what your daughter has described, that staircase is steep and straight. If you were to survive the fall, which is a big if, you'd break at least one hip." A gasp escaped me before I could stop it. He glanced at me but kept going. "You'd go into the hospital and be dead within a few weeks or months. You'd suffer acute pain during that time."

He paused. I realized my mouth was hanging open and I was breathing hard. I couldn't believe how descriptive and crass he was being.

"Don't do that to your family, Charlotte," he added.

My mother's lips were pressed together in a hard line, and she was furious. "No, you may not call me Charlotte," she snapped, pulling her hands away from him. "And if that's the case, then so be it. I'll move downstairs over my dead body."

He rolled back a little bit and looked at her. "You may get your wish, Mrs. Patnaude," he said softly, then looked at me. "I hope for everyone's sake that you're able to change her mind."

Shaken, I looked over at my dad as we all stood up to leave. He looked scared and I saw him swallow hard, fighting tears, which made me tear up. As my parents walked out, I caught the doctor for a moment. "That was a little harsh," I said softly.

He shrugged. "I know. I just hope it was harsh enough to get her to listen to reason about moving downstairs." He looked at me intently. "It really is imperative that that happen as soon as possible for her own safety."

I nodded my understanding. "We'll make it happen."

Still shaken, I followed my parents out.

Looking Back Now

Those last two doctor's visits had me reeling. I felt like I had even less direction and information about what to expect than I had when we'd thought my mom was suffering from Alzheimer's. Her refusal to even discuss the possibility of renovating their small house to make it possible for them to move to the main floor was simply one more battle I now had to have with her. My ever-present level of anxiety ratcheted up with this new information from the neurologist about how dangerous it was for her to have to navigate stairs. I kept hearing his words in my brain: *You'll suffer acute pain . . . imperative that that happen as soon as possible for her own safety . . . you may get your wish, Mrs. Patnaude.*

I was in a constant state of stress, worry, and overwhelm with feelings of inadequacy and hopelessness. I wasn't sleeping well. Looking back now, I wish I'd have realized and understood then what might've helped, even if just a little bit:

➤ There's no good way to prepare yourself to hear a diagnosis that's hard to hear. I don't think I could've done anything differently to prepare myself for those doctor's visits. Instead, if I'd realized that these appointments might affect me the way that they did, I might've scheduled some self-care after each one. For me, that form of self-care would've been making sure my brother was going to meet us for dinner that night and my work schedule was clear so that I didn't have to try to jump back into work when we got back. I also would've made time for a long walk with Dani to talk about everything.

➤ Think about what form of self-care helps you most when you receive difficult news or have had a really bad day. Before you go to any doctor's appointment (because you never know when a bomb will be dropped at one), build in some time afterward to engage in that self-care activity. Calling a friend, going shopping (even if you don't buy anything), or taking a nap can be helpful. The options are limited only to what helps you most.

➢ Resources for caregivers of loved ones with dementia are overwhelmingly focused on caring for people with Alzheimer's, as that type of dementia affects more than half of all people with dementia.[2] If your loved one is affected by Alzheimer's or something similar, those resources might be a little more helpful to you than they were to us. There was nothing I found at the time that specifically spoke to LBD and how to ride that roller coaster, which is a big reason I offer this guidance here.

➢ Advice like "be more patient" is bullshit. We all know we need to be more patient. The hard part is figuring out exactly *how* to do that in the middle of a stressful situation. What I came to understand is that being in the middle of it is exactly the wrong time to try to figure out what to do. Instead, use that journal I hope you're keeping.

➢ Here's an exercise I wish I would've tried at the time. It was inspired by a book called *Crucial Conversations*[3] and is designed to help you move from your emotional reactions to problem-solving:

  ✓ Write down your triggers for losing your cool with your loved one.

  ✓ Think about one example you can focus on. The more specific, the better.

  ✓ For that example situation, ask yourself what your goal is for the interaction. What do you want for yourself?

  ✓ What do you want for your loved one?

  ✓ What do you want for the relationship between you and your loved one?

  ✓ (And then here's the kicker) How would you behave if you really wanted those things?

If you can use these questions to help you think through the top three situations that cause you to react in ways you later regret, it might help you navigate them more successfully the next time.

➢ Not wanting to tell the doctor everything that's happening is a normal response of denial. If you know it will be difficult or uncomfortable for your loved one, consider speaking privately to the doctor to fill in some of the information, whether in person or by phone. Another option could be to talk to your loved one ahead of time about the need to share fully with the doctor in order to receive the best possible care. If they're able to remember that you plan to share things they may find uncomfortable, it might help. If they aren't, they may lash out. Stay grounded in why you're doing it: to help your loved one receive the best possible care. Speak compassionately and reassure your loved one in whatever way helps them feel calmer.

CHAPTER 8

A BATTLE OF BILLS

My mom had always paid all the bills and handled everything related to my parents' finances. So when we heard people in the ALZ support group talk about financial messes their loved ones had created, I paid attention.

"Have you noticed anything happening with the money that we need to pay attention to?" I asked my dad on our way home from a meeting. "Is Mom still handling your bills and such okay?"

He shrugged and said, "I guess so." Since my mom always handled all of that, he never paid attention to the bills.

I stared at him for a moment before looking back at the road. "I'm thinking maybe you should take a peek at the checkbook," I said, unable to keep the sarcasm out of my voice. "Just take a little look-see and make sure everything looks right." I felt angry at him that he was content to play ostrich on this issue. I knew if something terrible happened with their money, it would fall to me and Dani to help support them.

"How would I know what to look for?" he retorted, a little defensive. "Your mother has always taken care of all that stuff." He stared out at the road for a moment, then added, "She always said my job was to make the money and her job was to make the money go far." He half-smiled sadly. My heart sank. I realized he knew something was wrong but was more worried about protecting her dignity and keeping things the way they'd always been than he was about what happened to their money. I decided to do some checking of my own.

The next morning, I walked over to my parents' house unannounced. I hoped to keep the conversation casual, so I didn't warn my mother I was coming so that she wouldn't have time to get worked up and become defensive. My dad was washing their breakfast dishes when I walked in.

"Where's Mom?" I asked. He indicated with a nod of his head that she was in the living room. When I went there, I found my mom sitting on the couch. She was happy to see me.

"I wondered if we could take a look at your propane and electric bills," I started, keeping my tone as neutral as I could. "I noticed that mine have been higher than normal the last couple of months. I want to make sure they're splitting our two houses into two bills and not assuming that both should be billed to my address." None of that was true, but it was the best I could come up with as an excuse to take a look at their bills. She was defensive about her ability to continue managing their money and wouldn't let me look for the sake of looking.

My mom looked at me for a moment, the slightest hint of wariness in her expression, then said, "Well, ours have been normal, so maybe the boys are just leaving the lights on too much. Your house is always blazing, completely lit up with lights. I'm betting that's why your bill was higher this month." She pursed her lips in that mildly condescending way she had. I was immediately triggered, so I took a deep breath to calm myself. *I'm not here to fight*, I reminded myself.

"Yeah, they're the worst," I said. "But they've been like that for a while, so that isn't new this month." I looked at her coolly. "Can I just see those bills please?"

She shook her head, and I wasn't sure whether she was disgusted that I'd just insulted my kids or annoyed that I was asking to see her bills. She made a show of getting up off the couch and making her way over to the dining room table. It was piled with papers, leaving only enough space for their two placemats for eating. I waited, trying to give her space to be independent. After a few minutes, she went over to the little desk where there were more stacks of papers. My dad passed through the dining room, looked at us both, and went to sit on the couch, out of the way.

As my mom shuffled papers around for a few more minutes, I was starting to get irritated and finally spoke up. "Did you forget what you were looking for?" The bitchy comment came out of my mouth before I could help myself.

She snapped her head around, glared at me, then picked up a pamphlet from the desk and shook it at me. I could tell from the purple logo that it was a brochure from the ALZ. "You're not doing it right," she said indignantly. I was surprised and confused.

"Doing *what* right?" I asked with an incredulous laugh.

"Talking to me!" she shouted. "You're not supposed to lose your temper! You're not supposed to quiz me or talk down to me or be mean! You're supposed to be patient and calm! You're not being patient or calm!" She was screeching now.

The irony hit me hard, and I couldn't help but laugh again as my temper flared. "Are you serious right now?" I shouted back. "Are you quoting the fucking ALZ communication brochure at me?"

She glared in anger too, about both the conversation and the fact that I'd said the f-word. She hated when we said it.

I threw my hands up. "I can't!" I spat as I crossed the room to leave. "I came over here to try to help figure out our bills to make sure we're all paying the right amount, and you end up lecturing me that I'm not speaking to you correctly." I was furious now and spun around to face her. "How typical," I shot. "You've been telling me my whole *fucking* life that I'm not doing one thing or another correctly in your high and mighty opinion. What the *fuck* did you move up here for then, huh?" I was practically screaming now, shaking with rage and emphasizing my use of the f-word just to upset her more. I knew I was out of control and needed to get out of there. I threw up my hands again and stormed out.

It took us both a full day to cool down and recover from that exchange. My dad called me that afternoon to say they'd be eating at their own house for dinner that night, sounding tired and a little dramatic. I knew it was the right call for all of us, but I still couldn't help feeling hurt. He never said it directly, but I fully believed he felt like the whole thing was my fault. Ever since I was a little kid, when I'd be arguing with my mom he'd say to me, "If you could just keep your damned mouth shut, we could have some peace and quiet around here." It was never my mom's fault, not even a little bit, no matter how out of control she got. It was always mine. I carried that burden the whole time they lived at the farm. They relied on me for so much, yet they blamed me for not doing more, not being more, and for rising to my mother's bait.

A week or so later, my dad stopped by on his way back from taking the garbage cans out to the road. He came the long way around our house so he could stop and talk to me without my mom knowing. I let him in our front door, which we rarely used, and noticed he looked scared. "What's wrong?" I asked, immediately alarmed.

He pulled a bill from his pocket. "I think you need to look at the bills after all," he said quietly. "I think your mother just wrote a check for $1,403.60 instead of $140.36. Look at this bill." He handed it to me. It showed they had a huge credit on their account. I looked up at him quickly, my mouth hanging open.

"Did you have enough in the account to cover this?" I was immediately worried about overdraft fees and extra charges for this mistake. I knew they didn't have a lot of wiggle room in their budget.

My dad shook his head and shrugged, wide-eyed. "I don't know," he said. "Your mother handles all of that. I don't know how much there is in the account."

I frowned at him and narrowed my eyes, anger starting to creep in. "Well, I guess you better find a way to find out." He looked scared again, and I softened a little, but growled in frustration. "God damnit, Dad, you can't have it both ways! You either need to make her show me the checkbook and help me get a handle on things, or you have to do it yourself. You can't act like you're blameless for this situation. And you can't ask me to come help but then act like I'm the problem when she gets upset!" I was glaring at him.

He nodded sadly, hanging his head as he folded the bill carefully and put it back into his pocket. "When do you want to come over?" he asked.

I stared at him for a moment. "What do you mean?"

"When do you want to come over and look at the bills? I'll tell her we need your help with it." He still looked sad, like this meant admitting her further decline. I hardened myself to his sadness. I was hurt that he never came to my defense with her and was always more than happy to let me be the bad guy.

I shrugged. "I don't know," I said. "I'll have to look at my work schedule and see when I can make time. I'll have to let you know." I knew this couldn't wait long, but I stubbornly tried to hold onto some sort of boundary to keep myself from just running over there immediately and fixing this. "I think before I can come over to talk about this, you're going to have to tell her it's necessary. If neither of you is willing to admit you need some help, I'm not stepping in."

I looked at him defiantly, purposely hanging onto my anger to protect me from feeling sad too. He nodded and went back out the front door. As I closed it behind him, tears of frustration, sadness, and the weight of the burden caught up with me. I leaned against the door and cried.

"Your mother would like some help looking over the bills," my dad said over the phone the next morning, loud enough and in a tone that meant my mother was listening. "When do you think you could come over?"

From the background, my mom said, "To *help* me, not to simply yell at me and take over!" I could tell from her tone she was feeling defensive and hostile.

Feeling my own emotions triggered by her tone, I said, "I'm not sure. I'll have to take a look at my work calendar and get back to you. I know today I'm pretty busy."

My mom scoffed in the background. My dad said slowly, "O-kay . . ."

"I'll let you know," I said again. "I've got a call starting in a few minutes, so I've gotta go. I'll talk to you later."

I ended the call, feeling proud of myself for not jumping to go right then. I took a breath, got up from my desk, and went to the kitchen for more coffee. I didn't have a call starting in a few minutes. In fact, I had a pretty open schedule that day. But I wasn't sure I should go over right away. Part of me felt the urgency of the situation and wanted to fix it, knowing my mom was no longer capable of doing so. Another part of me was dreading the interaction, knowing it would be hard on many levels. I didn't want to have to do this for her because it meant she was losing capacity, which was hard to accept. But I also didn't want that kind of proximity to her. The more we tried to "work together" on something, the more we fought. The fact that she'd led with "to *help* me" meant she was going to fight me simply taking over the bills, which would've been the simplest solution. But I knew she would not let go willingly.

After looking at my calendar and putzing around my office for a little while, I knew I needed to get it over with. I called my dad back and told him I had some time free that afternoon after all and could come over after lunch. That seemed to suit them fine, so after my lunch, off I went.

Walking across the driveway, I felt a sense of dread in the pit of my stomach. I'm not one to shy away from conflict, but this felt like an unfair fight, like I was fighting dirty against an opponent half my size. My mother had always been my sparring partner for verbal jabs, and while she still sent them flying, my retorts were no longer met in the same way. I knew intellectually that I needed to be a better person than I felt capable of being. Emotionally, I was still hurting and simply overwhelmed.

I walked in the house and sang out "Hello-oo" with as much lightness as I could muster. I wanted to get this over with as quickly as possible, knowing that the longer it dragged out, the higher the likelihood of a fight.

"Hello," my mom responded, sounding guarded. "We're in here." I walked through the kitchen to the dining room.

"Found you," I said, smiling.

"In this huge house? What a feat!" my mom responded sarcastically. But she didn't look angry, so that was a good start. She was sitting at the dining room table with piles of papers in front of her. My dad was on the couch, reclining for his after-lunch nap. I knew he wasn't sleeping, but his eyes remained shut.

"Where would you like to begin?" I asked my mother as I sat down at the table with her.

She immediately looked flustered and gestured vaguely to the table. "Well, this is a bit of a mess. I'm having trouble finding things." I bit back the smart retort that came to me and nodded instead, trying to stay casual.

"How about those electric and propane bills as a starting point?" I offered, keeping my tone light.

She nodded and started sifting through some of the papers. "They're here someplace," she muttered, and I started sifting through a different pile to look for them.

"Don't!" she screeched, making me jump. "You'll mess everything up! I have it all organized!"

I stared at her, then at the paper in my hand. It was an old bank statement from three months prior. I looked back at her, frowning. "Mom, this is an old bank statement. What exactly am I messing up?" I kept my voice as calm as I could manage.

She was more frantically moving papers around now and stood up to reach more piles. "I have a system!" she yelled at me. I looked over at the couch to see my dad looking at us through half-open eyes. He saw me look at him, shook his head, then closed his eyes again, sighing. It lit me on fire.

I slammed the statement down on the table and shoved my chair back. "Alright, you two," I growled through clenched teeth, "here's how this is going to go." I pointed my finger at my dad, whose eyes were now wide open, though he didn't move from his position. "Dad, you're not sleeping, nor are you fooling anyone. You need to come in here and help." I turned my burning gaze on my mom. "Mom, you asked for my help. How exactly am I supposed to give you help if I'm not allowed to touch anything? We need to organize the papers on the table so we can get a handle on what's happening with the bills. Doing this alone clearly isn't working out for you. You can either accept my help, which means I'm going to touch things, or I can go back home and you two can figure it out on your own."

I stopped, glaring at them both. My dad was putting the footrest down and getting up off the couch. My mom was still moving papers around but less frantically now, avoiding my stare. "What's it going to be?" I held my ground.

My mom suddenly slumped back down into her chair, looking defeated and miserable, fighting tears. My heart went out to her, but I was still angry. I waited, biting my tongue so I wouldn't speak first.

"Fine," she said tearfully. "You win. I'm just a useless old lady who can't even manage a checkbook anymore." She covered her face and began to cry in earnest.

My dad was standing at the other end of the table now. We looked at each other. He began gathering up papers, and I followed suit. Neither of us spoke.

After a minute, my mom composed herself, found a tissue to wipe her face and blow her nose, and we just kept picking up all the papers. Once they were all in a pile, we started sorting which ones needed to go into their file cabinet and which ones needed attention or were at least current bills.

Once everything was organized, my mom went out to the living room and sat on the couch. I turned to her and calmly said, "Mom, I'm going to need you to pull it together and come back in here with me. You're the only one who's been writing checks and paying bills here for the past fifty-one years of this marriage." I stood my ground, watching her.

She looked at me defiantly for a moment, a retort clearly written on her face but unspoken, then stood up and walked back over to the table, her air of pride restored. "As I said, I wanted your help, not for you to come over here and yell at me," she said haughtily. She met my gaze, challenging me.

I stared back, then said, "I didn't yell, I growled. There's a difference." I kept a straight face only as long as she did. That broke the tension enough for us to sit down and begin.

It was a difficult afternoon. Though she got confused easily, I managed to keep my cool and repeatedly asked her to trust me when she did. As long as I stayed calm, that seemed to work. By the end of the afternoon, I was exhausted, as was she, but we got everything sorted out. I set up auto payments on every bill I could, which was everything except medical copays.

When I tried to get her to hand over the checkbook, that's where she drew the line. Her compromise was that she'd have me come once a week to "help" her write checks. That worked for a while. But then one day, she simply couldn't remember how to write a check. That day, my parents came over for dinner, and I could tell my mother had been crying. She tried to keep her dignity intact as she handed me the checkbook. I was caught off guard.

"What happened?" I asked, my voice reflecting my surprise and concern.

"I tried several times to write a check," she said, fighting back fresh tears, her tone clipped. "You'll see that it did not work." She handed me a bill. "I need you to write this check for me please."

Fighting tears myself, I took the bill and nodded my head. "Okay," I said softly. "No problem." I waited, but she didn't say anything else, so I asked tentatively, "Do you want me to hang onto this over here?"

She nodded once. "That might be easiest."

She turned away, in search of a tissue. I took the checkbook and bill and headed to my office. I didn't let myself open it then. Instead, I took a deep breath to calm myself and went back to the kitchen to make dinner.

Once my parents went home that evening, I sat down and looked at the checkbook. My mother had tried to write one check on the duplicate paper from a previous check, even trying to sign her name in the blacked-out area where the signature line is on an original check. One was made out to herself, and another had an explanation of what the check was for on the line where you write out the amount in words. I sobbed as I looked at them. This woman had taught me to write a check, manage a checkbook, invest, and create and live by a budget. To see in her own writing the struggle it had been for her mind to do this once-routine task simply broke me. It was one of the moments when

I sat helplessly witnessing as this horrible disease robbed this proud, capable woman of her dignity.

Nearly a month had passed since my mom had gotten the LBD diagnosis, and the fight to move my parents' bedroom to the main floor of the carriage house began in earnest. My mother was still adamant that she would not move to the main floor, and we were equally adamant that it needed to happen. Even if Dr. Bowman hadn't succeeded in scaring her, he'd scared the crap out of me. My brother David felt the same way, so we began to plot.

Though I'd talked to my parents many times about how to make the necessary renovations to their little house so they could move their bedroom to the main floor, my mother was no longer talking to me about it. If I tried to bring it up, she'd get aggressive or just leave the room. So I told my brother it was his turn, and he agreed to take a stab at it.

David hosted all of us for Christmas Eve dinner at his house. Dani and I were sitting in the living room after dinner, watching our kids and David's all play a game. My dad was sitting with us, and my mom and brother were around the corner in the dining room, within earshot.

"Hey, Mom," I heard David start. "I was thinking about coming up while we're on break and taking a look at that bathroom on your main floor. I think it would be good to put in a shower down there. What do you think?"

I smirked, waiting for the refusal.

"Oh, that would be lovely, David!" my mother exclaimed like an excited child.

I whipped my head around to look at Dani, my mouth open in angry shock. Dani stifled a giggle and held up her hands in a surrender gesture. My dad was within our line of sight, so he just looked at me, hiding a smile.

My brother got cocky. "I also could take a look at moving the wall of that bedroom a little bit so you could have more room in there," he continued.

There was a pause.

"Why would you do that?" my mom asked, sounding wary. I looked triumphantly at Dani. *Here it comes*, I mouthed.

David cleared his throat. "Well, I thought it would be good to make that a usable room. Right now, it seems like it's not big enough for much more than the one twin bed that's in there and some boxes. I thought it might be nice if it were big enough for two twin beds or a queen bed. That way, your granddaughters could come stay with you. Or me and Lauren."

I was back to being shocked, this time at his very clever approach. I waited. I think all of us were holding our breath.

"That's a good point," my mom said, sounding reasonable and calm. "I hadn't thought about that." She paused, then in a lower, conspiratorial voice said, "Your sister's been trying to bully me into moving down into that bedroom."

My mouth was agape, mostly in mock horror and feigned innocence, as I looked from Dani to my dad. Both were struggling not to laugh.

My mom continued, "But she's not going to win. I don't have to move to the first floor if I don't want to." She sounded like a petulant child.

"No, you don't," my brother said. "But this way, it'll be ready in case you ever change your mind."

There was another pause. I imagined my mother thinking this over while fiddling with a napkin. "You're right," she said finally. "I think that's a great idea."

I continued my over-the-top silent reaction of mock outrage to Dani and my dad, both of whom were having a hard time not laughing. I felt a mixture of relief, admiration, and appreciation for my brother, resentment that he'd been able to achieve what I hadn't, and irritation toward my mother for kindly responding to him while constantly fighting me. There was a small part of me that was deeply hurt that she'd said I'd been bullying her. One more way in which she just never thought I was doing anything right. I didn't know which emotion to let win. I settled on appreciation for David.

When we said goodbye, I whispered in his ear, "You're a fucking magician."

He chuckled and hugged me hard. "Happy to help. You're doing most of the heavy lifting over there." That brought a tear to my eye unexpectedly. I hugged him hard back.

Over the next six months, David and my dad got the work done. They converted the half-bath into a full bath, made a new laundry area, and moved the wall of the bedroom out three feet to make it big enough to fit my parents' bed and dressers. By June 2019, seven months after the neurologist had ordered it to be so, they were finally moved into their first-floor setup. My dad closed the door to the upstairs and put in a cat door so the cats could still move freely. After all the initial fuss, when it came time to move to the first floor, my mom acted like it had been her plan and idea all along. We let her have that one and kept our mouths shut.

Looking Back Now

This stage is when I really started feeling like I was losing my parent. Up until this point, my mom had so many lucid days that her dementia was almost like little time-outs from our "regularly scheduled programming" of interactions. She'd slip, hallucinate, and become confused, but she'd still been functioning with enough "normal" days that it hadn't hit me yet. At this point, it did. Hard.

The sadness and grief were the obvious parts of the journey. What I didn't expect was how unprepared I felt at the idea that my mom wouldn't be around and functioning the way she always had. It may sound childish (it does to me as I write it), but while intellectually I always knew that would be the case, emotionally I was caught off guard by how much that upset me. I'd been fighting for my independence from my mother my whole life. Once I could see clearly that her illness was becoming a reality, I wanted to stop time, roll back the clock, and have a do-over. But I wasn't going to get one of those, and that realization took me literally to my knees.

This wasn't a turning point, I'm afraid, as I still rose to her bait and she to mine. But it changed the trajectory of the journey. Looking back now, I see some things I wish I'd been able to see then:

➢ Many insights about caregiving come only with hindsight. Caregivers are so completely consumed with trying to keep their heads above water that finding time to sit and reflect on the experience can feel impossible. It did for me. Professionally, I'm a workplace communication coach, so reflection, gaining insight, and responding intentionally are my jam. And yet, I found it nearly impossible to apply those same skills to caregiving. There never seemed to be enough time or energy. Between working, raising kids, helping to run a farm, and caregiving, I had no bandwidth for sitting and processing what I was experiencing. As a consequence, sometimes revelations hit me hard out of the blue. That might've been different had I been more consistent about keeping a journal. I can't encourage you enough to start keeping one.

➤ Role reversals are hard. Taking over the finances of the person who may have taught you to do your own is a mind-bending experience. It's one of the many ways in which traditional parent–child roles get turned upside down because of this disease and others like it. And it's perfectly normal to experience it as a form of trauma. I didn't know to expect it, and I sure as hell didn't know what to expect in terms of how I'd feel in the middle of it. It can be a mashup of many feelings, including guilt, sadness, anger, resentment, overwhelm, anxiety, and loss. It was all those things for me. I'm pretty sure there's no way around those feelings, but had I known to expect them as part of the journey, I might've been able to take it in stride a little more. I might've also used other self-care tools (journaling, making space to have time alone to feel my feels, meditation) to help me work through the feelings. Instead, I just pushed them all away to keep fighting the fire.

➤ Caregiving is a team sport. Stay focused on the end goal rather than on which player takes the team across the finish line. I'm competitive by nature. Watching my brother step in and convince my mother so easily of something I'd been unsuccessful at doing for a full month was frustrating. Even though I'd asked for his help, I wasn't prepared for him to be successful. I lost sight of the end goal for a while, and it caused some tension in our relationship along the way. Remember to focus on the goal.

➤ If you find that you're beating yourself up for not being able to "just figure it out," you're not alone. I had more of those days than I can count. Feelings of guilt, shame, and inadequacy are totally normal while caregiving. They come from dealing with something completely unknown, unpredictable, and unexpected. You're constantly chasing that 8-ball, trying to keep up. If someone had been there to help me normalize or accept those feelings and see them for what they were, it would've helped me both during the awful journey and afterward. So, for what it's worth, let me be that person for you here. I see you. You're not alone.

CHAPTER 9

SMOKE AND MIRRORING

As the roller coaster continued, I'd call David periodically, usually from the car, ranting and raving about our mom's latest antics. I didn't mince words, and he could feel my frustration and burnout through the phone. At this point, my parents were coming to our house for dinner five nights a week as well as joining us with Dani's family for Sunday family dinners. And if we didn't have explicit plans to go out someplace, they'd often come for the seventh night too. We didn't get much of a break, but I hadn't asked for one. I felt guilty leaving them on their own. It was making me passive aggressive (or "aggressive aggressive," as Dani would say), and David picked up on it.

"Why are you letting them come for dinner every single night?" he asked me one evening as I finished my latest rant. "You don't need to feed them every night. And you need a break."

I sighed in frustration as I pulled into our driveway and parked. "I know I need a fucking break. I'm losing my mind! But I feel guilty every time I think about them fumbling around over there on their own. It makes me sad. They ate dinner every single night with friends and neighbors for so many years. I just . . . I can't." I felt guilty even saying any of this out loud.

My brother cleared his throat. "Well, you're the only one who can give yourself permission, but in case you need it, I'm giving you permission," he said. "Pick two nights and claim them for your family. Tell them which two nights they're on their own. They can take their asses out to dinner or make something at home. Dad's capable of making things. Worst case scenario, they can heat up TV dinners."

My shoulders slumped as I sat in the car listening to him. "I know," I said again. "I know you're right."

He went on. "I'm serious. This isn't fair to you. And if that's not enough to convince you, it's not fair to Dani or the boys. You need some time as a family. Two nights a week isn't going to kill them. They'll be fine."

I nodded in the dark car, even though he couldn't see me. "I know," I said yet again, sounding tired even to my own ears.

He waited for me to say more. I didn't, so he said, "So? Which two nights is it going to be?"

I laughed. "Seriously? You're going to make me pick them now?"

"Yeah, I'm gonna make you pick them now," he answered immediately. "Because if I don't, you won't do it. So pick. Which two nights?"

I laughed again. "Oh, I don't know . . . Friday and Saturday. Wait, is that fair? Should it be two nights that aren't consecutive?"

"It should be whatever two fucking nights you want!" he exclaimed, laughing.

"Fine!" I exclaimed back, laughing too. "Friday and Saturday!"

We laughed together for a moment, and then he said more seriously, "Okay, I'm holding you to it. I'm calling Dad, and if he tells me they're going to your house for dinner on any Friday or Saturday, I'm going to yell at you."

That made me laugh for real, then immediately caused me to choke up. My brother is my opposite in many ways. He's much calmer and more laid back than I am and will go to great lengths to avoid confrontation. He breaks out in a sweat just thinking about having to speak in front of a group of people, whereas that's a big part of what I do for a living. So the idea of him yelling at me for not honoring my commitment tickled me. It also made me feel very loved and supported.

The next day, I talked to my parents about it. I went over to their house, and we all took a walk down the road. I didn't mention that I'd talked to David. My mother had made it clear on many occasions that she absolutely hated the idea of any of us talking about her behind her back for any reason. It had the effect of causing her instant paranoia that was harder and harder to reason through with her. I took another angle instead.

"So, I think my little family might need a couple nights a week to just be together," I started.

My mom whipped her head around to look at me. She seemed startled. "What do you mean?" Always one to be anxious and expect the worst, she sounded alarmed.

I shrugged, trying to keep things casual. "It's no big deal," I said, smiling at her. "The boys are at a tricky age, and I just think it would be good for us to have a couple nights a week to just focus on them at dinner." I glanced over at my dad, hoping he'd pick up on what I was trying to say and back me up. I suddenly wished I'd talked to him about it first.

"Oh," my mom said, sounding hurt. "But you focus on them all the time at dinner. You always ask how their days went and what's happening. What else do you need to discuss?" She sounded concerned now, like there was a big problem brewing under the surface that needed addressing.

"There's nothing specific," I said, still keeping my tone friendly and hearing my brother's voice in my head. *Two nights a week isn't going to kill them.* "I just think there's stuff they might need to talk about with us that they don't necessarily want to talk about in front of their grandparents."

"Huh," my mom said, sounding genuinely surprised. "Well, I don't know why not. We're the same age as you."

I looked at her, thinking she was trying to be funny. Her face was serious. She looked at me. She looked normal; no dementia face. "Really?" I said, trying to feel it out without sounding too sarcastic.

She looked surprised and gave a little laugh. "Yes, *really*," she said with indignance. I looked over at my father. He was looking around at the fields, hoping to spot a deer and avoiding my eyes.

I kept walking, not sure how to respond. After a moment, she realized her mistake and said a little defensively, "Well, I mean, I know we're not the same age, of course, but I just forget that. You're an adult now and running your life so"—she waved her hands around, gesturing to the universe—"efficiently! I forget that you're younger than we are." I was pretty sure she did know that but was trying to cover her mistake.

"Okay," I said. "Well, the two nights we're going to just be on our own are Fridays and Saturdays. You guys can go out on your own or with some of your new friends from the seniors' group or make dinner on your own." I paused and glanced at my mother. She looked disappointed. Her head was down, and she was watching where she walked while hanging onto my dad's arm like she always did. Guilt hit me hard. They looked so vulnerable. I swallowed the lump in my throat and took a deep breath to keep myself from taking it all back.

We walked on in silence for a while, the sounds of the trees and birds soothing me but not taking away the sadness I suddenly felt. After a few minutes, my dad saw a deer in one of the fields, something he always got excited about, and the conversation returned to normal.

After finishing our walk, I headed back to my house. I turned around to tell them what time to come for dinner that night, but I stopped. They were ambling slowly back to their house. My mom was pointing at something back in the pasture behind their house, not in an alarming way but just telling my dad something she was seeing. I couldn't hear them, but the sight of them walking arm in arm, moving slowly, overwhelmed me with sadness. I had a sense of loss and grief. I clamped my hand over my mouth so they wouldn't hear the sob that suddenly bubbled up, then turned and went into my house.

By mid-2019, my mom's hallucinations were getting increasingly more elaborate. I'd get calls from my dad's phone only to hear my mom's voice on the line, shrill with anxiety and distress.

"Ellen, you need to come over here right now!" she exclaimed on one such call. "There's a man here who keeps trying to tell me he's your father"—her voice dropped to an urgent whisper—"but I know he's not! Your father left and this man appeared. He's trying to get me to go to bed with him!"

I was used to her hallucinations by now, but this was a new one. Was she forgetting who my dad was? Her husband of 52 years plus nine years of dating before that? "Umm," I said, unsure of how to respond, "I'll be right over. Try to stay calm. I'm confident he won't hurt you." I hung up and sighed, feeling exhausted from dealing with this tangled web and unpredictable behavior. But I got up from my desk and headed out the door.

As I walked across the driveway, I could hear my mom's shrill voice yelling, "Don't you touch me!" She sounded scared. I quickened my pace, worried for my dad as much as for her. Then I heard, "No!" I started running.

I rushed into their kitchen exclaiming, "What's going on?! What's wrong?"

My dad was standing at one end of the kitchen, his face a mixture of confusion, fear, and hurt. My mother was at the other end near the door I'd just come through, pacing around and highly agitated. "He tried to grab me!" she shrieked. She was on the brink of tears.

"Okay, okay, I'm here now, you're okay," I soothed, putting my arm around my mom and looking across at my dad with a questioning look on my face. "What happened?" I asked him.

He looked bewildered. "I don't know," he said, sounding just as confused. "One minute we were sitting on the couch. I was resting and she was fussing with something. She got up and walked over to the window, pacing like she does, and then she turned around and all of a sudden she thought I was someone else." He sounded scared and was fighting off tears. It had clearly shaken him.

I was still rubbing my mom's back, now swaying with her to try to calm her down. I turned to look at her. Dementia face. "Mom, that's just Dad," I said softly. "He's not going to hurt you. Like, ever. He's the same harmless nice guy he's always been." I waited, but she just kept looking around nervously. I kept gently rubbing her back, continuing to try to soothe her. "I promise you, you're safe." My heart went out to her. I swallowed a lump in my throat.

"Well, that's not who was here before," she said, her voice starting to calm down. She was still swaying back and forth, and I swayed with her. Her face seemed to be going back to normal. I was fascinated, heartbroken, scared, and deeply sad all at the same time. I continued to swallow hard and control my emotions. I knew it would only scare and upset her again if I started to cry.

"What do you mean, 'that's not who was here before'?" I asked gently.

"Just what I said!" She got a little agitated again, then pointed at my dad and said, "That's not who was here before!"

"Okay, okay," I cooed. "I'm sorry, I was just trying to understand what happened." I paused, making sure she was calming down again. "So, someone else was here with you and Dad?" I asked tentatively.

She clucked her tongue and gestured around the room with her arms. I stopped rubbing her back and stepped to the side to avoid being struck by her sudden movement. "No-o," she said impatiently. "Ron wasn't here! Another man showed up as soon as he left and then tried to tell me he was Ron, but I knew he wasn't. I'm not sure what his name was . . . maybe Dave? He looks a lot like Ron, but I know he's not!" She was a little agitated again but didn't seem out of control.

I nodded, and keeping my tone calm I asked, "Okay, well, is he gone now?"

She looked at me like *I* had dementia. "Don't you see your father standing right there?" Her voice was full of sarcasm and insult. "And you call *me* the one with dementia? Ha!" Her self-righteous and condescending attitude was back, and my empathy evaporated instantly. I stifled a sigh, my exhaustion immediately rushing back.

"Alright, that's enough of that," I said flatly. "I'll remind you that I came over here because you called and were upset. I was trying to help. No need to get nasty." I turned to my dad, who now looked more irritated than anything else, yet still a little shaken. "You guys good on your own for dinner tonight?" I asked. "It's Friday."

He nodded, still keeping his eyes mostly on my mom. "Yes, we're just going to make some TV dinners."

"Okay, sounds good," I said. "Dani and I are heading out to dinner with friends, so are you good to lock up the chickens for us tonight?" I glanced once more at my mom, who was now putzing around with something on the counter. I looked back at my dad as I started for the door.

My dad nodded as his face lit up with an exaggerated smile but genuine happiness. "Sure, no problem!" he exclaimed. He really did love helping us take care of the animals. I smiled at him in return, his demeanor endearing him further to me.

"Okay, well, then I guess if everyone here is all set . . ." I looked at my mom, waiting for her to look at me and acknowledge that she was fine now. "You alright now, Mom? You don't need me here anymore?"

She looked up at me, seeming to be lost in thought. "Yes," she said distractedly, then added with a more playful air, "You may go." She smiled at me, but it was forced.

"Well call if you need anything. We'll just be in Lapeer, so we can get home relatively quickly if we need to. The boys are all set up with food and movies, so they'll be fine on their own. If we don't talk to you again this evening, we'll see you tomorrow." I smiled, gave a little wave to them both, and walked out the door.

I walked back across the driveway, reliving the scene from when I'd first gotten there. I shook my head. It was so bizarre how these hallucinations showed up. Thinking my dad was someone else was a new twist and made me nervous. If she turned on him, we were all in trouble.

As Dani and I got ready to go a short while later, I told her what had happened. "Do you think it's still okay for us to go out to dinner?" I asked her. I felt uneasy, but I was also looking forward to having dinner with our friends.

She shrugged, not wanting to tell me I was worrying about nothing nor wanting to give up our plans either. "I think so," she said. "We'll only be in Lapeer. If anything happens, we can get back here within half an hour."

I still felt uneasy, but we got in the truck and headed to Lapeer. As Dani drove, I told her more about what had happened and the feeling I'd had watching the scene unfold. She was equally worried about what this new development might mean for the future and asked me, "Didn't Dr. Wendell say your dad needed to hide all the knives in the kitchen?"

I nodded. "Yes, but my dad's convinced they won't be a problem. He says she never cooks anymore or seems to even notice the knife block on the counter. I've tried to tell him to put them away anyway, but so far he hasn't."

Dani stared at me for a moment. "That's not good," she said in a low voice. "It's fine until it's not." That was always one of her favorite sayings. And it was very true.

"Yeah, I know," I said, looking out the window. "After today's incident, I'm even more worried about it. I'm going to talk to him again about it tomorrow."

About 30 minutes later, we arrived at a restaurant in Lapeer. We met friends for dinner, and for a couple of hours we laughed and enjoyed good company, trying to forget about my parents. I checked my phone every few minutes and was reassured by the lack of messages from my dad. Afterward, we stopped at the grocery store while we were in town to grab a few things, then headed back home.

It was dark by the time we pulled into the driveway. I could see into my parents' living room window as we parked. My dad was on the couch and my mom was at the window, rocking back and forth, watching us. I wasn't sure whether she could see us, but I waved. She didn't wave back. The uneasy feeling crept back into the pit of my stomach.

"I'm just going to text my dad and make sure everything went alright this evening," I told Dani as we headed into the house. "I just have this feeling."

I texted my dad: *How did everything go? Chickens all locked up?*

He texted back: *All locked up. Minor crisis but everything okay now. Will tell you tomorrow.*

"Well, that's not good," I said, reading Dani his text. "I wonder what happened?"

She shook her head and gave me a half-smile. "I don't know, but I know you, and you won't sleep worrying and wondering what happened, so I suggest you find a way to find out tonight if you can."

I knew she was right. I texted my dad again: *I'm not sure I'll be able to sleep wondering what happened . . . any chance you can call me or come over?*

He texted back: *Hang on.*

A couple of minutes later, my phone rang. "What happened?" I said as soon as I answered, putting it on speaker so Dani could hear too.

"I told her I needed to get something from the shed, so I only have a minute," he answered in a low, quiet voice. "We took out TV dinners to heat up. I told her I was just going to go lock up the chickens real quick so once we sat down to eat I wouldn't have to get up again. So I went down to the coop. I was only down there for maybe five minutes. I only sang one song." My dad loved to sing, and he delighted in singing to the chickens. I think he enjoyed the peace and quiet of the coop and the way the chickens cooed at him as he sang. It was really quite sweet and endearing to watch. Dani and I smiled at each other.

"So anyway," he continued, "I was heading back up the hill, not wanting to be gone that long after today's . . . incident, and as I came up the hill to the house, I heard the smoke alarms going off"—I gasped—"and saw smoke pouring out of the kitchen window."

Horrified, I stared at Dani, whose expression mirrored my own. "Oh no," I breathed. "What happened?"

"She had put the TV dinner on the glass-top stove and turned on the burner. She thought she was heating it up," his voice cracked with emotion. "But it was in a cardboard container, and it started to catch fire." He was upset but still trying to keep his voice low.

I felt my eyes prick with tears. "Oh Dad," I breathed again, looking away from Dani, my heart breaking for him. As hard as this was for me, I couldn't imagine what he must be going through watching his beloved wife transform like this. I looked back up at Dani and saw that she was also fighting tears.

"Luckily," he went on after regaining a bit of control, "I got back in there before it actually caught on fire. There was just a lot of smoke. And of course the damned alarms screaming didn't help any. I think the noise of those upset her more than the smoke did."

I let out a breath I didn't realize I was holding. "Oh Dad," I said again. "That's terrible. But everyone's okay? The house is okay? No real damage?" I wondered if he needed any help cleaning things up.

"No, no real damage," he said, sounding tired.

Then, from the background came a shrill "Ron?! Where are you?" She sounded scared.

"You better go," I said quickly. "I'll talk to you tomorrow. Call if you need us sooner."

We both hung up as he called to my mom, "I'm right here, dear, just getting something from the shed."

I looked at Dani, the events of the day catching up with me. I suddenly felt overcome with emotion and my face crumpled. Hers did too, and she put her arms around me. We just stood for a minute like that. I thought about how incredibly grateful I was to have her as my rock. And I couldn't help feeling overwhelmed by sadness for my dad as he watched his own rock disappearing under water.

One evening at the ALZ support group meeting, the facilitator of the group told us about an upcoming workshop being offered by the Area Agency on Aging. It had two parts: one part classroom learning and one part in an "experiential room." I was intrigued. Other members of the group had attended the workshop in the past, one gentleman saying, "It really gives you a sense of what they're experiencing." A few others agreed.

"I think we should go to it," I whispered to my dad. He shrugged and nodded, willing but not eager. He wasn't a workshop kind of guy, and the caregiver program he'd been through the previous fall hadn't done as much to help him as he'd hoped. In fact, it had turned him away from believing that any other workshop held any potential value. I looked at it differently. I figured if one wasn't effective, maybe another one would be. I signed us up.

When we arrived for the workshop a couple of weeks later, I wasn't really sure what to expect. There were about eight people in the group. We all signed in and sat down at a table to get started. I noticed a woman coming out of an adjoining room that had black plastic covering the opening where the door would've been. She smiled at me and quickly pulled the plastic closed behind her. Suddenly, I felt nervous. I looked at my dad. He'd seen her too and was watching her warily.

Another woman announced we were getting started and smiled brightly at everyone. "Thank you for coming today," she said, her tone upbeat and soothing at the same time. "As you may have noticed, we have two rooms where you'll participate in activities today." She gestured to the tables where we were all sitting. "This is where you'll be when you're not in the other room." She gestured to the room with the black plastic hanging in the doorway. "And this is our experiential dementia room," she said, turning back to us with a more somber expression on her face. "You'll be guided through this room one person at a time," she said more softly now. "One of us will help you get ready to go in, and then someone else will meet you inside and guide you through the experience."

The nervous feeling I had suddenly radiated through my belly. I had to take a deep breath to calm myself. I wasn't sure why I was feeling so rattled. I didn't know what to expect, but the older gentleman in our support group hadn't seemed bothered by the experience, so I was confused about why I was anxious. I tried to shake it off. The woman leading things was asking for a volunteer to go first. Everyone looked around at everyone else. One of the women sitting at the table raised her hand and said she'd go.

The leader started talking to us, but I still have no idea what she was saying. I watched the volunteer instead. She was given shoes to put on to replace her own and a pair of headphones that looked like the noise-canceling, big earmuff kind. Then they gave her a strange-looking pair of glasses. She stood up, needing a moment to find her balance and saying somewhat loudly to the woman helping her, "Ooh, these shoes feel spiky on my feet!"

She was then guided to the black plastic and given some sort of instruction I couldn't hear, and the woman guiding her stepped away. She felt around in front of her for a second, then pushed the plastic aside. I couldn't see into the room, as it seemed dimly lit. When the plastic closed behind her, I had the sensation that she was going into one of those haunted house attractions. It did not help my nerves. I waited, straining to hear anything coming from beyond the barrier, but I couldn't hear anything other than undecipherable talking.

I have no recollection of what the other activity was that those of us not in the dementia room were supposed to be doing. Neither does my dad. Our preoccupation with what was happening on the other side of that black plastic is the only thing either of us remembers. I do have the distinct memory of thinking that it was just something to keep us busy while we waited our turn to go in.

The leaders had a second set of shoes, headphones, and glasses for going into the room, and my dad got outfitted to go in next. The woman who'd gone in first came out, taking the glasses off as she did and seeming to wince from the way the shoes felt on her feet. While she was taking off the shoes and headphones, she said, "Those shoes were the worst part!" She didn't seem too traumatized, and I started to wonder if I was scared for no reason. My dad was guided up to the plastic and the process repeated. He didn't seem bothered by the shoes.

I decided to go next and got suited up in the set of equipment the first woman had just taken off. The shoes were very weird. They made my feet tingle and hurt a little bit as I tried to walk. The headphones blocked out nearly all noise from outside. I could hear the sounds of a radio station that wasn't quite tuned in all the way, so there was static mixed in with the faint sounds of a DJ. The volume was very low, so it was really hard to make out what they were saying. The glasses fit over my own prescription glasses and served to block out my peripheral vision completely, which made me feel like I was looking through a distorted tunnel.

I was standing, waiting for my dad to come out so that I could go in. He came out a moment later, looking a little disoriented from what I could see through my new weird glasses. Before I could talk to him or see if he was okay, I was led to the black plastic and told, "Just go into the next room. There's nothing to be afraid of."

The black plastic in front of me was distorted by the glasses. I couldn't tell how close or far away it was from me. Expecting it to be further away, I reached out and was startled at how close it was. I moved it aside and stepped through the doorway.

The room was indeed dimly lit. From what I could see with a quick glance around, it was set up a bit like stations representing different areas of a typical house. I turned my head too quickly and felt a wave of nausea hit me. The glasses took away my depth perception. I stood still for a moment, trying to get my bearings. A woman came up to me, approaching from the side so I didn't see her, and touched my arm. I startled again and felt tears prick my eyes. I didn't like this sensation. At all.

She took my arm, leading me to a table where a laundry basket sat with some towels in it. She was talking to me in soothing, low tones. I couldn't quite make out what she was saying, so I said, "What?" kind of loudly. She spoke again but didn't really raise her voice, so I still couldn't tell what she was saying. I began to feel frustrated and a little panicked. My feet hurt too. I wanted out of the room but tried to follow her lead. I couldn't make out what she said, so I just watched as she picked up a towel and folded it, then handed one to me to fold.

Taking my elbow again, which didn't startle me this time because I saw her coming, she then guided me over to what looked like a kitchen area with another table. There were stacked plates and a pile of silverware at one end. She was saying something again and gesturing to the plates, silverware, and table. I'd given up on trying to understand her with the noise in my ears, so I just picked up silverware and began setting the table. Apparently I wasn't doing it the way she wanted because she came over and moved the silverware into different positions at the place setting. I'd grown up setting a table with a very particular mother, so I knew I was doing it correctly. I moved the silverware back.

Tears again pricked my eyes and my frustration level rose higher. I couldn't see properly, I couldn't hear anything but this annoying staticky radio station, and my feet were killing me. I wanted to rip off the glasses and headphones and throw the shoes against the wall. My panic was starting to overwhelm me.

"I need to get out of here," I said firmly and loudly. "I get the point and I'm done. You need to let me leave!" I could hear the panic in my own voice. I tried to pull the glasses off, but they were stuck under the headphones and caught in my own glasses. The struggle only made me panic more. I managed to get the headphones off, then the glasses, and finally felt like I could breathe again. The woman was standing and staring at me, watching me intently, waiting to see whether I got it.

All of a sudden, it hit me like a brick wall. This was the whole point of the exercise. People with dementia experience the everyday world through a different lens, literally. Their vision can be affected, their hearing can be impaired, and they often develop neuropathy in their feet, making walking painful and causing them to shuffle. They don't know what's happening or why, and unlike me in that moment, they're not able to take off headphones or glasses.

Overwhelmed by emotion, I stood staring back at this woman and put my hand to my mouth. I suddenly felt a very strong urge to run home to my mom and hug her tight. I was instantly sorry for every moment of impatience, every harsh word.

"I get it," I sobbed to the woman. "I get it. Can I please go now?"

She smiled sympathetically at me and nodded. "I know this was hard," she said. "I hope that it was also helpful to you. I wish you the best with your loved one."

Unable to speak, I nodded, then pushed my way back through the black plastic. My dad was sitting at the table, watching for me. When he saw that I was crying, he welled up with tears too. As I took off the shoes and gave everything back to the woman, he stood up and made his way over. I noticed the other people still waiting to go into the room watching me with expressions that were a mixture of fear, concern, and discomfort. I'm not sure whether my emotional display was what made them uncomfortable, but it made me feel very alone, yet again. I felt like the only one who'd been affected like this by the experience. I tried to wipe my face and pull myself together.

"Let's go," I whispered to my dad, still fighting to stop crying.

We walked out together and headed back to the car. "That was terrible," I whispered to him. "Absolutely terrible. All I could think about was how much I wanted to rip off those headphones, shoes, and glasses and how Mom never can." I was crying again, my sobs causing me to choke on some of my words.

My dad walked beside me, trying to be stoic, stifling a sob of his own. Neither of us touched the other. I think we both knew that physical comfort would make both of us come even more undone. We got back to the car, each of us trying to regain our composure, and drove the 30 minutes home in silence.

The experience in the dementia room drove home for me that we needed respite care for my mom. Living with dementia was extremely hard on her, but it was also taking quite a toll on us. We all needed a break, my dad more than anyone. He was with my mom nearly 24/7. We watched him slow down considerably, unable to walk as fast or as far anymore, and simply running out of energy on any given day hours before he would have previously. I knew some of it was due to him getting older, as he had turned 78 that summer, but it also felt like at least some of it was from the unrelenting burden of caregiving.

My dad must've been feeling it too, because a couple of days later he showed up at my house under the pretense of getting some tool from Dani. Once inside my kitchen, he said, "Linda and Nancy from Seniors ["Seniors" being the shorthand way he and my mom referred to the local seniors' group] have volunteered to come sit with your mother for a couple hours at a time so I can have a break." True to form, he didn't preempt this with any small talk or context; he just said it out of the blue one day.

I nodded, used to his style. "I think that sounds like a great idea, as long as they know what they're in for." I was thinking of her endless pacing and often foul mood.

"Well, when we're at Seniors, she's always very pleasant to everyone," he said, reading my mind. "She's like that with everyone but us, just like she's always been." My eyebrows went up. That was the closest he'd ever come to admitting out loud that she was particularly nasty with us while acting like everything was perfect to the rest of the world.

I snorted. "Yeah, that checks out," I said sarcastically. "Well, it can't hurt to try, right? Even if they went over to your house and you just came over to my house and took a nap or something." I shrugged. "I think you should see when they're available."

My dad nodded once, the matter settled. "Okay, I'll call them this afternoon." He walked back to their house just as my mom came out the front door, throwing her arms up at him like he was a child who'd wandered off while she was busy with housework. I shook my head, wondering again how he put up with it.

Looking Back Now

The dementia room was deeply upsetting to experience because of the connection I'd made between my ability to take off glasses, headphones, and shoes to avoid pain and confusion and my mom's inability to do the same. And since my mom's behavior didn't indicate that she was experiencing most of those symptoms, my being in that room was also jarring and confusing. Though I know it wasn't the intention, the experience felt like a scare tactic.

I can look back now and see even more clearly what the intention was and why the experience was so upsetting. The intention was to give caregivers an experience that paralleled that of their loved ones as closely as possible. It was designed to create empathy and understanding and to help caregivers dig deep in moments of frustration to understand the importance of remaining calm and patient. It was also likely intended to make caregivers aware of the growing limitations to their loved ones' ability to understand and accurately perceive what was happening around them.

It did all those things for me. The unfortunate reality of my mother's reactions and nature, however, made for a different experience after leaving the dementia room. I came home that day and hugged her hard. While she seemed to appreciate the gesture, she was confused by it, which caused her to feel suspicious and paranoid. My clear distress caused her distress as well. Feeling suspicious, paranoid, and distressed caused her to lash out. It made her feel much the same way I'd felt when I got to the end of my rope in that room. Except that she didn't understand why.

So, all I could do was back away, try to soothe her, and realize that this was one more thing I could no longer share with my mom. As contentious as our relationship had always been, she had always, without exception, been there for me if I was upset or distressed about something. It didn't matter what it was. Her first instinct was to protect and comfort me and to seek to understand what was happening so she could help me problem-solve. Now the roles were somewhat reversed, with an important distinction: I couldn't problem-solve with her anymore. It only served to further upset and confuse her. For that, I now needed to turn to someone else.

It was a realization I fought for much of our journey through dementia. And it's one of the regrets I have now. Had I been able to shift my thinking in the moment, might I have reduced some of my mom's anxiety and stress? I problem-solved with Dani all the time, but in so many ways our relationship was different from the one I had with my mom, and Dani's personality was completely different from my mom's. I missed my sparring partner. And the dementia room made it clear to me that she was never coming back.

Looking back now, I wish someone had been able to say these things to me then:

> ➤ LBD is a completely different animal than Alzheimer's and other types of dementia. There's a much smaller percentage of people diagnosed with LBD than with Alzheimer's, but it's likely more prevalent than that, as LBD presents itself through a spectrum of varying symptoms and is referred to differently at varying stages.[4] I didn't realize until after it was all over just how different LBD is. None of the literature I saw at the time described what to expect. There were mentions of "possible aggressive behavior" but no examples or stories of what that

might look like. I'm sure it's different for everyone, but still. If your loved one has LBD, you might appreciate and benefit from reading some examples of what to expect, which is what I hope I'm providing now.

➤ We can all only do the best that we can with the information we have at the time. If you feel like you're just hanging on for the ride and barely keeping up, you're not alone. Give yourself a break from any negative self-talk you've got going on in there. I know right now it may not feel like things will ever be okay again. Your feelings, whatever they may be, are valid. It's okay to sit with them for a bit.

➤ Dementia room experiences can be eye-opening, but also deeply upsetting. If you choose to participate in one, ask what to expect. Ask what sort of support will be available to help you process what you experience. Use your therapist to help support you.

➤ When people offer help, accept it. And if they don't know how to offer what you need, find a way to ask for it. You cannot be at your best to care for your loved one if you're running on empty. Rest is not optional. It's mandatory for survival. Accept help where it's offered, and ask for it when it's not.

CHAPTER 10

IT'S FINE UNTIL IT'S NOT

By the fall of 2019, my mom's hallucinations were increasing in frequency as well as in how complex and elaborate they were. She was less and less able to settle herself and would pace endlessly in their house. She'd move from the living room to look out the big picture window, rock back and forth, then move to the kitchen to look out the smaller windows, still rocking back and forth.

One day, I was working away at my desk in my home office, which had windows on two sides that provided a beautiful view of the field across from our farm, our field and land to one side, part of our driveway, and the road. I saw my mom walking purposefully and quickly down the driveway toward the road. She had her tote bag that she always carried over her shoulder and was clearly trying to go somewhere fast. I leaned forward to look and see whether my dad was somewhere behind her, but there was no one else in the circular drive.

I got up, calling to Dani as I did. "Hey, baby? Where are you?"

My mom was really trucking down the driveway and I still didn't see my dad. Feeling alarmed, I went to the kitchen to see who else was around. There didn't seem to be anyone else in the house that I could see, so I went to the dining room and looked out the back windows to see if anyone else was aware that my mom was headed down the road toward town alone. Dani was out in the pasture with the horses and didn't seem to have noticed my mom walking by.

I was about to run to the back door when Sam came down the stairs, looking concerned. "Everything okay, Mom? I heard you yell—"

"Sam, run!" I interrupted. "Go down the driveway and go after Grandma! She's heading for the road! Go!"

He didn't hesitate, jumping down the steps with the agility only a 15-year-old has, and ran out the back door. I followed him out as quickly as I could, but he was much faster. He was down the driveway like a shot and caught up to her quickly. I watched him slip his arm through hers and turn to smile at her, as though they were just out for a stroll. I put my hand on my heart, suddenly choked up with emotion watching my boy just naturally know what to do.

My mother seemed startled by his presence but didn't push him away. I couldn't hear what they were saying, but she gestured urgently toward the neighbor's house. He looked in that direction, then back at her and smiled again. I imagined he was reassuring her of something. He looked back over his shoulder to where I was standing in the driveway, unsure of whether I needed to go after them.

Having seen the commotion, Dani came up from the pasture. "What's going on?" she asked, frowning.

"I was working in the office and noticed her trucking down the driveway," I said, turning to look at my parents' house to see where my dad was. "I sent Sam running after her. He seems to have her now, but she's pointing to the neighbor's house. I have no idea why. Where the hell is my dad?" I was exasperated.

"You go find your dad," Dani said, "and I'll go help Sam bring her back." She took off at a jog to catch up with them, and I took off at a jog to find my dad.

He met me at the door of the carriage house, looking concerned and a little disoriented. "Where's your mother?" he asked. "I just woke up and she's not here."

"She took off down the driveway," I said, "but I sent Sam after her. He's got her, and Dani's following them." I looked at him more closely. "Are you okay, Dad?"

He nodded sheepishly, then said, "I just sat down for a minute. I must've fallen asleep. We were cleaning all morning. Well, I was cleaning and your mother was moving things around. I didn't realize she'd gone." He looked anxiously around me, craning his neck to try to see where she was. I stepped back so he could come out of the house.

"She was heading for the road, out toward town," I said as we walked toward the road to see where they were. "I have no idea what she was doing or where she thought she was going, but it looks like they've got her now."

We watched as Sam and Dani walked with my mom, slowly heading back in our direction. My mom was still gesturing and pointing toward the neighbor's house. Dani noticed us watching and just shook her head. My dad and I walked toward them to meet them at the other end of the circular drive and see what had happened. My mom was speaking animatedly.

"Well I don't know how we're going to get the password then," she said, sounding unhappy about being overruled on a decision. "I'm telling you, he has it!" she exclaimed, jabbing her finger back toward the neighbor's house once more.

"It's okay, Grandma," Sam said, taking her arm again. "I've got the password. I'll share it with you. I'm sorry you didn't already have it."

Totally perplexed, I asked Dani as they approached what had happened.

My mom answered, looking and sounding annoyed that I hadn't addressed her directly. "I'll tell you what happened! I was on my way to get the password from the UPS driver. He has it and was stopping next door at your neighbor's house. I was trying to get there so I could get it from him before he leaves again! But Sam came and said he wanted to go with me, which slowed me down, and then Dani"—she jerked her thumb at Dani and said her name with disdain—"stopped us. She said we couldn't go up their driveway. But that's where the password is!"

Dani was scowling at my mom, not appreciating her disdain.

"Mom," I said, trying to smooth everything over, "the neighbors have two very big dogs. Dani was trying to stop you from being attacked. They're trained to guard the house and don't know you. They would've attacked you." It was all true.

My mom threw her hands up. "Well, then I guess we just won't have the password." She sounded totally disgusted.

"What's the password for, Mom?" I asked, genuinely curious how her mind was bending.

She stared at me for a moment, then her expression changed from irritated to scornful. "I dooon't knooow, El-len," she said, in a mocking slow tone. "I just know that was our last chance to get it and now it's gone." She threw her hands up again. "So I hope you're all happy!" And with that, she stormed off to her house.

We all stood for a moment looking at each other. "What in the fresh hell was that about?" I asked Dani.

Still angry at my mom's hostility toward her, Dani spat, "Who the fuck knows?" and stormed off toward our house. That was the first time my mom had ever spoken harshly to Dani. Usually, my mom acted like she liked Dani more than she liked me. *Welcome to the party*, I thought.

Nervous at the tension, Sam giggled and shrugged. "I tried to just reassure her, but I'm not sure it worked," he said sheepishly.

"It's okay, honey," I said quickly. "You did everything exactly right. Thank you so much for running after her so quickly." I gave him a hug, then he walked back to our house too.

My dad stood with me, staring at their house. He heaved a deep sigh.

"You okay?" I asked. "You want me to come over and see if she's okay?"

He shook his head. "No, you better head home. I'll go." I noticed his shoulders looked more slumped than normal as he headed back to their house. That was worrying. I was seeing more and more signs that this ordeal with my mom was starting to have some physical effects on him.

"Okay," I called softly after him. "We'll see you for dinner. Holler if you need me sooner." I watched him for another moment, then turned and headed back to my own house, suddenly exhausted.

The very next day, the scenario damned near repeated itself. I was working in my office when suddenly my mom went trucking past. I jumped out of my chair and ran to the door, ready this time to just intervene. I yanked open the heavy front door, which we almost never used. "Mom!" I yelled as she got to the corner of the driveway.

She stopped and turned, looking surprised. "What?" she replied, as though this were normal.

"What are you doing?" I asked, shouting so she could hear me as I walked onto the little front stoop.

"I'm going to catch the bus," she said like I was stupid. "What do you think I'm doing?"

I frowned. That was a new one. "Umm, I'm not sure the bus comes this way," I said, trying to figure out what to do. I hadn't even grabbed my phone before running out the door.

"Of course it does!" she exclaimed impatiently. "But you're going to make me miss it!" She turned to head down the road.

"Wait!" I shouted. "I'm coming with you!" I just had house shoes on, but I picked my way quickly over the stones and wild grasses to try to catch up with her.

She frowned back at me. "Well, hurry up! This Greenfield bus only comes once an hour!"

Greenfield Road is in Detroit. I knew she'd caught that bus as a teenager to go to work in the flower shop where my parents had met. My mind was racing, trying to figure out what to do to get her turned back around. I was coming up blank. "I'm hurrying!" I said. "Where are we going?"

She made a face at me that suggested I really was stupid. "Downtown, of course!" I hadn't quite gotten to her, but she didn't wait for me. She turned and headed for the road.

Suddenly, I remembered that I was supposed to try to redirect her in moments like this. It was a tactic they'd talked about in the ALZ literature as well as in one of the workshops. The idea was that when your loved one is caught in a repetitive or harmful behavior, redirect them to something else in the hope that they'll focus on the new thing and forget the former.

"Hey, Mom, I just realized I left dinner in the oven!" I exclaimed. "I think we need to go back so I can get it out." I put my hand on her arm and tugged gently.

She frowned at me. "Why did you do that?" she asked.

I wasn't sure what to say. This redirection felt like lying, because I *was* lying, and it wasn't comfortable. "I-I don't know," I stammered. "But we need to go back. I don't want my house to burn down!" I said more urgently. "Can we please go back?" I felt like I was pleading now.

She sighed in frustration. "Fine," she said flatly, like I was a bratty child nagging at her. But she turned and headed back toward the house. I breathed a sigh of relief.

As we came back up the driveway, my dad was hurrying out of their house, looking scared. I wasn't sure how much more of this he could take. I felt like I was watching him age before my eyes. When he saw us, his pace slowed and his face relaxed.

"We're good," I called to him. "I remembered I left dinner in the oven, so we're going to take it out." I turned to my mom. "Do you want to go and make sure Dad is okay?" I said to her, making sure she could hear the concern in my voice. "I think he looks worried."

She pursed her lips in annoyance but nodded her head. "He's fine," she said. "He's just overreacting, as usual."

I barked out a harsh laugh, and said, "Well, if that's not the pot calling the kettle black!" It was out of my mouth before I could stop myself.

Before I could do any more damage, I turned back to the walkway leading to our back door and went inside. I glanced out the window to see my parents walking slowly back toward their house. Dani met me at the stairs up to our living room.

"Everything alright?" she asked.

"Yeah," I said. "She was on her way to catch the bus." My eyebrows raised. "You know, the one on Greenfield."

Dani raised her own eyebrows. "Where's that?"

"Detroit."

"Oh," she answered, nodding like it was a perfectly normal thing to do. We looked at each other and smiled at the absurdity of it all.

"That's not the best part," I said, a laugh bubbling up. "She said my dad was 'overreacting, as usual.'" I was laughing so hard I could hardly speak. "Oh my god, I can't take it!"

We were both laughing now. Finally, we stopped, catching our breath.

"I feel like a bad person for laughing at this shit," I said. "It's not funny. It's terrible."

Dani smiled sympathetically at me. "Babes, you gotta laugh some days to keep from crying. It's okay." And with that, we held each other's hands and walked into the living room toward the kitchen.

Later that afternoon, I called Dr. Wendell. This behavior was new, and I wanted to see whether we needed to go in to have my mom checked out. I didn't think there was necessarily anything that could be done, but my instinct was to call the doctor, so I did. It was nearly the end of the workday, so I didn't expect an answer, but I didn't know what else to do. I left a message for him, saying that I was concerned about this sudden uptick in erratic behavior. To my surprise, he called me back a while later. It was 7 p.m.

"I'd like you to take her to be tested for a UTI," he said without preamble. "A urinary tract infection."

I waited to see if he'd explain why. He didn't, so I asked, "Sorry, why? I don't understand what that has to do with this strange behavior."

"UTIs can affect behavior in anyone over the age of seventy-five," he explained, "whether they have dementia or not. But especially if they have dementia. So it's the first thing we check when there's a mental status change like what you're describing."

I was confused. "'Mental status change'? What does that mean?" I felt like maybe he wasn't understanding what I'd explained was happening with my mom.

"A mental status change is the term we use when there's a sudden change in behavior, like what you're describing with your mom," he clarified. "She wasn't taking off down the road by herself for weird reasons before, right?" He didn't wait for me to answer. "So that's a mental status change. And the first thing to check to understand why that's happening is to see if she has a UTI. Now, what's the closest lab to you? Quest down in Lapeer?"

I was still trying to wrap my brain around this. "Yes," I said. "I think so. I don't think there's anything up here in North Branch."

"Okay," he said. "I'll call in the order right now. Can you get there first thing tomorrow morning? They're closed now."

"Yes, we'll make sure she gets there," I answered.

I thanked him for calling me back outside of office hours and we said goodbye.

My dad took her the next morning, and her urine test was positive for a UTI. Dr. Wendell called in an antibiotic prescription, and things settled down for a couple of weeks. When we saw another spike in strange behavior a couple of weeks later, I was sure she couldn't have another UTI that fast. But the cycle repeated. I called Dr. Wendell, he ordered a urine test, it was positive again, and he called in another antibiotic. This time, he prescribed a stronger one. About two weeks later, the cycle repeated itself yet again. This went on for four months.

Dr. Wendell saw her in his office a couple of times during this period, suggesting that the repeated infections were due to her not being able to properly clean herself anymore. She completely fought us on accepting any help with her hygiene. My dad started having her shower every day, but that didn't seem to help. It was one more twisty turn on the roller coaster.

The more paranoid my mom's hallucinations caused her to be, the more she tried to "escape" from their house. She also started experiencing signs of sundowner's syndrome, a disorder that caused her to be awake all night and sleepy during the day. Between that and the hallucinations, we were all exhausted, particularly my dad.

When we brought up these challenges in our ALZ support group, several people recommended getting alarms for the doors to the carriage house. Others suggested inexpensive cameras to watch what my mom was doing when no one was home. Since she'd already gotten out a few times during the day without my dad knowing, none of us wanted to imagine what might happen if she snuck out in the middle of the night without any of us knowing.

Feeling exasperated and exhausted from making all the decisions all the time, I called my brother and told him about the recommendations.

"I don't know which one would be better," I said. "What do you think?"

"I think we should get both," he said. "We have cameras in our house to keep an eye on the dog when we're not here. They aren't expensive."

"I don't really know if we need to watch her *in* the house," I said, not wanting to invade my parents' privacy like that. "Dad rarely leaves her alone at this point. But it would be very useful to mount one on the shed, pointing at the back door. That way, if she does manage to get out, we can see which way she goes at least."

"M-hm," he said. "I think the ones we got came with two cameras, so we can set them up to cover two angles outside the house."

"Okay, what about these door alarms?" I asked.

"Yeah, we can get one of those too," he answered. "They don't ever use that front door, do they? We could probably just put one on the back door and be fine."

I thought about it for a second. "Well, that's true, but what if she decides to use that front door? Dr. Wendell has warned us several times now that if we can't imagine her doing something, we should plan that she might do it. Her behavior is just totally unpredictable at this point. I'd rather just get two and put one on each door." I could just imagine her going out the front door, walking around the far side of the house, and being out on the road without ever being seen on camera.

"Okay, it's up to you," he said.

Sudden anger flared in my chest. "And why is that?" I said bitterly. "Why is everything up to me?"

He chuckled nervously, just like our dad. "Because you're there," he said simply.

I swallowed hard, trying to focus on the matter at hand. "Alright, well, when can you come do this? I may make the decisions, but I'm sure as fuck not going to try installing all this shit. That's your department." Dani could handle it, I was sure, but I was still mad about the comment and realization that I really was the one who had to make all the decisions. We did enough. David could come take care of this.

"I can come up next weekend," he said. "I'll just have to check with Lauren and make sure nothing's going on. I can meet Dad at Home Depot to buy the right stuff and then follow him up there to install everything."

My anger flared. "Well, hopefully your calendar isn't too busy," I said sarcastically. "It's just our mother with dementia trying to escape and slowly killing our father in the process. No big deal." I made myself stop. I wanted to unleash on him about his lack of urgency living an hour away, while we couldn't escape it living across the driveway.

He chuckled again, avoiding confrontation as usual. "I'm sure I can find a way to make it work," he said in a tone that I'm sure was intended to reassure me but came out sounding like he was just trying to pacify me. It only made me angrier. We said goodbye before I lost my temper.

David did make time that next weekend, meeting my dad at the store to buy the right things and coming up to install everything. He even helped me and Dad get the app set up on our phones so we could monitor the cameras and alarms remotely. My mom always responded well to my brother, so having him there also meant a brief reprieve from the crazy.

During this period of time, my brother and I felt strongly that my dad needed to start looking for a facility where my mom would eventually have to live. It was clear to me and Dani from our front row seat that his health was suffering a general decline under the stress of caregiving, and David could hear it in his voice every time he talked to him.

I'd heard high praise from three people I trusted for a local nursing home called Sunrise. They had a special dementia care unit. After encouraging my dad for two months to let me make an appointment for a tour, he finally relented. By that time, my aunt Dolores had started staying with my parents for a week or so at a time to help with my mom. She was in agreement that we should at least go take a look, which seemed to help.

We all visited one afternoon in the fall of 2019. Walking through the nursing home section to get to the director's office reminded me of visiting my grandparents. The smells of a nursing home are hard to describe, but they're the same anywhere you go. They seem like a combination of cleaning supplies not quite doing the job of covering the smells of bodily fluids, the products elderly people use on their skin, and sadness. I felt immediately heartbroken and resistant at the idea of my mother living there. I knew it would be her absolute worst nightmare.

The director, Maude, was a lovely woman. She ushered all of us into her small office and started by giving us some basic information about the facility, then took down information about my mom.

"It sounds like Charlotte would be best served in our memory care unit," Maude said when we'd finished telling her about my mom. "Would you like a tour of that area so you can see what it's like?"

We all agreed that would be helpful, so we filed out after her. As we walked down the hallway to the locked memory care unit, I wanted to cry as I looked at all the elderly people. Not because they weren't being well-cared for but because my heart broke at the idea of the lives they'd had nearing their natural end. I felt too young to have a parent ready for this. My mom was only 76 at the time, and I was 46. Nursing homes were supposed to be for people in their late 80s and 90s. Even my grandmother hadn't lived in one until she was in her late 80s, regardless of her Alzheimer's. I had a sudden rush of emotion at this thought. Guilt, sadness, and panic all mingled, giving me a sense of feeling, once again, like I wasn't doing enough. Like I wasn't doing it right.

Maude unlocked the door to the unit and led us into another hallway. The residents of that section were more animated than those in the general area. Several were walking up and down the hallways, one woman tracing her finger along the plastic railing that lined the wall as she walked. She looked at us with mild curiosity, then went back to walking. In one large room we passed, a group of people were sitting around tables, doing an activity of some kind.

"That's our craft room," Maude said. I tried to imagine my mom sitting in there, but I couldn't.

Maude led us to another room. "This is one of our resident rooms," she said, ushering us inside. There was a twin bed that looked to be electrically adjustable, a nightstand, a sink with a mirror above it, a chair, and a dresser with photos and knickknacks on it. The bed was neatly made, and everything was very orderly. I again tried to imagine my mom here. Tears pricked my eyes as I became emotional. Aunt Dolores noticed and squeezed my hand, smiling sympathetically at me.

"These areas are set up like a clover leaf," Maude continued. "There are four private rooms like this with a full bathroom at the center." She led us to the bathroom. It had another sink and mirror, a toilet, a shower, and a tub. There were half-walls between the shower, tub, and toilet. I imagined there might sometimes be a need for more than one resident to have use of the facilities at the same time. My chest started to feel heavy, and I wanted to run out of there. I could not imagine my mother here, and trying to was making me feel nauseous.

Maude finished the tour, pointing out some of the other common areas and talking about the activities of a typical day. I was only half-listening by then, feeling numb. My dad looked uncomfortable, and my brother's face was neutral and hard to read. Aunt Dolores was listening attentively, asking a few questions and nodding. I was glad she was there, as I felt like she might be the only one who could retain any information.

We went back to Maude's office and sat down again in a small circle of chairs. I tried to swallow the lump in my throat. I hated that I felt so emotional all the time.

"What questions do you have?" Maude asked, smiling at us kindly. I liked her. She seemed very competent and compassionate.

"What does it cost for someone to live in the dementia unit?" Aunt Dolores spoke up. I think the rest of us were too overwhelmed and avoided looking at each other to keep our emotions in check.

"Well, the private pay rate is close to ten thousand dollars per month," Maude said.

A gasp escaped my lips before I could stop it. "Holy shit," I breathed. "I had no idea what it cost." My brother and father both looked shocked.

"Do you have an elder law attorney?" Maude asked. "They would be able to help you look at your estate, find out what sort of assistance you might qualify for, and help you manage your assets. There are ways you can protect your community assets"—she looked pointedly at my dad—"while spending down Charlotte's assets to help her qualify for more assistance sooner. You might have to pay more of the cost at the beginning, but then you will qualify for having the whole cost covered after a few months. An elder law attorney would be able to go over all of your options and help you navigate the system."

I shook my head dumbly. "No, we don't know any elder law attorneys. My parents did estate planning last year, but not specifically with an elder law attorney. What's the difference?"

"Elder law attorneys specialize in helping seniors manage their affairs and assets," she replied. "Not all estate planning attorneys specialize in that."

I felt like a deer in headlights. "Umm, okay," I said, glancing at my dad and brother. They both looked at me expectantly. I knew they fully expected me to take the lead. "Can you make any recommendations for someone we could talk to?"

Maude nodded and reached up to a rack of papers and brochures on the wall. She took down a sheet of paper with a short list of names, firms, and contact information on it and handed it to me, saying, "This is a list of a few that we recommend in the local area."

I looked at the list, not sure how to decide who to call. I looked up at Maude and asked, "If it was your mother, which one would you call?" The lump in my throat made my voice catch.

She smiled at me reassuringly, leaned over, and pointed to a name. "I'd call her," she said softly. "But I need to be clear. That's me personally telling you that, not the facility."

I nodded again. "I understand, and I really appreciate that, thank you."

"Is there a waiting list to get into the dementia unit?" Aunt Dolores asked. Again, I was grateful for her presence of mind.

Maude nodded. "Yes, there is," she said. "Would you like me to add Charlotte's name to it?" She directed her question to my dad. His eyes welled up with tears and he looked over at me. I knew he was looking for my guidance. My own eyes teared up and I gave him a small shrug, my head tilted to the side, indicating that I thought we probably should. But I could tell he wasn't ready.

"Can we take the paperwork and think about it?" I asked Maude.

She nodded again, reaching for a folder from her desk. "Absolutely," she said. "Here's the folder with all the information we talked about as well as the intake form we need filled out to put her on the waiting list. Once she was admitted, our team would assess her to decide if she needs placement on the dementia unit or can be well-served in the general area. I know she has a Lewy body diagnosis, so we'd have to evaluate her current status at that time. Lewy body can be tricky, and we need to make sure all residents stay safe."

I took the folder from her, feeling completely overwhelmed. "Okay," was all I could manage. The strong urge to run out of there was coming back.

Maude looked at all of us, then said softly, "You know, my dad had dementia. We placed him here. This was before I worked here. That first night, after we'd gotten him settled here, my mom and I shared a bottle of wine. We cried, and we both admitted that we felt relieved. We were relieved that my dad was in a place where he was safe and well-cared for and that we could finally breathe. We both slept better that night than either of us had in years."

Unable to hold back my tears anymore, I was now wiping them away. I glanced over at my brother and dad and saw they were in the same state. Even Aunt Dolores was reaching for a tissue to dab her eyes. We all knew the day would come when we'd have to place my mom in a facility, probably sooner rather than later. We also knew how much she'd fight us and be miserable in her moments of lucidity.

There's no other way to describe how I felt in that moment other than completely overwhelmed with sadness and anguish, weighed down by the very heavy burden of trying to make the best possible decisions for everyone involved when there were simply no good options. None of us wanted to be in this position, least of all my mom. And I knew she wouldn't be able to process it that way, and her wrath would land squarely on me and my dad.

I heaved a deep sigh and tried to collect myself. I gave a weak smile and said, "Maude, thank you so much for your time today and for all this great information. We have a lot to think about and do before we'll be ready to move forward. But when we are, this is clearly a very good option." I stood up to leave, needing to get out of the small space and into the fresh air.

While we pondered the information Maude had given us, the two women from Seniors who'd volunteered to come sit with my mom to give my dad a break started to visit a couple of times a week. They were wonderful. But one had serious health challenges of her own, and the other had a husband who was quite ill. My dad didn't feel comfortable asking them to come more often than they'd offered, and it was clear to all of us that he needed to take more breaks from my mom.

Through networking for my business, I'd met a man who owned a company called Comfort Keepers, which provided home health care and respite care. I decided to reach out to him to see what was possible. Since my parents were on a fixed income and had always been very frugal, my dad was worried about the cost. But I reasoned that if we didn't get some help, we'd be putting both of them into an early grave.

After making the call, I found respite care to be something my parents could afford to have a couple of times a week. The agency would send a certified nursing assistant to the house twice a week for four hours at a time. She (we specifically requested women) would keep my mom company during that time and could help with bathing, toileting, and keeping her safe. My dad was worried how my mom would respond to people she didn't know coming into the house, but I felt we didn't have a choice. The more time passed, the more worried I was becoming about my dad's health.

It wasn't easy to find caregivers who were willing to drive all the way out to where we were. Our options were limited by the location of our farm and the small population in the area. North Branch is a little town 30 minutes north of Lapeer, a city of only about nine thousand people, and the town itself had only about nine hundred people. But Comfort Keepers was determined to help us, and they found a couple of people willing to make the drive.

With respite care, family members are supposed to be able to leave their property to go get a cup of coffee, do their grocery shopping, get their hair cut, or take care of other errands that are difficult to do with their loved one. My dad couldn't bring himself to do anything except be at my house at first. Too worried about what would happen, he parked his car on the other side of our house so my mom wouldn't be able to see it and came in our front door. He then either watched their house from a protected view or sat on my couch. He wasn't really relaxing.

"You know you're sort of defeating the purpose of respite care right now, right?" I said sarcastically and with a smile. "What do you think is going to happen? That lady they sent seems very nice and quite competent."

He didn't say anything for a minute as he kept watching their house. "I'm not sure what's going to happen," he finally said, "but I don't have a good feeling about it. I can't just sit down and relax." He sounded worried.

"Well, try," I said. "Let's at least go into the kitchen. Do you want some coffee or something to drink? A beer, maybe?" I was only half-joking. It was only 2 p.m., but I wasn't sure how else to get him to calm down.

He laughed and shook his head. "No, I'm fine," he said, following me to the kitchen.

We chatted in there for a little while, my dad sitting at the kitchen counter where he could still sort of see out the living room window and over to their house, me washing dishes and putzing around. Dani soon came in and joined us, and we all speculated on what was happening over at the carriage house.

"I think Mom is probably happy to have someone paying attention to her," I said. "She's probably telling her stories and showing her pictures of all her grandkids."

"I think she's probably bossing the lady around," said Dani, smiling. "I'll bet she's got her reorganizing the pantry, Ron."

My dad smiled back and shook his head. "I don't know what they're doing," he said, "but I hope Charlotte isn't getting upset. This won't work if she gets upset."

His somber words sobered all of us. "Well, let's hope it works out," I said. "You really need a break, Dad. We can see how exhausted you are."

He nodded, not looking at us, and I could see he was fighting tears. "Yeah," was all he could muster.

A little while later, it was time for him to go back home. "Good luck," I said. "Let us know what happened when you can."

We didn't need to wait for him to give the report. We got it from her that evening at dinner.

"I didn't like that woman," she said, frowning and looking disapproving. "She kept telling me I had to sit and do my puzzle. I didn't want to do my puzzle. She was ordering me around like I'm a child!" She sounded upset.

My dad looked over at me, disappointment all over his face.

"I'm sure she wasn't trying to tell you what to do or make you feel like a child," I assured reasonably. "Did you tell her you wanted to do something else instead?"

"She just kept following me around everywhere!" my mom said, getting more agitated. "She was watching my every move. I felt like a prisoner." She took a bite of her food, then said, "I don't want her to come back."

I looked at my dad again. He was focused on his plate, looking resigned. He'd expected this.

"Well, we have a contract with them to try this out for a month," I said, trying to remain calm. "Today was just the first day. How about we try it for a little longer and see how it goes?"

She pursed her lips and shook her head, saying, "I don't know. I don't understand why I can't just go with your father into town. Why do I have to stay home?" She sounded hurt and my heart went out to her, but I also felt very protective of my dad, who I was worried was going to die quietly while trying to keep up with her demands and never-ending movement. Resentment won.

"Because Dad needs a break!" I blurted out. "He's exhausted! You don't slow down enough for him to have a proper rest! I'm starting to worry you're going to put him in an early grave!" I knew I shouldn't be saying any of this, but I couldn't help myself. I was angry.

She looked at me with confusion on her face, then concern. She turned and looked at my dad and said, "Am I doing that, dear?"

He smiled at her. "No," he said, then went back to eating.

I threw my hands up, furious with them both. I pushed my chair back from the table and slammed down my napkin. "I can't," I said flatly. "I just can't." I got up from the table and walked away, heading to my office.

After closing the door, I threw myself into my chair and let out an exasperated breath. I was angry with my mom for a lifetime of demanding, controlling behavior toward my dad, and I was just as furious with him for not standing up to her and doing something about it. I was bitter about the consequences their tendencies had on me as a child and resentful that they were continuing to affect me as an adult living next door and trying to help. And I was disgusted with myself for not having better control of my temper and leaving my family at the table to suffer in the wake of my outburst. Steeping in my self-loathing and indignation like a bag of bitter black tea, I let my anguished tears fall.

When my mom turned 77, her brother and his wife, Raymond and Pauline, decided they should come visit from Colorado. We decided it would be a great opportunity to invite their three cousins with whom my mom had grown up. Two of them came with their husbands, and it was the first time in many years that they'd all seen one another. In addition to the older generation, my brother and his family came. We were 17 people in total gathered at our farmhouse on a beautiful but cold November afternoon.

When the cousins arrived, my mom greeted them warmly, but I could tell (and likely so could everyone else) that she wasn't quite sure who they were. She seemed to recognize them but wasn't able to place them or come up with their names. After a couple of minutes, she came over to me with a broad smile and whispered, "Clearly these lovely people know me, but I'm not sure who they are." There was no trace of fear or malice on her face. I was struck by her ability to be diplomatic and aware even while not remembering exactly who they were. Her presence of mind served to keep us all firmly in the roles we'd always been in with her, and it fascinated me.

It was a lovely day. We took lots of photos, laughed a lot, and shared stories. My mom smiled and laughed more than I'd seen her do in a long time. She often wasn't involved directly in the conversations, which was the most definite change any of us noticed, but she was always in the periphery smiling and laughing along with everyone. I found myself watching her affectionately a lot that day. It seemed to me that she was smiling with genuine fondness and happiness at being there with everyone. But her laughing seemed to be because she was taking cues from everyone else, not because she was following the conversation. At one point, Raymond leaned over and whispered to me, "She seems to be having a really good day today." I nodded in agreement and felt protective of my mom, as though she were a fragile vase.

Near the end of the day, we took several group photos. My parents sat front and center, with the other members of the older generation around them and my family and David's family on either side. I noticed my mom wasn't smiling in any of them. She didn't seem to really understand why she should.

After the cousins and my brother left, Raymond and Pauline helped us clean up while my mom rocked back and forth, looking out the windows at the pastures and animals. My dad settled on the couch to have a little nap while the boys played on their gaming devices. I kept watching my mom. She seemed content but not really present with us. Though it made me feel sad that she was missing out on the jokes and banter with us and her brother, which she'd always loved, she was content, and that's what was most important.

That was the last time any of the older generation saw her.

About six weeks later, my mother's behavior was once again causing us to suspect yet another UTI. I put in a call to Dr. Wendell, asking if we needed to consider some other way to treat these chronic infections. The next day, on December 18, 2019, I was on-site with a client, conducting back-to-back one-on-one meetings with eight members of a team, with 15-minute breaks in between. Dr. Wendell called me back during one of those short breaks.

"Dr. Wendell," I began, pacing around the room, "I'm just wondering if there's anything else we can try doing to knock this infection out once and for all or some sort of preventative medication she could take that might help. I'm not sure what to do, but this has now been four full months of back-to-back infections. That can't be good, right?" I was exasperated.

"Yes, there's a medication called methenamine we could try," he answered. "It's not something we'd normally put someone on for a long period of time due to the long-term effects it can have on the kidneys and liver, but I'm not concerned about that for your mom."

Unease pricked at my stomach, and I stopped pacing. "No?" I asked.

"No," he confirmed. "I think we have bigger issues to worry about."

I waited. "You do?" I finally asked, the knot in my stomach growing. I started pacing again.

"Ellen, I think you need to be aware that in my clinical experience of more than forty years of working with elderly patients with dementia, your mom has about six to twelve months left."

A wave of nausea swept through my belly. I reached for the chair to steady myself. "Excuse me?" I managed.

"I'm sorry to say it but, given the behavior and patterns we've seen in the last six months, I believe that's the prognosis," he said matter-of-factly.

I glanced at my watch, suddenly aware that I had another team member coming in to talk to me. "'Six to twelve months' for what exactly?" I asked, my breathing quickening.

"Until she passes away," he said more gently. "I'm sorry to say, but that's what my clinical experience tells me."

I took a breath, trying to steady myself. I held on tight to a chair, frozen. I couldn't quite wrap my head around it. My mother was walking, talking, feeding herself, bathing herself, and toileting herself, and she never stopped moving. It was surreal to think that she'd be gone inside of a year. Tears tried to fight their way to the surface, but I was determined to shut them down before my client walked into the room.

"Okay, I need to go," I finally said. "I'm with a client today and can't process or deal with this right now. I'm going to call you back next week, after I've had a chance to talk with my dad and brother. Thanks for the call back."

I was reeling from the news. I could not believe he would drop something like this on me so casually, and over the phone. His bedside manner had always been lacking, but this was unbelievable. I was shocked. I also couldn't accept what he'd told me as the truth. My grandmother had been blind, deaf, and unable to speak or walk at the end of her journey through dementia. I knew intellectually that

LBD is very different from Alzheimer's, but emotionally I couldn't stop comparing their experiences. In that context, my mom was a very long way from death.

My next client appeared at the door, which was closed, so he waved to me through the window. He frowned when he saw me, looking concerned. I held up my hand and gave a weak smile as I went to open the door. "I just need to run to the restroom for a minute, okay?" I said. "I'll be right back. You can have a seat anywhere you like."

I practically ran down the hallway to the bathroom, making it just in time to throw up in the toilet. Shaking, I pulled myself together, splashing some water on my face and being grateful that this client kept mouthwash in their ladies' room. Taking several deep breaths to calm myself, I looked in the mirror. "Put it away," I whispered fiercely to my reflection. "You just put this shit the fuck away and pull yourself together." I smoothed my hair, wiped my face, fixed my makeup, and with one more deep breath, went back to my client and finished my day.

Looking Back Now

Denial gave me the ability to "put it away" and carry on working with my clients that day. I knew Dr. Wendell was an expert and hadn't been wrong about anything else thus far, but I wasn't ready to accept his prognosis in the face of watching how my mother still functioned. She wasn't slowing down. In fact, we'd started joking by then that she was turning into the Energizer Bunny, perpetually in motion and moving faster than she had before. The full force of what Dr. Wendell had said didn't hit me until later when I talked to my dad about it.

As for my growing irritation with David, I realize now what was plaguing me during our conversation about how everything was up to me, simply because I was there: envy. I wanted my old life back—the one in which my wife and I lived on our beautiful farm with the kids, caring for animals, running a business, and having free time to relax without worry. Given the extremely contentious dynamic that had always existed between me and my mother, caregiving for her was the last thing I'd wanted to do. I knew she triggered me in the ugliest of ways and that it felt nearly impossible to be kind and compassionate with her all the time because of it.

Meanwhile, David was continuing to live his best life. He and Lauren (who is now his wife) were sharing custody of my two nieces with his ex-wife, working and enjoying life as they always had. He slept well every night. He had his girls only half the time, which left him plenty of time to socialize, go out, and relax without worry. They even scheduled time to relax. I was bitter, jealous, and anguished at how differently we were living our lives.

I'm pretty sure David is still oblivious (although maybe not now, if he's reading this) to how I was feeling then and how I feel now. Sharing my feelings with him at the time wasn't an option for me. Not only could I not fully articulate then what I can see now, but I was also worried that if I made him mad or caused him to feel like he'd be attacked whenever he came up, he'd stop coming altogether. I couldn't imagine not having him on the other end of the phone to support me or not coming up when he did to help take some of the burden off me and Dani.

That doesn't mean that I was always able to hold my tongue. I did make some nasty comments to him as well as to Lauren, but I never unleashed on them. Instead, I swallowed my anger in the moment and vented it out to Dani and to friends.

At this stage, I still felt behind the 8-ball and like I was perpetually trying to get out in front of everything. But it got significantly worse during this period of time. I indeed felt like a fly that had been trapped in a spider's web. The more I struggled to break free and find a path forward, the more tangled up and trapped I became. I was flying blind but at a much more accelerated pace, and things were starting to spin out of control. Yet the worst was still to come.

Looking back now, I would've benefited greatly from having someone to talk to then who'd been through something similar to what we were going through. If I'd had someone like that, I would've loved to hear them tell me these things:

- ➢ That I'd be okay.
- ➢ UTIs are very, very common in older adults, and that includes the population affected by dementia. Some people don't experience any symptoms beyond behavior change. Unlike when we're younger and may notice burning, pain, an odor, or other symptoms, for some reason those symptoms aren't always present with someone affected by dementia. Your loved one very well may not be able to tell you that something is wrong because they won't realize something is wrong. Having a standing order at a lab where you can have your loved one tested as needed is very helpful and saves a lot of time when you notice behavior changes.
- ➢ There's nothing wrong with putting door alarms and cameras up to help keep your loved one safe. I struggled with some shame and guilt about this because it felt like spying on my parents. It was one more way in which the role reversal messed with my head. But being vigilant 24/7 isn't possible, and trying to be is exhausting and unsustainable.
- ➢ Caring for someone with dementia is a lot like caring for a very young child. They may be walking and talking, but that doesn't mean they're necessarily making sense or are able to tell you what's wrong. They just get upset or show signs of behavior changes, and it's up to you to figure out what's causing them. At the same time, they may still demand autonomy and independence, also like a strong-willed young child might.

Though having the mindset that you have to reverse roles with a parent can be very challenging, it can be helpful to you and your loved one.

➤ One thing our experience with the ALZ support group taught us is that it's not only perfectly fine to find moments of humor on this journey but essential to your mental health. It doesn't mean you're heartless, insensitive, or anything else negative you might be telling yourself. It means that you're human. Humor is a release valve for stress. Don't be afraid to use it.

➤ We do what we have to do to survive. You're not a monster for putting aside your emotions in order to be able to focus on tasks that help you pay your bills. And if you can't do that, you're not broken. You're enough, just as you are. You're doing the best that you can, and that's enough.

PART 3

FALLING OFF THE CLIFF

People often call Alzheimer's and dementia "the long goodbye." I imagine it comes from the way in which most dementias go on for many years before the person either passes away from something else or the dementia causes their body to shut down. I think it also might come from the slow, steady decline that most dementias cause. You're watching your loved one fade away piece by piece. That certainly was the case with my grandmother. She started showing symptoms of dementia in her early 70s, and she passed away when Alzheimer's finally shut her organs down at the age of 96.

This was absolutely not the case with my mom. She started showing signs a few months before she turned 74, and she passed away four short years later, one month after her 78th birthday. Like I said, Lewy body is a whole different animal. There's no long goodbye. Instead, you and your loved one are on a roller coaster from hell, finally crashing and burning.

This is the story of the end.

CHAPTER 11

REALITY CHECKS

The prognosis from Dr. Wendell didn't really sink in. I understood what he'd said, but I just couldn't believe it. I knew I had to share the news with my dad and brother, but I also knew I had to do it when my mom wasn't around and when my dad would have time to process it all.

I chose a day when Comfort Keepers came to the house and my dad and I went to the grocery store in Lapeer. Once we got to the parking lot, I told him I needed to talk to him before we went in.

"I called Dr. Wendell a couple days ago to ask about Mom's never-ending UTIs," I said. My dad waited, watching me. "I wanted to ask if there's anything we can do to prevent them, since they keep happening over and over."

He nodded, waiting for me to continue.

"Well, he called me back while I was working at my client's office the other day," I went on, feeling the tears start to prick at my eyes.

My dad looked alarmed and started to well up with tears because I was. He looked away, out the window.

"He said there's a medication we can try that they don't usually like to use long term because of the side effects," I said, no longer able to keep my voice from rising with emotion. I swallowed hard, trying to stay calm.

My dad stared studiously out his window, his chest hitching with a stifled sob. He didn't know what I was going to say, but my emotional response triggered his.

"Well, he's not worried about those long-term effects on Mom because he said, based on his clinical experience, that she only has six to twelve months left," I finished, no longer able to hold back the sobs.

My dad whipped his head around, a horrified and disbelieving look on his face. He shook his head, unable to speak, then looked away again, his hands going up to his face as he sobbed. I put my hand on his back in an attempt to console him. We sat like that for a little while, both of us grieving. I looked around for some tissues and got both of us a few. Once we both pulled ourselves together a little bit, my dad was the first to speak.

"I want a second opinion," he said gruffly, still calming his tears.

"What?" I said, surprised. I hadn't been expecting that.

"I want a second opinion," he repeated, his voice stronger now. "I don't ever want to see that doctor again. I never liked his manner anyway, but now I never want to see him again. He doesn't know what he's talking about."

I wasn't sure what to say. I, too, didn't want the prognosis to be true and didn't much like Dr. Wendell's bedside manner at times, but I absolutely trusted his medical expertise. He hadn't been wrong yet. But I wanted to respect my dad's wishes above all, so I agreed.

"Okay," I said. "I'll ask around and do some searching for another doctor we can see." I felt exhausted all of a sudden. My dad's request felt like another wave of denial about my mom's dementia. More than three years into her illness, it was clear to me that this wasn't going away. His denial was another brick in the backpack I already felt I was responsible for carrying.

I asked a friend named Missy, whose mother had been in Sunrise, whether she knew of any local doctors who might be able to see my mom. I did some looking online too, but the list of names didn't mean anything to me. Missy was well-connected in town and knew a lot more locals than I did. She recommended a doctor named Dr. Baleen who worked through the hospital in Lapeer. While that hospital wasn't my first choice for care, I didn't see many other options locally.

Dr. Baleen was able to see us just a couple of weeks later. I gave my dad the date of the appointment, but we agreed it would be best to not tell my mom about it until the day before. I didn't want the endless questions on repeat that she was prone to asking once we introduced a new activity to the daily routine, and my dad didn't want to be berated or grilled about why we were going to a new doctor. It turned out that neither of us had anything to worry about.

The day before the appointment, I went over to the carriage house to tell my mom about it. As I walked up to their kitchen door, my mom met me. She looked angry and a little scared.

"I'm glad you're here, Ellen," she said loudly, like she was trying to make sure someone else would hear us. I peeked around her into the kitchen and saw my dad standing at the other end of the room, looking worried. His face instantly changed to relief upon hearing my name and seeing me. My mother went on. "Maybe you can stop this madness!" I felt wary.

"What's going on?" I asked cautiously, stepping into the kitchen.

My mom gestured to my dad. "This man is trying to arrest me! You can't let him take me down to the station. I don't want to go!" She was angry, but I could tell it was only to cover her fear.

I looked at my dad, who was now shaking his head and looking distraught. "Charlotte, stop it!" he pleaded. "It's me, your husband,

Ron." He sounded desperate, and I wondered how long this had been going on. She was clearly hallucinating.

I looked at my mom. Dementia face. "Mom," I said urgently, "that's just Dad. He's not going to arrest you, I promise. He has no power to do so, nor would he want to. It's okay. You're okay." I took a step toward her to put my hand on her arm and try to comfort her.

She swatted my hand away and yelled, "Don't you take his side! That's not your father! Have you lost your mind? You talk about *me* having dementia, ha!" She glared at me.

Fear tingled my spine. It was incredibly unnerving to watch these hallucinations play out, and they were only getting increasingly more elaborate. "Mom, I'm on your side, I promise," I continued. "I'm here. I won't let anyone take you away, I promise." I spoke soothingly to the best of my ability, trying to cover my own fear, which was for a completely different reason than my mother's but no less intense.

My mom was rocking back and forth, standing with her hands on her hips. She looked like she was ready to run if anyone tried to touch her. I was desperately trying to think of how the hell to get her out of this hallucination. I stepped between her and my dad, trying to block her view of him at the other end of the kitchen. She craned her neck to look around me at him.

"Dad, go in the other room," I said sternly to my dad over my shoulder. He hesitated, then turned and walked into the dining room. "Mom, look at me." She did, suspicion in her eyes. She continued to rock back and forth.

"What?" she said.

"I came over here to tell you about a new doctor we're going to see tomorrow," I said.

She continued to eye me warily. "O-kay," she said slowly, waiting for me to say more. She glanced over my shoulder, watching the doorway to the dining room. She still looked ready to run.

"It's a lady doctor," I went on. "She specializes in elder care and came highly recommended by Missy," I continued. "Do you remember Missy? From the library?"

She stared at me for a moment, thinking, still rocking and still with her hands on her hips. "The nice little library lady?" she said. "Of course I remember her." That last comment was said with disdain, like I was ridiculous for even asking.

I huffed out a breath in annoyance. "Oh, good," I said sarcastically. "I was afraid your memory was failing you. Silly me." I raised an eyebrow at her.

"Where is your father?" she said suddenly, sounding alarmed. "He's been gone a long time."

I turned toward the dining room and called, "Hey, Dad? Are you out there? You want to come in here please?"

My dad grunted as he pushed himself out of whatever chair he'd been sitting on. "Yes, I'm coming," he said, sounding tired and mildly annoyed. He walked into the kitchen. "You called?"

"Ronald, where have you been?!" my mother shrilled, startling me with her sudden outburst. "There was a sheriff here trying to arrest me! I kept telling him he couldn't take me down to the station, that I had to wait for you to come back, but he was really insistent! Thank God Ellen came in when she did! Where were you?" She was animated, waving her arms around and yelling at him.

I turned to look at my dad, astonished at the sudden outburst and mind-bending situation. His mouth was hanging open slightly in disbelief, and I could see anger in his eyes. He'd been taking the brunt of everything from my mom. I turned back to her and held up my hand.

"He's here now," I said firmly. "Stop yelling at him. There's no need for that. He's doing the best that he can." My anger was rising.

She threw her arms up, and I could see she was really upset. "Well, his best almost got me arrested," she hissed. "I would say his best might be lacking." My mom was glaring at us, and we were both glaring right back at her.

"Okay, well, that's enough," I said sharply. "The other man is gone now, and Dad is here. Let's focus on the present." I looked back and forth between them. My dad's anger diffused quickly, and he just looked exhausted. I thought again about the toll this was taking on him. Physically, my mom stayed just as she had been, but she said nothing else and was still rocking.

"So," I said with a forced brightness in my voice, "who wants to walk with me to get the mail?" I looked between them again. "Mom? How about you come with me to the mailbox?" I thought she might need a physical change of location to keep her from slipping back into her delusion.

She frowned, suspicious. "Why do you need me to come with you to the mailbox?"

I glared at her. "Why do I have to be the one to collect your mail?" I shot back. "Your mailbox is right there too, you know."

That got her attention. She was very controlling of the mail and hoarded the store ads that came. "Fine, let's go," she said, moving toward the door.

I mouthed to my dad, "You stay here" as my mom opened the door and started to go out.

"Mom, it's cold outside," I said quickly. "You need a coat." It was below freezing outside.

She didn't say anything but moved obediently to the coat tree next to the door and put on her warm winter coat. When she fumbled with the zipper, I noticed her hands shaking more than they had before. I softened.

"Mom, do you want some help with that?" I asked softly. I moved toward her to help.

She yanked her jacket away from me. "I can do it," she mumbled angrily, concentrating.

I frowned and hardened again. She continued to fumble, unable to get it. I looked away and took a deep breath, digging deep to find some patience. My dad was watching us silently. He shook his head at me in sympathy.

"Dammit," my mother whispered in frustration. "They just don't make these zippers properly anymore. They don't work on any of my coats!" She kept fumbling but wasn't having any luck.

I waited another beat, then said, "Can I please give you a hand?" I sounded like I was pleading. I was.

She looked up in exasperation and heaved a big, dramatic sigh. "Fine!" she snapped. "But it's not me! It's the damned zipper. It doesn't work right!" Though she was furious, she let go of it and waited for me to help.

I gingerly approached her and reached for the zipper, half expecting her to swat at me again. I pushed the pieces together and zipped up the coat, then smiled at her and said, "There. I fixed it. Let's go get the mail."

It was cold but bright and sunny outside, the brisk air delightful after the stuffy kitchen. I put my scarf over my nose and mouth to protect my asthmatic lungs and deeply breathed in the cold, fresh air. More unsteady on her feet than she usually was, my mom was stepping very gingerly, so I offered her my arm to hang onto. She took it, and we made our way slowly down the driveway toward their mailbox.

"What a beautiful day," I said. "Cold, but beautiful."

My mom was concentrating on walking carefully. Every now and then her foot would slip ever so slightly and she'd jerk on my arm a little to steady herself. "Yes, it is," she said distractedly.

We made it to the mailbox, and she carefully reached inside to pull out the mail. To make sure the hallucination was over, I was trying to think of other things to talk about. I was so used to talking about everything very directly and frankly with my mom, so it was difficult for me to avoid mentioning what had just happened. But I knew enough by then to know it not only wouldn't help at all but might actually put her back into the hallucination.

"What should I make for dinner tonight?" I blurted out, unable to come up with anything else that didn't feel totally fake and random.

She gave me a look like *Seriously?* And then said, "How should I know?" again, like I was ridiculous for asking.

I shrugged. "I just wondered if there was something you were particularly in the mood for." Though I kept it at bay, my annoyance at her response was just under the surface. She seemed to completely take for granted that I cooked for them most nights and, even when they didn't eat with us, gave them leftovers half the time.

After walking slowly back up the driveway, we reached their door and I said, "Alright, well, I'm heading home then to get some work done. That doctor's appointment is tomorrow at two p.m., so we'll leave about one fifteen."

"Okay," she said distractedly as she carefully opened the door and stepped inside. I followed her into the doorway, just to make sure she'd recognize my dad. He was at the sink washing their breakfast dishes and looked up when she came in. He smiled at her, but I could see his wariness.

She smiled back in a forced way. I wasn't sure whether she recognized him. She turned, looked at me expectantly, and asked, "Yes?"

I looked back and forth between them, unsure of how to test this out. "Who's that?" I blurted out, pointing at my dad.

She looked at him, then back at me like I was being absurd. "That's your father," she said slowly. "Who do you think it is?" I couldn't tell whether she was annoyed because I'd quizzed her or because she remembered having mistaken him for the sheriff earlier and didn't want it pointed out. I didn't ask.

"Okay, just checking. I'll see you later for dinner." I shut the door, huffed out a breath I didn't realize I'd been holding, and headed home.

When we arrived at the doctor's office, my mom hadn't fully grasped why we were going to see a new doctor, but she didn't ask any questions either. My relief at the lack of battle was suffocated by my sadness at the clear sign of her loss of cognition.

Dr. Baleen was very soft-spoken, so much so that both my parents had a hard time hearing her. She took my mother's history from me, listening very attentively without interrupting. Her manner was completely different from Dr. Wendell's. Even though I knew my mom couldn't hear much of what she was asking and saying, she seemed relaxed with Dr. Baleen. That counted for a lot.

She did some movement assessments with my mom, speaking loudly enough to ask her a few questions directly. I recognized the memory screening by now. "Who is the president?" Dr. Baleen began.

My mother frowned and rolled her eyes. "That clown, Donald Trump," she said with disgust. I frowned at her. Normally her filter would've enabled her to do a slightly better job of hiding her disdain for a politician in front of someone she didn't know.

Dr. Baleen just smiled in amusement. "And what year is it?"

My mother kept frowning, staring at the doctor for a moment and thinking. "2020, isn't it?"

Dr. Baleen nodded and smiled again, then gestured toward me and asked her, "And what's her name?"

When my mom turned to look at me, she smiled affectionately in a way she didn't often do. It brought tears to my eyes. "That's Ellen, my wonderful daughter."

Dr. Baleen smiled at me, and I gave a little laugh, embarrassed that I was tearing up. She then sat back and looked at us for a moment. After looking down at the notes she'd been taking on my mom's medical and behavioral history, she looked back up at us again, then settled her gaze on me.

"Has anyone talked to you about what to expect with Lewy body?" she asked softly. I was suddenly grateful that my parents couldn't hear everything she was saying. I shook my head, feeling more tears pricking my eyes, and took a breath to try to calm myself.

She nodded. "Okay," she said. "Let's get you some more information about that. Do you have support in place? Like palliative care and respite care?"

I glanced at my parents, then looked back to the doctor. "Well, we have Comfort Keepers coming in twice a week for four hours at a time to give my dad a break. For now, anyway. Is that what you mean?"

She nodded. "Yes, that's part of it. What about any palliative care for your mom?"

"I'm not sure what the difference is, to be honest," I admitted sheepishly. I'd heard the term before but never bothered to find out what it was; I'd had too many balls to juggle as it was. But now I was embarrassed that I didn't know.

She smiled kindly. "It's okay, I'll explain. Respite care is more directed toward the caregiver. Palliative care is more directed toward the patient. Respite care is what can give your dad a break and allow him to focus on taking care of himself. Palliative care is what we can do to support your mom by making sure she's not in pain or suffering. It's aimed at helping manage the symptoms of terminal illness."

The words "terminal illness" landed heavily on me, and I felt a knot in my stomach. I swallowed. "No, I don't think we really have any palliative care," I said. "Well, we did use pot gummies for a while to help keep her calm, but now they seem to make her hallucinate more often and more aggressively, so we stopped using them. So no, we don't have any palliative care for her." I paused. "What would we do to help her? She doesn't seem to be in any pain."

"That's alright," she said with a kind smile. "There are some drugs we could try if she's agitated, but she seems fairly calm to me. Is this how she normally is?"

I looked at my parents and they looked back at me quizzically. "What is she saying?" my mom whispered. I chuckled. She seemed to think that because she couldn't hear the doctor, the doctor wouldn't be able to hear her whisper.

"She's just asking me about how we're supporting you," I said, smiling reassuringly. I turned back to the doctor and said in a lower voice, "No, this is pretty calm right now. She can get pretty agitated at times, especially when hallucinating. She's also been suffering from sundowner's syndrome quite a bit recently. The melatonin helps with that. For now." I was trying to keep my mother from feeling like I was attacking or criticizing her in case she could hear what I was saying.

Dr. Baleen looked down at her notes again, then back up at me. She smiled sympathetically and softly said, "I don't see anything here that leads me to disagree with Dr. Wendell's prognosis. I'm sorry."

The tears immediately came back, stinging my eyes. I nodded, pursing my lips together like my mom did, trying to hold the tears in. I suddenly wanted to lie down. I looked over at my parents and tried to smile, but they could see I was upset. My dad hadn't heard the doctor clearly, but he read my face. I saw tears well up in his eyes too as he guessed what she'd said. My mom looked concerned.

I don't remember anything else the doctor said after that. I still have a booklet about LBD that we got from her that day, but that's all I remember. We scheduled an appointment for April 2020. We never made it back.

Looking Back Now

While seeking a second opinion didn't change my mom's prognosis, there was value in getting one. If nothing else, it was confirmation from a doctor whose style was completely different from Dr. Wendell's, which made it feel less like a bomb had been dropped and more like what it was: difficult news we needed to process.

Our experience with the kind and understanding staff of Comfort Keepers lasted a total of two months. By the end, my mother was so agitated upon the arrival of a caregiver that we knew she wouldn't make it through the whole visit. She'd come storming out of the house, waving her arms around like she was trying to shoo away a fly. The caregiver would follow, keeping a respectful distance but appearing to be trying to reason with her. As we stood watching the shit show from my house one day, my dad and I realized this was no longer a tenable situation. I ended the contract and apologized for my mother. They were all very gracious and understanding.

At this point, we were still in the middle of an ever-accelerating progression of my mom's disease. It's only with hindsight that I realize I was probably too exhausted and overwhelmed to do much more than try to keep up. Looking back now, I think it would've helped ease at least the feelings of guilt, shame, and inadequacy if I could've heard someone say these things to me:

➢ Seek guidance from your doctor about what sort of care is appropriate for your loved one. You might need respite care, palliative care, or both. Your doctor can help direct you to resources available in your area. Your local Area Agency on Aging may also be able to help. In some areas, there are abundant resources for aging seniors, specifically those affected by dementia.

➢ The ALZ website can be a little overwhelming at times because of the vast amount of information available on it. However, not taking some time to look for what you need to know (where to find resources, what your loved one's form of dementia is about, what to ask a doctor, etc.) will leave you blindly navigating this path like we did. Start small. Set aside 15 minutes and pick a specific topic/question to research.

➢ Denial is real and can show up repeatedly throughout the journey. Denial is a defense mechanism that protects us from painful, strong emotions like grief. But the more it builds up, the harder it can be to break through it. It might be helpful to ask yourself a question about why you're struggling with something, then journal about it. Or, if you prefer to do your processing in your brain, take a walk and let yourself think about what's happening and really feel all the feelings.

➢ None of us could keep this up for long. Something had to give. In a moment of crisis, someone (I cannot remember who at this point) recommended taking my mother for a "geriatric psychiatric evaluation." As it was explained to me, this evaluation is a specific process that isolates your loved one and takes them off all medications under close supervision in order to determine what the root cause diagnosis might be. It's a drastic step, one we were never able to bring ourselves to put my mom through, mostly because she was still lucid some of the time and we were afraid the process would destroy her. But in some cases, if your loved one is in danger of hurting themselves or you, it might be necessary. Talking to your doctor about options for your loved one might be helpful, but I'm skeptical that it's ever an easy or clear decision. That's a huge lesson for me from this experience: it's messy. Despite what some of the experts say, there are no clear answers about "right" and "wrong" ways to handle things. Talk to your doctor and listen to your gut instinct. Then make the best decision you can in the moment.

CHAPTER 12

DOPPELGÄNGERS AND DEATH MARCHES

A few short weeks later, everything shut down as the COVID-19 pandemic swept across the world. I'd been planning to be gone for two weeks to work in Belgium with a longtime client. Dani often went with me on those international trips, but we'd decided she needed to stay home to take care of the kids and the farm and to help my parents. The day I was supposed to get on a plane to leave was the day the global shut down was announced. Though I wasn't at the time, I'm so grateful now for a small silver lining: I was home.

A few weeks into the pandemic, my parents headed out for their daily walk. Compared to how hard it had been for my dad to get her to go for a walk when they'd first moved up to the farm, my mom's energy level was astonishing. Her speed was also surprising. Though she'd previously been walking slower and slower, relying more and more on my dad to hold onto and seeming like a wind-up top that was running out of juice, something changed. As her dementia symptoms got worse, she sped up. My dad was now using a cane on their walks because he was still slowing down, following the normal aging process. He'd commented to us more than once that it was getting harder to keep up with her, both in speed and endurance. It really was like she was the Energizer Bunny.

On this particular day, I didn't see them head out. I was working in my office, which faced the part of the road leading to town. They usually walked in the opposite direction, following the road along fields and forest until they came to the river where the road ended. Roundtrip, the walk was about two miles. When my dad texted me to say they were going for a walk, I thought nothing of it and continued working.

A little while later, I got up to get a snack and decided to see whether they were back. I looked at my phone to check for a missed call or text from my dad, as they came frequently at that point, but there was nothing. I realized it had been over an hour since they'd left. It was April and spring was flirting with us. The snow had melted and the sun was out. Dani was working out in the barn, so I decided to go out to see how she was doing and check in on my parents at the same time.

They weren't at home. I frowned. That was odd. Their car was still there, so I knew they couldn't have gone far. I walked to the edge of the road and craned my neck, standing on my tippy toes to see if I could spot them. Nothing in either direction. Getting a little concerned, I went into the barn and headed down the stairs to the lower level where our horses sheltered from the elements.

"Hey, baby," I said as I got downstairs. "Have you seen my parents or heard from my dad?"

Filing one of the horse's hooves, Dani was bent over, a tool in one hand and the horse's leg in the other. She looked up at me, panting slightly from the exertion. "No," she said. "Why?"

"My dad texted me over an hour ago saying they were going for a walk, but they aren't back yet," I said. "I'm starting to get a little worried. That walk doesn't take them more than thirty or forty minutes at this point, the way my mom trucks down the road."

She'd gone back to filing. "Did you call your dad?" she asked.

"No," I said, heading for the stairs. "I was just checking around first. I didn't want to be paranoid. I'm going up so I can get a signal to call him now."

I jogged back up the steep stairs, pulled my phone from my pocket, and walked to the open doors of the barn to stand in the sunlight and get a better signal. As I opened my phone to dial my dad's number, he called me.

"Hey," I said, trying to keep the concern out of my voice. "I was just about to call you. Where are you guys at?" He sounded breathless and my heart dropped. "Dad, what's wrong?"

"I think I need you to come pick us up," he said, sounding like he was still walking, his breath and voice labored.

"Where are you?" I tried not to raise my voice, fighting the panic as I ran from the barn back toward the house to grab my keys. "What happened?"

"We're down the road," he answered, still struggling to talk.

"That doesn't help!" I shouted in frustration. "Down the road by the river? Is Mom okay? Are you okay?"

"No, the other way," he said.

I stopped in my tracks, cold fear washing over me. "What do you mean, 'the other way'?"

He struggled for a minute to breathe while I struggled to contain my panic.

"Dad, can you stop walking? It sounds like you're still walking. Just stop for a second and talk to me so I know where to go to help." Though I made an effort to sound calm, I wasn't.

"I can't," he said. "She'll get even further ahead of me."

Holy shit, I thought, no longer able to contain my panic. "I need to know where the hell you are!" I yelled.

"Head down the road toward town. Cross whatever that road is and keep going," he panted. "I'm not sure how far down we are, but I can't get her to turn around." He stopped, breathing hard again. "And I can't keep going."

Panic surged and I choked back a sob. "Do you need an ambulance?!" I yelled, climbing into my car and starting it up. As I looked behind me to back up, I saw Dani coming out of the barn, looking concerned. She must've heard me yelling because she raised her hands in a gesture of *What's happening?* I backed out of my spot and swung around, lowering the window.

"No," my dad said. "I just need you to come pick us up." More panting. "I'm going to keep walking so I can keep my eye on her."

"Okay, we're on our way," I said, motioning to Dani to get in. "We've gotta go," I said to Dani urgently. "He's in distress."

Dani jumped in and I flew out of the driveway, racing down the road toward the main road. "What happened?" she asked, also sounding alarmed.

I shook my head, trying to keep my emotions under control. "I don't know," I said. "They must've gone the other way down the road and I didn't see them go past." I shook my head again, guilt washing over me like a wave. "How did I not see them go past my office down the road?" I reached the main road, paused without fully stopping, looked both ways, and shot across. "Now my dad sounds like he's dying because she's moving so fucking fast! I have no idea how far they've gone. He couldn't tell me." I slowed my driving down, not wanting to come up over a hill too fast and risk hitting them. I had a death grip on the steering wheel.

"Geezus," Dani breathed, straining to look ahead to try to spot them. Suddenly she pointed. "There they are."

I slowed even more, swerving to the left side of the road to give them space. My mom, looking irritated with her hands on her hips in her classic disapproving stance, was standing with my dad, who was leaning heavily on his cane, looking like he was about to pass out. She saw us and her expression changed to one of surprise.

Dani rolled down her window. "Hey, kids," she said, her tone light and playful. I still don't know how she did it. "You two lovebirds lost?"

My dad gave a weak smile and looked relieved. Dani got out of the passenger seat to help them as I sat behind the wheel, not wanting to get out in case another car came along and I had to move. She helped my dad first, guiding him to the car and helping him get into the front seat next to me. He looked over at me, his expression a mixture of embarrassment, relief, and fear.

"Just in time," he said, softly, his breathing still labored. He was wheezing and sounded like I did when I was having a severe asthma attack. I gave him a feeble smile, my own relief and fear still mingling.

"What the hell happened?" I said in an urgent whisper. He shook his head, either not yet able or not willing to say, as he looked around to see what my mom and Dani were doing. I tried again. "Are you okay? Do you need medical attention?" I was instantly frustrated at how he still seemed more worried about my mom than he was about himself. "Dad!" I said more loudly, my frustration now evident.

"No," he said with a stronger voice. "I'm fine."

Behind us, Dani was talking to my mom, trying to get her into the car. "Why did you come pick us up?" my mom asked, sounding critical and irritated. "We were perfectly capable of walking back."

"Well," Dani responded, "we were in the neighborhood and saw you two, so we thought it might be fun to ride back home together." She didn't miss a beat, and her tone was still light and playful. I wondered again how she did it. My dad and I exchanged a glance that told me he wasn't sure how she did it either.

Once both my parents were back in the car, I turned around and looked at the odometer so I could measure how far they'd gone as we drove back.

"Didn't you guys head to the river, like normal?" I asked, still not sure how they'd gotten past the house without me seeing.

My dad nodded. "We did, but then your mother wanted to go the other way, so we turned around."

"How did you get past the house without me seeing you?" I asked, incredulous.

He shrugged but said nothing. I simmered in my frustration at the lack of information.

"We walked!" came my mom's voice from the back, sounding chipper and a little sassy.

I glared at her in the rearview mirror, but she didn't look at me. I don't think she could see me in the mirror at that point, as her vision had started to deteriorate. "Ha, ha," I said sarcastically.

As I pulled into the circular drive to let them out at their house, I looked at the odometer again. They'd gone three miles down the road, plus however far they'd walked toward the river before turning back. That would've meant a walk of at least six miles had they turned around where they were to head back. I shook my head in frustration.

Dani got out and ran around to the side of the car to help my dad. Though his breathing seemed to have returned to normal, he was moving slowly and wincing, appearing like he was in pain.

"Are you sure you're okay?" I called as he labored to straighten himself back up after climbing out.

He turned back and looked at me. "Yes, I'm okay," he said. "Thank you." His eyes glistened. "That was close."

I knew he meant he'd come close to collapsing. I felt like we'd narrowly dodged a bullet. My father is not a man who can ask for help; he is one of the men they're talking about on the billboards that say, "This year, thousands of men will die from stubbornness." In fact, if he'd read one of them, he would've responded, "No, we won't."

Dani got back into the front seat, and we watched my parents walk slowly to their house. My mom seemed more aware now of my dad struggling, and she held his arm and walked with him. I saw her look over at him with concern on her face, then shook my head and looked at Dani. She'd seen it too and shook her head as well. We drove back over to our house and parked the car.

"Holy fuck, what the hell was that about?" I spat, my anger and frustration returning. "And how in the hell did I miss them coming back past the house?" I was dumbstruck and still didn't understand.

Dani shrugged, smiling sympathetically at me. "It's not your fault, baby," she said softly.

Her comment cut right through my anger and frustration into the heart of what was really bothering me, which was the feeling that it actually *was* my fault somehow. My face crumbled as I looked at her. Her eyes welled up too, and she patted my arm. "Come on, love," she said. "Let's go in."

My mother's hallucinations were increasing in frequency and fantasy. Days after what Dani and I called "The Attempted Death March," my dad took the trash cans down to the road. He always put their cans out with ours, so he'd drag them from their driveway along the road to our end of the circular drive. Then he'd usually walk back by way of the circular drive so he could look at and often talk to the horses and other animals in the pastures on his way back.

This day, he started up the driveway but came to our rarely used, always locked front door. I was working in my office and saw him walk past, but I startled when he knocked on the door. I jumped up and let him in, then Dani came out of the kitchen and met us at the door. He looked terrible—haggard and tired with bags under his eyes. I looked at him with concern, and his eyes welled up with tears.

"Oh my god, Dad, what's wrong?" I breathed, ushering him inside. "What's happened?"

Motioning all of us to come further into the house, Dani said, "Come on in, Ron, and you can tell us what's going on." She led us to the dining room table where we sat down.

My dad wouldn't look at us, instead staring out the bay windows at the pasture. He was trying to control his emotions and losing. My heart beat faster and I felt scared as I watched him. I could tell something big was going on.

"Dad, talk to us," I said softly, reaching over to touch his arm. "What's wrong? Did something happen?"

He shook his head and laughed. "Yeah, the last three years." He tried to play it off, but I could almost see his heart breaking. He put his face in his hands and started to sob. "I can't do this anymore," he said, his hands muffling his voice.

Dani and I were also crying, and we both reached across the table to put our hands on his arms and try to comfort him. "It's okay, Dad," I said through my tears. "It's okay. We're here. We've got you." I had a terrible, sinking feeling. This was it. It was time for my mom to live in a facility. I felt a mix of fear, profound sadness, and the tiniest bit of relief.

We stayed like that for a few minutes, giving my dad time to grieve and collect himself. Dani got up and grabbed a box of tissues for us all. After we'd all wiped our faces, I said as gently as possible, "What do you want me to do?" As much as I already knew, I needed to hear him say it's what he wanted. I did not want to be in the position of being blamed for making a decision he regretted. I'd told him months prior that if it was going to happen, he'd have to be the one to ask me to do it.

He looked at me then, his face full of misery, and said softly, "Do you think you can find a place for my sweetheart to go?" His voice broke on the last words, and his face crumpled. My heart broke for him.

I nodded. "Yeah," I whispered. We were all back to crying.

After we'd pulled ourselves together again, I said, "I'll start making some calls. It's going to be tough with the pandemic, but we'll figure something out. I promise."

After a couple of more minutes, we all got up. "I've got to get back," my dad said, suddenly worried. "I can't leave her for more than a few minutes now."

"What are you going to tell her about where you were?" I asked, knowing her tendency to be paranoid about us plotting against her.

"I don't think it will matter," he said, his voice full of sadness and defeat. I waited to see whether he'd say anything else, but he didn't. I didn't ask why.

Dani and I walked him out and then went back inside. I turned to her, tears overwhelming me again, leaned into her open arms, and cried.

We'd seen this coming for a while, even if my dad insisted on clinging to denial and the hope that my mom would somehow snap out of it or get better. I couldn't blame him for that, but since I face life very differently than he does, I still found it frustrating. As a way to cope with my anxiety, fears, and sadness, I turned toward finding solutions. Although the moment for implementing them might be months or even years away, I needed to know what our options were when that moment finally came.

I'd connected with an agency in our area that helps find placement for seniors and toured a few facilities with my dad before everything shut down. They'd all been depressing. None of them felt like the right fit. But now we were desperate, and in-person tours were off the table. I started with the people I knew.

"Hi, Cathy," I said when the director of Daleview answered the phone. We'd worked together a few years before on a community project, and I liked her very much. She was such a calm presence and strong advocate for her residents. Daleview had independent living apartments in one building and assisted living and memory care in another. "I think it's time," I said. "We need to find a place for my mom."

"Oh, Ellen, I'm so sorry to hear that," Cathy said, her voice full of empathy. "And what a time to be trying to do this. Oh, my heart just goes out to you, Dani, and your family." She'd met Dani a few times, and they'd shared jokes about how short they both were. "What did you have in mind?" she asked.

"Well, I'm just trying to figure out my options here," I answered. "You know she has the diagnosis of Lewy body. I suppose one option would be to see if my parents wanted to live in an apartment on the independent side together, but I think my dad is going to die from exhaustion. So I'm starting to think we need placement just for her." I was trying not to let my voice crack with emotion.

Cathy waited a beat, then said, "Honey, I'm so sorry, but we can't take her here with a Lewy body diagnosis. Does she have that actual diagnosis, or is it just what you suspect?"

I had a feeling she was trying to work with me on it, but I couldn't lie. I respected Cathy too much and I knew how erratic my mom's behavior was. "She got the actual diagnosis last November," I said sadly.

"I'm so sorry," Cathy repeated. "I can't help you. Have you tried Sunrise?" Sunrise was the local county nursing home and dementia care facility that we'd toured with my aunt.

"We visited them last fall when my brother and I started to suspect this would be necessary at some point," I said. "I talked to Maude, the ED, in January to see where my mom was on the waiting list, but she told me they wouldn't be able to take my mom while she was so out of it. You remember, Dani and I talked to you and Maude around the same time. My mom was having those UTI's one after another and was really off the wall until we got it under control. She's not loopy like she was then, but she's like the Energizer Bunny now and my dad is at the end of his rope." My voice finally broke and I couldn't hold back the tears.

Cathy made soft, sympathetic sounds, then said, "I do remember, and I'm so, so sorry, honey. I wish I could do something to help. You should call Maude again and see if there's any change, and if she can't help you, I'd call Sapphire." Sapphire was the other well-known, private (a.k.a. expensive), upscale facility in Lapeer.

"Thanks, Cathy," I said, trying to pull myself together. "I'll try them both and see what happens."

"You keep me posted," she said. "And if I think of something else, I'll let you know."

I thanked her and we said our goodbyes.

I tried Sunrise next. Maude didn't answer. I left her a message, unable to keep from crying as I did. I pleaded for her help.

Pulling myself together again, I looked at a folder from Sapphire. I'd requested information from them a few months prior when I started getting worried we'd need placement sooner rather than later. I didn't think my parents could really afford Sapphire, as they didn't have any special insurance and it was a private facility. That meant that once they ran out of money, my mother would have to leave. I didn't like the idea of that, but I didn't know where else to turn, so I called. I was connected to a woman named Jessica.

"Hi, Jessica, my name is Ellen, and I'm looking for placement options for my mom," I started. "She has dementia, so she'd need to be in your memory care unit." I left out the Lewy body for the moment.

"Hi, Ellen, it's nice to virtually meet you," Jessica said. "I'm sorry to hear about your mom. And this is such a difficult time, even more than it normally is, to try to find placement. My heart goes out to you and your family."

She paused, so I murmured a thank you.

"Unfortunately," she continued, "we're at capacity at the moment. I would be able to add you to our waiting list, if that might help?"

I was secretly relieved but also felt my options dwindling, which made me afraid we'd have to go with one of the not-so-great places we'd toured. "Oh," I said, hoping my disappointment showed more than my relief. "That is unfortunate." I paused, then with a surge of desperation, said in a rush, "Jessica, we're sort of at the end of our rope over here." My voice broke, of course. "My dad is at his limit, and I'm worried about his health. That in turn makes me worried about my mom's safety because he's exhausted and can't care for her properly. Do you know of any other places I could try? Also, you should probably know that she's been diagnosed with Lewy body, in case that matters." I sounded as desperate as I felt. All I could picture was my dad at our dining room table the day before.

"I'm so sorry," Jessica said again. "I understand. This is such a difficult time for all of us, but even more so for people in your position. My heart really goes out to you. And thank you for telling me about the Lewy body. That actually does matter, and we wouldn't be able to accommodate her here either." She paused and I heard papers rustling. I swallowed my bitterness at her last comment, feeling hopeless. Then she asked, "Have you talked with Mandy at Cedarland?"

I perked up slightly. "No . . . I don't think I've heard of it."

"Cedarland is dedicated to memory care only. It's a small facility, I think somewhere around twenty to twenty-five beds. The director there, Mandy, is fantastic. And she's very experienced with all kinds of dementia, so if she can't take your mom, she might have other resources for you."

My hope returned in a flash. "Thank you so much, Jessica," I said. "Do you have a number for Cedarland by any chance?" She gave me the direct line, I thanked her again, and we hung up.

I sat back and took a deep breath. I wanted to call Mandy right away but was also scared. What if she didn't have room either? Or what if she wouldn't take my mom because of the LBD? I was afraid to know, but not knowing was worse. I picked my phone back up and dialed.

After getting her voicemail, I left a message, telling her that Jessica from Sapphire had recommended I call and asking that someone call me back. I left my number and hung up, sinking back into my chair, thoroughly drained.

A couple of hours later, Mandy called me back. Her voice was calm and reassuring without being gushy. "Hi, Ellen, this is Mandy from Cedarland," she said. "I do have a space for your mom."

That simple statement was my undoing. I began to weep with relief. I'd never seen this place, but I felt so at the end of my rope that her casual response was a life raft. "I'm sorry," I said through choked sobs. "I'm just so relieved. You have no idea."

She laughed softly and said, "Oh, I can imagine. And I understand. We actually have two open beds right now. Tell me a little about your mom."

I took a deep breath and tried to get myself under control. "Well, she was diagnosed with Lewy body back in November," I began, bracing myself for rejection. "Is that going to disqualify her?" I squeezed my eyes shut, coming as close to sending up a prayer as I get.

"No, not at all," she said. I burst into fresh tears. "I've had several clients here with Lewy body over the years."

"Oh my god, I can't tell you how relieved I am!" I choked out through my tears. (I'm not an elegant crier.) "I've been turned away by three other facilities for that."

"Well, then they weren't the right place for your mom," she said simply. I think I fell in love with her a little bit right then and there. She asked for my mom's information, which I gave her, then said, "I obviously can't bring you in for an in-person tour, but would you like to do a virtual one? We can FaceTime if you have an iPhone, or we can use Zoom if you don't. I can walk you through the facility, show you a resident room, things like that."

With a deep breath, I went into logistics mode. "I'd like my dad to be part of that call," I said. "I know he'd like to see it too."

"Of course," she said.

We organized the call for the next day, at a time when I thought I could get my parents to come over and Dani would be able to distract my mom. We discussed the cost and process for moving my mom in if we were in agreement once we did the virtual tour.

"How soon would this happen?" I asked. "Can we talk through the logistics of the move?"

"Sure," she said. "It will take a few days to process the paperwork and get the room set up for her. From there, we can set your move-in date."

We finished the call and I hung up, flooded with relief.

Looking Back Now

During this period, my mom's hallucinations were lasting longer, sometimes for hours, and my mom would sometimes reenter the same one over and over during a period of days. She became increasingly agitated and upset by them, and she often perceived my dad to be a doppelgänger of himself who tried to hurt her, sexually assault her, arrest her, or kidnap her. In the most benign of the hallucinations, she'd think my dad was making her life miserable or was a con artist trying to sell her on something. He of course never did any of those things. It was her mind playing elaborate and convincing tricks on her. But my dad paid the price.

At this point, my mom was also suffering with incontinence and would fight us tooth and nail against wearing any type of absorbent undergarment. Because of her hallucinations and general confusion, she'd often get up in the night to use the bathroom but get lost. My dad would sometimes find her on their couch relieving herself, and at least twice he caught her falling down as she tried to squat over the waste basket.

Sundowner's syndrome was also still affecting my mom and, in turn, my dad. There were many nights neither of them slept at all or for just very brief periods. My mom would often "escape" to our house in the middle of the night. If I was awake enough to hear my phone, which was set to accept all calls and texts from my dad at any time of day or night, he'd try to warn us she was coming. Other times, we'd wake up startled to the sound of her screaming and banging on our back door, which was directly below our bedroom windows. And sometimes, before we got alarms for the doors, she'd sneak out without my dad realizing she'd left. He was exhausted all the time. When David and I were babies, my dad was the one who awoke to hear us crying at feeding times. When we were teenagers, my dad was the one who heard us come home from being out with friends or working. Now he was sleeping through nearly everything.

My mother also became aggressive and sometimes violent. She'd hit or at least swing at my dad many times during hallucinations when she believed him to be someone else trying to hurt her. His instinct was always to go to her to try to calm her down, but that only made things worse.

Due to her tendency toward violence, our ALZ group and Dr. Wendell had warned us to put away all knives and any weapons. Despite my pleading, my dad had brushed off those warnings. His reasoning was that she'd stopped doing any kitchen work or food prep and never went anywhere near the knife block on the counter. Until she did one day when she took a knife from the block and put it somewhere "for safety" in a place she wouldn't disclose. He hid the rest of the block after that, and we found the knife in a dresser drawer a few days later.

Those moments were some of the hardest for all of us, especially watching my mom turn against the man she'd loved since the age of

16. It was hard on us, for sure, but no one suffered as much as my dad. For him, it was three years of pure, unadulterated hell. Looking back now, I wish I'd known these things so that I could have better supported him:

> ➤ Sundowner's syndrome is very common in older patients with all kinds of illnesses, but it's especially common in all types of dementia. It's basically the reversing of day and night. As the sun goes down, the person's level of agitation increases, sometimes causing endless pacing, inability to settle, and sleeplessness, often lasting through the night. At the first signs of it, please consult with your loved one's doctor to understand what medications or remedies are appropriate for their specific case.

> ➤ Caregiver exhaustion is real, and it causes premature death in spouses who are caregiving more than anyone else. For up-to-date statistics, please visit the ALZ website at www.alz.org. They have a wealth of information you'll wish you didn't need to know but just might help you in very real ways.

> ➤ It's totally normal and acceptable, even expected, to have very mixed feelings about moving your loved one to a care facility. I personally battled between guilt, relief, sadness, and extreme stress over the placement of my mom. All feelings are valid, and having negative ones doesn't mean that you don't love your loved one. In my case, I needed to believe that I wasn't a bad daughter for doing the exact thing my mother begged me not to do. Caregivers act in what they believe to be the best interests of their loved ones and do so without malicious intent. Those who don't are called something else, not "caregivers."

> ➤ It's important to ask the right questions when looking for a facility for your loved one. The type of dementia they're

diagnosed with sometimes matters, as we found out the hard way. Some facilities are simply not equipped with the right staff to handle the unpredictability and typical aggression that are common with LBD. Does your loved one need a skilled nursing facility? An adult foster care home? In-home care? Hospice? Make those assessments with your loved one's doctor, ask lots of questions, and get recommendations from people in your community who work with the aging population. And it's never too early to start that search. You may not realize the moment to make the transition has arrived until it's happening.

CHAPTER 13

IT'S NOT FINE ANYMORE

After a video tour of Cedarland, my dad seemed numb. I knew he was struggling with tremendous guilt at placing my mom, having promised her that he'd keep her at home until the end. That promise was foolish to make, we now know. It had been based on the false assumption that her journey through the disease would mirror that of my grandmother's. We had no idea how differently my mom's disease would progress.

The promise had also been based on the desire to comfort and reassure my mom. Her pleas with us to help her die with dignity and to keep her at home until the end were based on my mother's terror. In a different state, we would've been able to honor her wish to die with help and dignity before the disease had ravaged her so completely. But that wasn't an option in Michigan. In my darkest hours, all I could see was the selfishness of her requests and the danger fulfilling them would put us in. It's only now that I can have empathy for her desperation.

The facility had just 20 beds and was an adult foster care home rather than a skilled nursing facility. I later learned how important that distinction was. For the time being, all I cared about was that they had space for my mother and experience with managing patients with LBD. It was a private pay facility but affordable for the moment at $4,200 per month. I knew my parents wouldn't be able to sustain that for the long term, but they could handle it for a few months until the elder law attorney was able to help them restructure their estate to have Medicaid kick in.

I was more worried about how we were going to convince my mom to go without physically forcing her into the car and back out of it. She still had moments of lucidity often enough that she wasn't just living in her own world. And we couldn't always tell when she was lucid and when she wasn't, so we had to constantly be on our guard about what we said in front of her. She'd turn on us in a heartbeat and was very unpredictable.

Mandy was a huge help during this process. Once we'd gotten all the paperwork taken care of and set a move-in date for a couple of weeks out, she said I could call anytime with any other questions. So I did. She always answered, even if we played phone tag to do it.

"Mandy, this is Ellen, Charlotte's daughter, again. I'm not sure how to tell my mom that we're moving her. I'm pretty sure she's going to fight us tooth and nail on this."

"In situations like this," Mandy replied, "I find the less information you give your loved one, the better. I know it probably feels wrong and uncomfortable to be less than honest with her, but in my experience, if you can think about it not as a lie but just as not sharing all the information with her, that will help keep her the calmest and be the least afraid. It might help."

I swallowed hard. Because of how often my mom was still lucid, this was a tough one for me. It definitely felt like I was lying to her. But I could see Mandy's point. "I don't even know what to say," I stammered.

"Well, you don't have to tell her that this is a permanent move," she offered. "That makes it seem scarier to people with dementia. The fear of the unknown is almost always present for them. Instead, you could try telling her that this is just for a little while. The goal is to get her here. If you focus on that as what's in her best interest, the rest will follow."

I nodded, tears welling up again as they did nearly every day now. "And how far in advance should I tell her she's moving?" My voice broke.

"I would not advise telling her until the day you're going to bring her," Mandy said more firmly. "If you can pack a bag of some of the initial things she'll need and want to have without her knowing, that would be the best option. You can bring more of her things later. We'll need to have you and your dad and brother come in to meet with us once she's here and can be evaluated. Our medical staff will evaluate whether she needs to be in hospice care and make recommendations about her care that we'll need to discuss."

I was both comforted and panicked by what she said. It was all moving so fast. Hospice? She couldn't be ready for that, could she? I managed to squeak out, "Okay, thank you," before the tears overwhelmed me.

Mandy paused, then said more softly, "You're doing the right thing, in case you need to hear that. Your dad can't manage her care anymore. The threat to his health is real. We're here to help."

Making matters worse, I was terrified of what I didn't know. The COVID-19 pandemic was in full swing by then, and I was fully in charge of these decisions for my mom. I just wanted to be able to talk to her about them. In spite of our combativeness, I'd run nearly every important decision I'd ever made past her. If nothing else, I was always looking for her approval and reassurance that I was doing the right thing. Even if she didn't agree with my decision, we always fully discussed it, even if that discussion was in the form of arguing. Faced with this huge decision, I just wanted to be able to talk to the very person I couldn't. I never felt so alone in my life, before or since.

I talked to Dani instead, seeking her ideas on what we could tell my mom to get her to go with the least resistance possible. "What if we tell her your dad needs to go somewhere for treatment for a few weeks? Do you think she'd buy that?" she suggested.

I thought about it, feeling skeptical. I was struggling mightily with not being completely honest. "I don't know," I said slowly. "I'm worried that would backfire and she'd want to go stay with him."

I asked my brother and my dad to weigh in. Neither of them had any ideas to offer. My dad was like a zombie, moving through the days just trying to keep up with my mom, clearly near the end of his rope. My brother thought Dani's idea would work but didn't seem too concerned about it. It all made me feel more alone, trapped under the weight of these decisions.

As the date for bringing my mom to the facility drew closer, I decided to go with a version of Dani's idea, which was as close to the truth as I could come. I started making comments at dinner, and to my mom.

"Wow, Dad really looks tired," I'd say in a worried tone to my mom. "Do you think he's sleeping okay?" I was hopeful she'd worry more about him and managing his health, like she always had in the past.

She'd look in the direction I was indicating, usually to my dad doing something nearby. Sometimes it seemed like she was lucid for a moment, and she'd say, "I don't know," sounding mildly concerned. Other times she didn't seem to understand what I was saying. Once she turned on me. "Why are you so worried about him?" she snapped. "Why aren't you more worried about what's happening with me?" *Oh, Mom, if only you knew,* I thought to myself. *That's all I think about these days.*

I talked to my dad and Dani about the plan privately. "I think our best bet is to tell her that you haven't been well, Dad," I said with genuine worry. "I mean, that's the honest truth, after all. I think we should say that you're going to have some tests done and will need to be away to be evaluated and get some rest and that she needs to stay someplace where she can be cared for too." I paused, looking at them both for a reaction.

Dani nodded encouragingly, and we both looked at my dad. He shrugged. "I guess so," he said quietly. "But I don't like lying to her." His eyes welled up as he looked away. Fighting tears was our new normal. It was exhausting, which only made fighting them harder. I felt trapped in a vicious cycle.

"I know," I said, my own tears close to the surface. "Me neither. But Mandy said we need to think about this differently. We can't think of it as lying because Mom's no longer capable of consistently living in reality. What we're doing is giving her a story that she can hopefully understand and accept because it's critical for you both that she live somewhere else. If she doesn't, I don't think you're going to make it, Dad." My voice broke at the end, and I could see him lose his fight too. Dani put a hand on his arm in reassurance. Her eyes were also wet.

I took a deep breath. "Are we agreed then? This is our story, not to be told until the day we take her?"

Dani looked at my dad, who was still looking out the window. He nodded in a daze. His state only caused me more anxiety, worry, and fear, which made me antsy.

"Okay, I'll go call David and share it with him," I said, then turned and walked away toward my office, eager to have something to do.

We planned to take my mom to Cedarland on Thursday, May 21, 2020. Since everything was still shut down due to COVID, we didn't have to compete with work and school schedules, so a random Thursday fit the bill. We decided that David and Lauren, along with David's two daughters, would come over for a nice brunch so we could all be together once more. We didn't know whether we'd have another chance for that. The level of uncertainty was just another layer of stress that was adding to our collective exhaustion and anxiety. After brunch, David and I were going to drive her to the facility. My dad couldn't bear that, so we didn't think it would be a good idea.

Per Mandy's guidance, we didn't tell my mom anything in those 10 days leading up to her departure. I was on edge, struggling to make sure I didn't give anything away to her. She grew suspicious but wasn't sure why. She'd always picked up on my moods and energy. That was true even in the throes of this awful disease, though she couldn't articulate anything about it. I was having a really hard time not telling her what was happening. It was breaking another deeply ingrained pattern of communication between us.

The day before she was set to leave, I couldn't take it anymore. I felt very strongly, deep in my bones, that we needed to tell her something about what would be happening the next day. Not telling her anything and pretending like it was just another Wednesday was making me feel physically ill. I couldn't see how we'd get a bag packed for her without her knowing what was going on, at least in part.

It was a rainy day, overcast and gloomy, as I hurried across the driveway to my parents' house. It fit my mood, which I thought was cliché, and I nearly laughed out loud as I jogged along dodging puddles.

I burst into their kitchen, making more of an entrance than I'd intended. My dad was at the sink and looked up at me, a little startled. He waited for me to speak as I shook the rain off my jacket and then hung it on their coat tree near the door. I smiled at him, trying to assess him as I did. He looked exhausted. My mom was nowhere to be seen. "Where's Mom?" I asked softly.

As he started to say something, she walked into the kitchen, frowning. "What's going on?" she demanded in her strident way. I couldn't tell what her state of mind was.

I forced myself to smile brightly and replied, "Nothing! I just wanted to come and see how you guys were doing today." It sounded lame, even to me.

She snorted, and I decided she must be somewhat lucid. Not great for my plan. The more aware she was of what was happening, the harder she'd fight for control of the situation. Sensing that I had an agenda, I saw my dad tense up. I hesitated, suddenly doubting myself. My mother's frown deepened. She was still staring at me but was standing still for a change. I swallowed.

"I just wanted to get out of the house for a minute," I blurted out. "The boys are driving me a little crazy and I just needed a change of scenery for a minute."

Both of them seemed to accept that. My mom looked away, resuming her constant movement at the far end of the kitchen. My dad visibly relaxed and went back to rinsing the dishes in the sink. I watched them both, still torn. I felt the weight of all the decisions I was making heavy on my shoulders, and I knew I was going to cry. Turning away from them so they wouldn't see my face, I grabbed my wet jacket from the hook and put it back on.

"Where are you going?" my mother asked, surprised and disappointed that I was leaving so soon. "I thought you said you needed to get away from the boys." *So she's indeed more lucid today,* I thought. *Even more important that I get out of here.*

"I just remembered I have a call to make," I said, forcing my voice to be strong. "I'll see you guys later on."

I didn't wait for them to reply but rushed back out the door into the rain, tears overflowing and running down my face. I choked on a sob. I didn't remember ever having felt so alone in my life. I cried openly, looking up at the sky and letting the rain soak me, the sound of it muffling my heartbreak. My chest heaved as the pent-up emotion came rushing out. I ambled through the rain, suddenly desperate to get back to Dani for comfort.

The rain stuck around the rest of the afternoon. As dusk crept in early, I was in the kitchen thinking about putting dinner together. The immense weight from earlier had subsided, and I just felt drained. I was standing at the fridge, staring inside and feeling listless, when my phone rang. I pulled it out of my pocket and saw that it was my dad calling. I sighed as I answered.

"Hi, Dad. What's u—"

"Is your mother over there?" His voice was urgent and full of fear as he cut me off, and he was a little out of breath. I was instantly on high alert.

"No," I said, going straight into crisis management mode. I walked briskly out of the kitchen, through the dining room and into the living room, looking for Dani and any sign of my mom being there that I wasn't aware of. Dani was on the couch and looked up at me. She read my expression and got up, watching me to see what I needed. "She's not here," I confirmed. Dani shook her head, her eyes widening in alarm. We both looked outside at the gathering darkness and unrelenting rain. I felt my insides churn.

"Shit," my dad swore under his breath, which he didn't often do. "She's not here either."

"What happened? What's the last thing that happened?" I demanded as I put the phone on speaker.

"I must've fallen asleep in my chair," my dad said, sounding shaken and ashamed. "I don't know when she got out, but I've searched the whole house and she's not here."

My heart dropped and I turned back to Dani, eyes wide in panic. Her face was grim, and she headed for the back door. "Okay," I said to my dad, rushing after her. "We're coming!"

I hung up and shoved my phone back in my pocket, then jumped down the three steps and jammed my feet into my muck boots. "Holy fuck, this isn't good," I said to Dani, panic starting to take over.

"Let's have a look around outside," she said with a reassuring voice. "We'll find her. She hates rain. She won't have gone far. I'll look in the barn. You go see if your dad is okay and look around outside the house."

I pulled on my damp jacket and nodded, fear curling around the edges of the nape of my neck. Dani and I ran out the door, her sprinting across and to the left to go into the barn and me dashing across the driveway toward my parents' house. My dad was pulling on his jacket as I got to the back door. I was struck by how exhausted, sheepish, and old he looked.

"Why didn't the door alarm go off?" I asked, suddenly remembering that there was one.

He didn't meet my eyes, instead looking around for something. "I turned it off," he mumbled.

"Wait, what?" I stared in disbelief. "Dad! This is exactly why we have them!" I was stupefied.

He finally found the flashlight he'd been looking for and turned around to face me and head out the door. "I know," he said quietly. The look of pain and grief on his face stopped the tirade of words I wanted to rain down on him.

We went outside into the pouring rain just as Dani was running toward us from the barn. "Nothing," she shouted over the rain. "She's not in the barn. I'm going to get in the truck and drive down the road."

I felt bile come rushing up into my throat. If my mom had gone onto the road, she could've fallen into one of the deep drainage ditches that ran alongside it, made it out to the main road where traffic whizzed by at 55–65 miles per hour, or made it down to the river. I turned to my dad.

"Do you have any idea how long she's been gone?"

"No," he said, then paused. "I don't think it was that long, but I-I'm just not sure."

I could hear the panic and fear in his voice. "It's okay," I said loudly over the rain, as much to reassure myself as him. "We'll find her." I turned back to Dani. "Okay, you go down toward the road first, just in case she's gotten to Jefferson, and I'll take a look around the pastures just in case she went that way. Dad, maybe you should stay here in case she comes back?" I was worried about him falling himself.

We all agreed to the plan and split up. My dad gave me his flashlight as he headed back to his house, and I took off down the side of the pasture, swinging it wildly to try and spot her. "Mom!" I yelled, quickly realizing it was useless but unable to stop myself from crying for my mother.

As I got to the end of the tree line and pasture, I somehow felt that it wasn't where she was. I cut through the long grass, around the pine trees where our chicken coop was, ducking under the low branches. Something told me she hadn't come that way. The chickens were already roosting in their coop. They stayed quiet as I came crashing past, assuming I was a predator.

As I came up the hill from the coop, out of breath from both the exertion and the fear, I came face to face with my parents' car. I stopped dead in my tracks. The yellow-orange parking lights were on. Wondering whether my dad had gone out in the car to look for her as well, I broke into a run again and went right past it up to their house. I really thought someone should stay at the house in case she came back.

I burst into the kitchen with even more force than I had earlier that day, only to find my very startled-looking dad hurrying into the kitchen from the living room. "Did you find her?" His voice was full of hope.

"No, but did you decide to go out in the car to look for her?"

He frowned at me. "No, you told me I should stay here." He started patting his pockets for his keys. "But I can, if you think I should."

I stared for the split second it took me to realize that if he hadn't gone to their car, maybe my mom had. Not bothering to close the door behind me, I turned and ran out, sprinting to their car. As I came up to the passenger side, I saw that the door wasn't closed all the way. I made myself slow down. Relief, fear, and hope mixed in my stomach, causing me to feel nauseous and like I wanted to cry. I looked into the passenger seat window and saw her. She was crouched down in a ball, trying to wedge herself down into the footwell but not succeeding very well.

I gently opened the car door. "Hey, Mom," I crooned softly. "There you are. It's me, Ellen. Are you okay?"

I put my arm out to touch her shoulder gently. She jerked violently away, cried out, and threw her arms over her head like she was protecting herself from a blow. She was shaking and whimpering.

"Hey, hey, it's okay," I said, trying to calm her while fighting back my own tears. "I'm here, you're safe, I promise. Can you look up at me, Mom? Can you look at me and see that it's just me?" I was afraid to touch her again, but I couldn't stand not to, so I reached for her hand covering her head and gave it a gentle pat. "Momma," I said softly.

She jerked her head up, then looked around, trying to locate where I was. When she saw me, her whimpers turned to sobs. "Oh, Ellen, I'm so glad you're here!" she choked out. "I was so scared! Did they find Sam?!"

My blood went cold. "What do you mean, Mom? Sam is in the house, he's fine. It's you that scared us half to death!" I managed a little laugh.

"No, Sam is missing!" She was shouting now. "There's been a search party out looking for him because there were bad men after him!" She was agitated and gesturing wildly from her crouched position.

I nodded reassuringly and took her hand. "Well, he's safe now, and you are the one we couldn't find. Can you climb out of there? You look like your legs are going to fall asleep in that position. It's raining and I'd like to get you back inside. Give me your hand." I kept up a constant stream of encouragement, instructions, and cajoling as

I helped her unfold herself and get out of the car. "There you go," I soothed as she finally stood upright, wincing in pain. I didn't know how long she'd been like that, but long enough to become stiff. I put my arm around her and guided her away from the car and back to the house, struck by how thin and bony she'd become.

Dani came back in the truck just as we were walking to the back door, so she pulled into my parents' end of the driveway and rolled down her window. "All good? Is she hurt?" she shouted.

"All good!" I confirmed. "I'm just going to get her inside."

My mom finally seemed to notice the rain, which she hated being out in, and started making noises as though the raindrops were hurting her. I tightened my grip around her shoulders and hurried her inside.

Having seen what was happening from the kitchen window, my dad met us at the back door. He was ready with a bath towel to put around my mom. She started telling him the story again.

"I was so scared, Ron! Sam was lost and there was a search party out looking for him. I could see their flashlights and hear them shouting. But some of the men looking were bad men and they were trying to hurt him. I knew I should help look for him, so I got in the car, but I was scared, so I hid instead." She paused, looking at my dad and crying openly. "I didn't know what to do, and then Ellen came and found me. I was so scared!"

My dad and I were both crying too, and he wrapped his arms around her. I stood awkwardly, not knowing what to do. I rubbed her back, struck again by the vivid details of her hallucination and her apparent ability to recall it after it had happened. She'd always been able to describe what she was seeing or experiencing when a hallucination was happening, but it was rare to hear her talk about one after it was over. I wondered whether she was still stuck in it.

"It's all over now, Mom," I said gently. "You're safe, Sam is safe, and the search is over."

Dani came running in the back door then. Her eyes were wide. We all needed some reassurance. I smiled weakly at her. "She's okay," I mouthed. "Thank you."

Fresh tears welled up as I looked at my wife, feeling profoundly grateful that she was by my side for this nightmare. She squeezed my arm fiercely, looking intently into my eyes. "I got you," she mouthed back.

No one was hungry, so we decided my parents should just rest at home for the evening and we should go back to our house as well. I knew the next day would be traumatic for all of us, and I needed to regroup before then. We hugged my parents goodnight, then ran back through the rain to our warm and cozy house.

The next morning, I woke up early, unable to sleep. My stomach was churning, my emotions a jumbled mess of grief, sadness, fear, and a tiny bit of hope at the relief that might come from this move. It was a toxic brew that made me queasy. After an hour, I couldn't lie there anymore and crept out of bed, trying not to wake Dani.

"You can't sleep either?" the mound of blankets spoke. I smiled affectionately at it, leaning back over and draping myself over my wife's form.

"Nope. I'm heading down to make coffee," I said. "You in? Maybe catch the sunrise on the deck before all hell breaks loose?" I felt better already, just knowing she'd be with me.

We got up, dressed, and headed downstairs. She started a fire in the wood stove in the living room to take the chill off the morning while I went into the kitchen to make coffee. I loved this time of the day, and I loved our farmhouse. My spirits didn't exactly lift, but I definitely felt more at peace.

We made our coffee and headed outside in jackets to sit on the deck and watch the sun come up. There were about a dozen deer grazing in our largest pasture. I couldn't see the cows from the deck but knew the three of them were out there too. The horses huffed in our direction. The farm was peaceful and calm as always. I breathed deeply, trying to take it all in as though it were salve on a wound.

Eventually, we saw movement at my parents' house across the driveway. "Well," I said, feeling my stomach begin to churn again, "it's showtime." I stood up slowly, feeling like my body was fighting me, all the dread I was feeling pooling in my legs and making them heavy.

Dani looked over at their house, then back at me. She smiled lovingly and said, "It's going to be over soon, baby. You just have to get through today. We'll all sleep better tonight."

I hoped she was right but felt skeptical. I knew I'd worry about my mom even when she wasn't there anymore. But I nodded, trying to accept her encouragement as I went back into the house.

As I walked slowly over to my parents' house, I tried to figure out what to say. I needed to get her packed to go but wasn't sure exactly when or how to break the news to her. My dad must've been watching for me because he opened the kitchen door as I approached. He gave me an exaggerated smile and a warm, "Well, hello there, and how are you this lovely morning?"

I smiled back, shaking my head at his ever-present desire to make light of things. I used his own line on him as I stepped into the kitchen. "I'm just ducky. And how are you?"

He rolled his eyes and jerked his head toward the living room and bedroom where I guessed my mother was still getting dressed. In a low, more serious voice, he said, "How do you want to do this?"

I shrugged, feeling helplessness and mild irritation at being in charge of my parents. "How the hell should I know? I've never done this before. I'll wing it like I usually do. Seems to work most of the time." I paused, listening. "Is she still in your bedroom?" I asked more quietly. "I have to figure out a way to get her packed."

He nodded. "She's getting dressed. She's already thinking something is happening. When I told her David was coming for brunch today, she was immediately suspicious."

"Great," I said, then gave a long sigh filled with dread. My stomach was churning up my coffee, so I put my hand on my belly and rubbed it. "This is giving me indigestion."

"You want some Pepcid?" he said as he moved toward the counter.

I chuckled. "No, I don't take that shit," I said. "I'll be fine. But thank you." I paused again, trying to decide what to do. "Maybe I should wait until David gets here. He can distract her over at my house, and I'll sneak back over here to pack a bag. I'm worried if she's involved in packing the bag, we'll have a serious fight on our hands." I was practically whispering now.

My dad nodded just as my mom came around the corner into the kitchen. She looked surprised, then wary at the sight of me. "Well, hello. What are you doing here so early?" she said.

I looked at my watch. "It's not that early. It's already nine a.m. We've been up for hours."

"Well, what are you doing here?" She eyed us suspiciously, looking back and forth from my dad to me. "What are you two hatching up in here?"

I smiled at the expression. It was a glimpse of the mom I used to know. I swallowed the sudden lump that formed in my throat, then cleared it. "I wanted to make sure you hadn't forgotten that David and Lauren and the girls were coming over for brunch and that you weren't just sleeping away the day over here," I quipped, trying to goad her and distract her from her paranoia. It worked.

"Of course I didn't forget," she spat, immediately haughty, her nose in the air. "Don't go writing me off just yet."

I laughed too loudly, and she looked at me sharply. *Damn, of all the days to be suddenly "with it,"* I thought. I needed to get out of there before I said too much.

"Alright, well, now that I can see for myself that you're up and dressed and moving, I guess I'll go back to my house and help Dani get the food ready. Just come on over whenever you're ready. We've got coffee." I pointed at my dad with that last comment. My mother had never been a coffee drinker. He nodded appreciatively. I turned my finger and pointed to my mom. "Don't dwadle around over here," I said, intentionally mispronouncing the word as I always had, which she'd always found funny.

She just frowned at me, still suspicious, not responding to my attempt to make her laugh.

"Alrighty then," I breathed as I headed for the door. "See you soon!"

I headed back to our house, breathing deeply to calm my nerves, still not sure how we'd pull this off. I pulled my phone from my pocket and texted David: *Please get here as soon as you can. This is going to suck and I need support.*

He replied a minute later: *Leaving in a few minutes.*

David and his family got there before my parents did, even coming from an hour away. I ambushed him as soon as he walked in.

"Okay, this is the game plan," I said in a rush, looking over his shoulder out the living room window to their house. I could see them in the kitchen putting on jackets. It was warming up outside, but my mother was perpetually cold and made my dad wear a coat if she was cold. "You're going to distract her over here while I sneak over to their house and pack her a bag. If she's at all involved in that process, shit will go sideways."

He chuckled his nervous laugh, cleared his throat, and said, "Okay."

My parents walked over, and we all met out on the deck. None of us had been going out anywhere unmasked, and none of us had been to work, so we all felt relatively sure none of us was sick. But we stayed outside most of the time just to be safe. Frankly, everything else was so overwhelming and all-consuming that we felt really far removed from how COVID was devastating more densely populated areas.

My mom sat down on one of our patio chairs. She shivered, then said, "Ron, can you go get me my sweater? I should've put it on under this coat." She gave me a side-eye. "I didn't realize Ellen would make us stay outside." Her tone was disgusted. My jaw dropped. Her nasty little comments never failed to amaze and irritate me. But I also saw an opportunity.

"I can get it," I said quickly, jumping up.

"Well, you don't know the one she wants," my dad said, struggling out of his own seat. "I'll come with you." He gave me a meaningful look.

Catching on, I looked at my brother. He nodded. I turned back to my dad. "Fine," I huffed, feigning irritation. I made the mistake of glancing at my mother. She was watching me, frowning.

"What are you two up to anyway?" she asked, sounding very suspicious.

"Charlotte, will you help me bring out the silverware?" Dani said, stepping in to try to redirect her. But my mom was lucid.

"Yes, but that doesn't mean I don't know that these two rascals are up to something. Probably no good," she grumbled.

My dad and I headed over to their house. "Unbelievable," I breathed as we walked briskly. He just chuckled softly.

"I figured you might not know which bag to get or where to find them," he said softly as we approached the house. I glanced at him and saw that he was tearing up. I patted his arm.

"Thanks," I said, my voice thick with emotion. "Upstairs in the closet for the suitcases, right?" He nodded.

Once we were in the house, I raced up the stairs and moved quickly. It was stuffy up there, the air stagnant from no one being up there anymore. The smell of my parents' soap and distinct scents threatened to overwhelm me with sadness. I swallowed hard and forced myself to focus on the task. Given her lucid state, I knew if we were gone too long that my mom would get even more suspicious. I grabbed a small suitcase and ran back down the stairs.

"I just got the small one because Mandy said we'll need to bring all her things later when we go meet with her," I said to my dad. "I'm just supposed to pack enough for a couple days." He nodded, then followed me as I ran toward their bedroom.

I put the suitcase on the bed and hurriedly opened it up. I opened her drawers and pulled out a few clothes, some socks, and some underwear, enough for three days. He carefully folded her nightgown and robe, placing them gently into the suitcase. He was fighting tears and losing, and I couldn't look at him.

"I'm going to need you to pull it together, Pops," I said, forcing my voice to sound flippant. I couldn't let my emotions well up or I wouldn't be able to go through with it. Through gritted teeth I said, "I have to drive her, remember."

He cleared his throat and made an attempt to pull himself together. We finished packing the basics, including her toiletries bag and slippers, and I closed up the suitcase. "I'm going to leave it here for now," I said. "One of us can come back for it when we're ready to go." He nodded. "Ready to go back?" I asked. "You have to stop crying. She's going to know something is going on." I sounded stern, but it was as much aimed at myself as it was at him. He nodded again.

I left the suitcase in the kitchen, and as we started to leave I exclaimed, "Her sweater!" I suddenly remembered we'd forgotten to grab it. After my dad went back to the dining room and grabbed it off the back of a chair, we headed out.

The meal was relatively uneventful, except for the suspicious way my mom kept looking at all of us. She could sense something was happening but didn't know what, and she knew we weren't being honest with her. Finally, everyone was done eating and it was time to go.

"Mom, remember how I've been telling you I'm worried about Dad?" I started, bile rising in my throat as my stomach did gymnastics. I was nearly overwhelmed by my nerves all of a sudden. She frowned at me but didn't say anything. "How I've been noticing how tired and run down he is?"

She eyed me, still frowning. "Ye-es," she said slowly.

"Well, he needs to go into the hospital to have some tests run." I didn't really plan any of this, but it's what came tumbling out. "He's going to be there for a couple weeks. As you know, Dani and I are working, so we can't take care of you, so we've found a place for you to go and stay while he's getting the tests done and resting."

Her frown deepened and she looked at my dad. I thought I could see betrayal in her eyes. "But if he's having tests done, shouldn't I be with him?" she asked. "Who will talk to the doctors? You know *he* won't." She scoffed that last part, which took away the sting of emotion I was feeling. It was easier when she was bitchy.

"Well, that's part of what will keep me busy, I guess. I'll have to be there with him some of the time." I waited to see if she'd say anything about where she'd be going. Realization dawned on her face slowly, and it nearly broke my heart. The betrayal was clear now. My dad choked back a sob.

"It's just for a couple weeks," I said softly, fighting hard to stay calm and reaching over to touch her hand.

David cleared his throat and started gathering plates up, recognizing we needed to get moving before we all backed out. I took his cue and said to my mom, "I packed a few things for you already, so you don't need to worry about that. I can bring you anything else you might want."

We all got up from the table, my mother saying, "Well, someone will have to take care of my flowers, so I'll need to show whoever that will be how to do it. I don't want to come home to dead flowers."

I nodded, not expecting that but trying to roll with it. David said, "Why don't you show me, Mom? I'll be happy to do it for you." I think he was trying to give my dad a minute, as he was clearly struggling. He took her arm and walked slowly with her down the steps and across the driveway.

Dani and I cleared the table while my dad tried to pull himself together. The kids, who were all sitting at another table on the deck and watching this silently, began moving around, helping to clean things up. I heard Sam say something to the others that made them all laugh, and I was grateful for his maturity and instincts, even at age 16.

We tried not to make a huge deal out of the goodbyes and got my mom into my car as casually as possible. David sat in the back seat, my mom in the front passenger seat. I made myself look straight ahead as we pulled out of the driveway. I didn't trust myself to look at anyone else. When I made the mistake of glancing in my rearview mirror, I caught my brother struggling to fight back tears. I immediately looked away.

As we drove, my mom said, "You know, I had the strangest thing happen yesterday. I was sure that Sam was lost and there was a manhunt for him."

All the hairs on my neck stood up and I looked over at her sharply. "What?" I asked incredulously.

"You were there too, at the end," she continued. "There was a lot of yelling, and it was raining I think. There was a bad man trying to hurt Sam, and he had run away to escape from him. So there was a manhunt to try and find him because he was lost. I was scared and confused, so I hid, and then everyone was looking for me."

I glanced in the rearview mirror at my brother again. I'd called and told him about the previous day's events, and his eyes were as wide as mine. This had never happened before; she had never recounted a hallucination like this a full day after it had happened. "Oh, yeah?" I managed. I had goosebumps and was trying not to be freaked out.

She paused, thinking, then looked at me and said, "Was that a hallucination? I think I might've been hallucinating. Do you know? You were there too, right? Didn't you find me?"

I was speechless and realized I'd forgotten to breathe. I took in a big gulp of air and tried to steady my voice, keeping my eyes directly on the road. "Yep, I did," I said. "I'm astonished that you remember all that, Mom." I glanced over at her. She was looking out the window.

"Me too," she said softly.

It was a 40-minute drive to Cedarland. We'd never been there, but Mandy had given me clear instructions on where to go. She wanted me to pull through the circular drive and stop to let my mom out at the main entrance. She'd meet us there and guide my mom inside. We were to make it as casual and quick as possible.

And that's exactly how it went. Mandy was masked and standing there when we pulled up. David got out of the back seat to help my mom out and get her suitcase, which Mandy took from him. She was warm and doted on my mom, who lapped up the attention with a spoon. David gave our mom a brief side squeeze and said he'd see her soon. I just waved at her, not trusting myself to get out and say goodbye without bursting into tears. David got into the front seat with me and shut the door. My face crumbled.

"Not here," he growled. "Drive."

I sucked in air and pulled away from the curb, forcing myself to drive without looking back. I made it to the edge of the parking lot before I fell apart. He gave me a minute, then we both felt the urgency to get back to the farm and our families.

It was done.

We had an appointment to meet with Mandy at Cedarland the following day. We needed to complete some paperwork and hear her assessment of my mom. We were also to bring the rest of my mom's things to help her feel more at home. We wouldn't be allowed to see her, both because of the COVID-19 pandemic restrictions and because Mandy had said that residents had the easiest time adjusting to their new "home" if families stayed away for the first week or two. Since no one knew when visitation restrictions would be lifted, it was one more layer of stress from the unknown that we'd already been feeling.

As my dad and I drove down together from the farm, there wasn't a whole lot of conversation. But at one point my dad said, "I hope this will be a good place for her to rest and get better while I have a break."

I looked sharply over at him. "What?" Was he really thinking this was temporary? My anger flared.

He looked at me innocently. "I said, I hope this will be a good place for her to rest and get better while I have a break."

I stared ahead at the road, trying to control my emotions. I didn't trust myself to respond. I was instantly furious at his denial of reality, angry at being the only one responsible for all these decisions and the only one seeing reality for what it was, and completely alone. I felt like the only person in the world who was in this position; no one else could fully understand what I was feeling and going through. Finally, I brought myself under control enough to say quietly, "I'm not sure that's going to happen, Dad. I don't think she's going to get better."

He didn't respond, instead looking out the window. A moment later, I saw him wipe his face. I felt terrible for being the reality check, but it felt like a necessary thing for my own sanity. I could not be the only person reckoning with this terrible situation.

When we arrived at Cedarland, my brother was already there waiting in his truck. We all gathered and went into the main lobby, which was empty, and waited for Mandy to come out. No one spoke as we waited, the feelings of trepidation palpable among us. Finally she appeared, her eyes smiling. She greeted us all and then led us into a meeting room that had a small, four-person table with chairs around it and a couch up against one wall. There were doors leading to other places but no windows. I glanced at my dad. We're both claustrophobic, but he's much worse than I am. It was hard to read his expression from behind his mask, which I knew didn't make his sensitivity to enclosed spaces any easier.

After we all sat down around the table, Mandy said, "I've asked the nurse who does most of our hospice care to join us, if that's alright." She looked around at all of us but focused on me. I shrugged, not wanting to be the one who had to answer but manners prompting me to give some indication that I'd heard her.

She walked to the door at the far end of the room, punched in a code and opened it just far enough to say something to someone on the other side. A moment later, a woman dressed in black scrubs came in, bringing another chair. They both joined us at the table.

My stomach had been doing flip-flops since we'd arrived in the parking lot, and my heart rate went up as the two women looked at us. I could see the sympathy in their eyes. The air in my mask started to feel hot. I glanced at my dad. He also seemed to be struggling. Only David had a poker face that gave nothing away.

"Thank you all for coming in today," Mandy began in a clear, strong voice. I could tell she was used to communicating with elderly people. "We haven't met formally, Ron. I'm Mandy. I'm the director here at Cedarland. I had the pleasure of meeting your lovely wife, Charlotte, yesterday." She paused, waiting to see if he'd say anything. He just nodded.

"I've invited Amber to join us because I've had her talk with Ms. Charlotte and evaluate her for hospice care. We both agree that she should be placed in hospice care at this time."

I stared, my heart hammering in my chest, tears welling in my eyes. Out of the corner of my eye I could see my dad having the same reaction. My brother shifted in his seat and cleared his throat but didn't speak. After a moment, I said, "I'm not sure I understand what that means. I thought hospice was for people who had less than six months to live." My voice caught on the last few words.

Mandy and Amber both nodded empathetically. Amber said, "Not necessarily. I have a gentleman in my care who has been in hospice care for nearly three years. Care needs are determined by a few factors. Given your mother's diagnosis of Lewy body dementia, her recent weight loss, and my assessment with my doctor of her health, we feel she would benefit from the extra support that hospice care can provide."

I looked at Mandy and said with confusion, "'Recent weight loss'?"

Mandy nodded. "We weighed her yesterday when she was admitted. Her records say that she weighed 151 pounds at her last doctor's appointment in February. As of yesterday, she weighs 132."

I gasped. I knew she'd seemed bony, but I didn't realize she'd dropped nearly 20 pounds in three months. My brother and father were shifting in their seats, also struggling with the news. I looked at my dad. He was crying openly and seemed to be having a hard time breathing. I put my hand on his arm. Mandy pushed a box of tissues across to us and gently said to him, "Ron, you can take your mask down if you need to."

He yanked his mask down and gulped in air while I grabbed some tissues for him. "Breathe, Dad. It's okay," I said, trying to sound soothing but hearing my own distress. I turned back to the two women. "He's also claustrophobic, so I'm sure that's not helping right now."

They both nodded sympathetically again, watching him carefully. No one spoke for a minute. My dad started to regain his composure, so I turned back to them. "So . . ." I stopped, realizing I wasn't sure what to ask. My mind was reeling.

"There are some cost benefits to placing your mom in hospice care," Mandy offered. "Hospice treatment is covered by Medicare. All of her medications will be covered completely, as will her disposable undergarments and other medical supplies she may need. If she needs a walker or wheelchair, those will all be covered."

"She doesn't really take any medication," I said. "Since she was weaned off her Paxil and Premarin, she just takes vitamins, but I'm not even sure she's been able to take those for a while." I glanced at my dad, who shook his head. "She was taking pot gummies for a while, until they started making her worse, and CBD oil helped for a while, but I don't know that she's taking anything now, is she, Dad?"

He cleared his throat and said quietly, "Just her pill for the UTIs."

"That's right," I went on. "Dr. Wendell put her on a preventative medication to keep the UTIs from coming back. She was getting them one right after another for four months straight. He said this medication would help."

They nodded and Amber said, "Once you decide if you'd like to place her in hospice care and choose the hospice team you'd like to care for her, that doctor will evaluate her and make recommendations of what medications and treatments will keep her most comfortable at this stage. That's the goal of hospice, to keep the patient as comfortable and pain-free as possible through the end of life."

I heard my dad stifle another sob at that statement. Given our conversation on the way there, I knew this was one hell of a reality check for him. I took a deep breath to calm my nerves, nodded to Mandy and Amber, then looked at David to see whether he was going to participate in this conversation at all. He nodded.

In that moment, all the emotions I'd be warring with on the drive to Cedarland came rushing back. The isolation and heavy weight of being the one everyone seemed to be relying on to make all the decisions, ask all the questions, and take the lead was overwhelming, and I was partly numb from the trauma I, too, was experiencing in these moments.

"Well, where do we go from here?" I finally asked, trying to keep my bitterness out of my voice.

"You first need to decide if you want to place your mom in hospice care," Mandy began.

"I think that makes sense, based on what you've shared," I cut in. "Dad? David? Any disagreement?" I knew I sounded impatient, but I couldn't help it. I was suddenly eager to get this over with and get out of this small room. They both shook their heads. I looked back at Mandy who was watching me carefully.

"Alright," she said slowly. "Then the next decision is who you'd like to provide that hospice care. We have Amber's team, who are based here in the McLaren clinic building we're attached to. They're on-site, which means there's always someone here on call, and they're here in Cedarland every day. But there are many hospice organizations in the area, and you're welcome to use any one you choose. They all partner with us."

I nodded. "Well, given the COVID situation and"—I gestured around vaguely—"just the general fucked up nature of everything at this moment, I'm frankly at my limit of researching options. So I think we should just partner with Amber's team." I looked at my father and brother again. "Any thoughts? Different ideas?"

They both shook their heads again. "Dad," I said, "I'm gonna need some verbal agreement or disagreement on this. I don't want to make all these decisions alone, please." My voice broke, my anguish fully on display.

My dad looked at me with eyes full of sorrow and anguish, red-rimmed with more tears and exhaustion. A wave of shame washed over me and I dug deep for some empathy. "I'm sorry, but please don't make me decide this alone," I whispered, my own tears taking over.

He nodded, took a shaky breath, and said, "I think that's fine."

I turned to David, and he nodded at me too. Turning back to the women across the table, I said, "Well, I guess that settles it then. What do we do now?"

Amber opened a folder in front of her and pushed a few papers across the table to me. "I have a few more forms I'll need you to sign, and then we'll get her set up with us immediately."

After we took care of the paperwork, Mandy gestured to the suitcase we'd brought in with us. "Is that for your mom?"

"Yes," my dad and I answered in unison. I chuckled, releasing some of the tension.

"Alright, well, that takes care of everything for now," Mandy said. "I'll be in touch with you after hospice evaluates her."

She and Amber stood up, so we followed suit. Mandy came around the table to usher us toward the door we'd come in. I suddenly didn't want to leave, anxious to see my mom. "Wait, any idea when we'll be able to see my mom?" I asked, unable to swallow the tears that immediately surfaced again. I sounded like a small child to my own ears.

Mandy nodded sympathetically. "Unfortunately, that's out of my hands. We're under restrictions like everyone else caring for the elderly right now. But I'm hopeful we'll be able to have outdoor visits in a month or so."

I was devastated. Intellectually, I knew what was happening and how reasonable that sounded. But emotionally, I was a little girl who just wanted to be able to see her mom. In spite of our often-difficult relationship and the exhaustion we all still felt from the last few months, I was loath to leave the building where she was just a few feet away on the other side of the wall. I made myself turn toward the door, put one foot in front of the other, and numbly followed my father and brother out.

At the farm, life got a little quieter. There were no more unexpected disruptions at all hours of the day and night. My dad reported sleeping somewhat better, but he was now struggling with my mom's absence, worrying about how she was faring and whether she'd be happy to see us again once we got the chance. He was consumed by guilt at "sending her away," as he'd say. Gently reminding him of reaching his breaking point was of limited value.

I also wasn't sleeping as soundly as I imagined I would once my mom was no longer living at the farm. I remembered Maude from Sunrise telling us how she and her mom had gotten the best sleep of their lives after her dad had moved to Sunrise. I wondered why I couldn't let go of my anxiety. And then it hit me. It's because I couldn't see her. We were blocked by COVID restrictions.

Though most of the conversations are a blur to me now, I talked to Mandy several times in the 10 days that followed. Hospice formally evaluated my mom and found her to be doing relatively well in her adjustment to living at Cedarland. Mandy reported that some days she was fine and calm, and others she was asking where I was and why she couldn't see me. She didn't ask about anyone else. I was anxious to see her, but I was also fighting guilt at feeling relieved that I didn't have to see her yet. I wasn't sure what we'd encounter when we saw each other.

And then, it wasn't fine anymore.

I got a call from Mandy one day that my mom was becoming increasingly angry and agitated. She'd been refusing to eat, saying that the food was poisoned.

"And your mother appears to be quite the woman of influence, as she's now got some of the other residents convinced that the food is poisoned." Mandy tried to laugh it off, but I could tell she was concerned. "Luckily, she's still drinking water, but only if she watches us open a fresh bottle. Otherwise, she says that's poisoned too."

"Oh, no," I breathed, feeling relieved that I wasn't there along with guilt and urgency to see her. "Anything I can do? Any sign of the restrictions being lifted anytime soon for outdoor visits at least?"

"Unfortunately, no sign of that, but I am starting to think I should have you talk to her on the phone." Mandy paused. "I don't usually like to do that while a resident is still adjusting, which your mom clearly is, but I'm hoping maybe she'll listen to you."

I was nervous but willing. "Okay, I'm happy to talk to her. When?"

"How about now? I can walk out there and find her."

My stomach flip-flopped. "Sure, that's fine," I said, then got up to go find Dani. I didn't want to talk to my mom without having her nearby. I found her in the kitchen, put the phone on speaker, and whispered to her, "She's going to put my mom on the phone." Dani nodded, her eyes wide.

I heard Mandy get up from her chair, open a door, and walk into the hallway. She greeted a couple of other residents as she approached my mom. "Miss Charlotte," she sang. "I have someone on the phone that would love to talk to you."

"Who?" I heard my mother bark. She sounded angry.

"It's Ellen, your daughter."

"I know who Ellen is," she snapped. "She's the one who dumped me here." My blood went cold. She sounded angrier and more lucid than I expected. I swallowed hard.

"Well, she's on the phone and would like to speak with you if you want to talk to her." It sounded like Mandy was holding out the phone to her. "Do you want to talk with her?" She kept her voice patient and calm without being patronizing. I admired her.

There was a moment of fumbling and then, "Ellen? Is that you?" My mother's strident and angry tone filled the room.

"Hey Mom," I said, making my voice upbeat and happy while trying to sound soothing. "How are you?"

"How do you think I am?" I could imagine her face contorting in anger as she spat the words at me. "You dumped me off in this hellhole and now I'm a prisoner here! They won't let me leave or call you, I'm not allowed to go outside, and now they're trying to poison me!"

"Mom, I promise you that they're not trying to poison you. And as for not being allowed to leave, that's because you're staying there while Dad has tests done and rests. Remember?"

"Don't patronize me!" I was grateful for my decision to put the phone on speaker as she screamed. Dani's eyebrows went up. "Of course I remember! There's nothing wrong with my memory!"

I took a breath. "I'm sorry, Mom. I'm not trying to patronize you. I'm trying to help you understand why they won't let you leave."

"Well, that doesn't explain why you haven't been here to visit me!" She dropped her voice and hissed, "You dropped me off in this seedy place with these unsavory people and you don't even visit?! What kind of a daughter are you anyway?!"

My gut twisted as though she'd stabbed me with a knife. I tasted bile. She was speaking directly to my shame, guilt, and ever-present worry that I hadn't made the right decision. Dani put her arms around me and held on tight as my eyes welled up with tears. I took a deep breath and tried to calm myself.

"Mom, I'm sorry. If I was allowed to visit, you know I would. But the coronavirus is still running rampant, and no one is allowed to visit anyone in a care facility. I'm sorry you don't like Cedarland, but I know they're doing as well as they can in taking care of you. I promise you I'll visit the second they tell me I can."

She muttered something I couldn't hear. It sounded like she was far away from the phone. Mandy's voice returned. "Okay, Miss Charlotte, I'll be right back. Sharon, will you help Miss Charlotte to the bathroom please?" We heard Mandy walking back down the hallway. I took another deep breath, trying to hold off the tears.

"Bear with me, Ellen, I'm walking back to my office so we can have privacy."

We waited, heard a door close, and then Mandy said, "Okay, I'm back. How are you doing? I know that was probably rough. She wasn't very kind."

I snorted a laugh. "Yeah, that's sorta par for the course for Miss Charlotte," I said, my voice heavy with sarcasm. "She doesn't do 'kind' very often or very well. And certainly not under these circumstances."

"Well, I am concerned enough about the poison theory she has that I think you might need to come here."

I waited, looking wide-eyed at Dani. "Okay . . ." I held my breath.

"We're breaking the rules here, and possibly the law, but I'm worried about her hunger strike. I'm also worried about the effect it's having on some other residents. So, if you're able and willing, I'd like you to come here with some food. If you want to make her a favorite dish or stop and pick up her favorite takeout, whatever you want. But you need to be the only one that comes, and you need to bring her the food. I need you to get her to eat."

I was alarmed at how bad this sounded. "Of course," I said quickly. "I can stop and grab some Wendy's, which is one of her favorites. When do you want me to come?"

"You tell me when it works for your schedule."

"I mean, I can come today if you want, or tomorrow. Anytime, really."

"Let's have you come this evening. Park in the employee lot and come to the main entrance, which will be locked. Text me when you're here and I'll come out and get you."

"Okay. I'll be there around five p.m., if that works?"

"Perfect. That's when they're eating dinner anyway, so I'll keep her busy when dinner starts, and once you're here, hopefully she'll eat dinner with you."

We hung up and I looked at Dani in disbelief. "Holy shit," I breathed, overwhelmed by all of it.

Dani tried not to laugh.

"What?" I said, unable to see what was funny.

"A 'seedy place with unsavory people'?" She tried again to stifle her laugh.

I'd taken my mom's description in stride, as I was used to her colorful vocabulary. "Yeah, well, she should know, with her hoity-toity upbringing and all," I said sarcastically, smiling now too. Dani took my smile to mean it was okay to laugh about this and let loose. Soon we were both howling with laughter, and I felt myself relax.

Before I left for Cedarland, I finished putting everything in the pressure cooker for our dinner. My dad watched me, rocking slightly back and forth, a nervous tendency he has. I'd told him about the conversation my mom and I had, and he'd recognized the same humor in my mom's comments that Dani had. But I'd also seen how sad it made him that she wasn't asking for him.

"Consider yourself lucky," I said while setting the timer on the cooker. "I'll be the recipient of any nastiness she wants to dish out." I looked at him. "You're welcome." I smiled in what I hoped was a reassuring way. He smiled back but it didn't reach his eyes. "I'll take pictures and video for you," I said softly. "And we'll be able to visit her together before you know it." I don't think either of us believed that, but I felt compelled to say it.

As I drove to Cedarland, I listened to music, singing loudly in an attempt to steady my nerves. I wasn't sure what I'd find when I got there. I drove through Wendy's and ordered my mom's usual hamburger meal, along with a large chocolate Frosty, which was her favorite. Once I arrived, I parked in the staff area as instructed and texted Mandy. I waited in my car until she waved to me from the main entrance, then I hurried up to it, carrying the bag of food and the Frosty. We were both masked, but I was pretty sure she was smiling at me.

"I feel so cloak-and-dagger," I said as she ushered me through locked doors and into the same meeting room where we'd talked to her and Amber just 12 days prior. I was nervous.

Mandy chuckled. "Yeah, I could get in a lot of trouble for this, so please don't tell anyone outside of your family about it. No posting it on Facebook or anything."

"No, no, of course not," I said. I didn't want anyone seeing my mom in this state anyway.

Mandy indicated the table I should sit at and encouraged me to sit down while she went to get my mom. My stomach was in knots. A couple of minutes later, I heard my mom's voice outside the door as Mandy was unlocking it. When my mom came in and saw me, she frowned, not recognizing me at first. "Lower your mask," Mandy said. "Show her your face."

I did, and my mom's face lit up. "Ellen, you came!" She walked over to me, and I stood up to hug her.

"Of course I came, Mom." I swallowed back my tears. I was so relieved to see her, and doubly relieved that she seemed happy to see me instead of angry as I'd feared based on our conversation just a few hours before. When she hugged me, I could feel how frail she was. We sat down.

"I'll leave you to it and be back in a little while to check on you," Mandy said, motioning for me to put my mask back up, which I did.

My mom looked at me and frowned again. She looked confused. I pulled the mask back down and smiled at her. She relaxed again. The mask seemed to be a problem, but I didn't want to get myself or anyone else in trouble. Mandy was already breaking the rules for us. But I hadn't been anywhere outside the farm in weeks, so I was pretty sure I didn't have anything to pass on. I kept the mask around my chin.

"I brought you some Wendy's, Mom." I pulled the hamburger and fries out of the bag.

"Oh, good, I'm starving." She noticed the Frosty and smiled widely like a child. "And a Frosty? Is it chocolate?"

"Of course," I said with feigned indignance. "Like I would bring you anything else."

She touched my arm and smiled warmly at me. "You're so good to me. What would I do without you?"

My eyes welled up at this rare warm praise and I smiled at her affectionately. "Thanks, Mom," I said softly, meaning it. "So how are you doing?"

"Oh, I'm fine," she said, no trace of our earlier exchange in evidence. "But the food here is terrible, and I'm pretty sure it's poisoned, so I haven't been eating. When they've tried to force me, I just put it in my mouth and then spit it out into my napkin." She smiled mischievously at me, like a kid. "I don't think they know."

A laugh escaped me before I could stop it. I marveled again at the ways in which her moods could swing so completely and was amused at her belief that she was pulling one over on the staff. "Oh yeah?" I asked.

"Well, they aren't exactly the brightest bulbs in the box," she said conspiratorially, continuing to eat.

I chuckled again, embarrassed by her insults toward the staff who were trying to help and care for her but happy to see this glimpse of her real personality shining through. I heard the door being unlocked, so I quickly pulled up my mask. Mandy poked her head in.

"How's everything going in here, ladies? Are you enjoying your Wendy's, Miss Charlotte?"

My mom nodded, gave Mandy a big, exaggerated smile, and said, "Mm-hmm!" Turning back to me, she rolled her eyes and winked at me, something I don't remember my mother ever doing before. "See what I mean?" she whispered.

"We're doing great, Mandy, thank you," I said, giving her a thumbs up. Mandy nodded and backed out of the room again, closing the door behind her.

I was afraid to talk about my dad, the farm, or my family because I wasn't sure whether it would upset my mom or cause her to start asking when she was going back, so I stuck to the present. "So, what kinds of things are there to do during the day here?"

We chatted while she ate every bite of the food I'd brought. I wasn't sure how much of what she was describing was true, but it didn't matter. She was happy and calm while I was there, and she was eating, and that's all that mattered to me. I took my mask down again and snapped a few pictures of us together. She made funny faces, patting under her chin and saying she looked fat. I told her she was actually way too skinny.

After about 20 minutes, Mandy came back and saw that my mom had finished her food. "Okay, Miss Charlotte, we're starting a movie in the other room. Won't you come and join us?"

I knew it was my cue to leave. I gathered up the wrappers and empty cup, reluctant to leave. The visit had gone so much better than I thought it would, and I wanted to linger in my mom's good mood. But I knew it wouldn't help anything for me to resist.

"Ooh, that sounds like fun, Mom," I said, trying to sound encouraging.

"Why don't you come with me?" she asked, looking at me hopefully. My heart broke a little.

"Oh, I wish I could, but Dani needs me to help feed the animals, and the boys are waiting for me to get back to tuck them in, so I have to go, unfortunately. Another time?" I turned to pick up my things so she wouldn't see the tears in my eyes.

"Ellen will come back and visit again soon, Charlotte," Mandy said, ushering my mom toward the door. I knew I wasn't supposed to hug my mom, but I was bereft at the reality of it. Before I could protest, Mandy had whisked my mom through the door, saying to me over her shoulder in a stage whisper, "Be right back."

Tears overcame me and I slumped back down into a chair. A minute later, Mandy was back, so I stood up, reaching for the same box of tissues my dad had used just a couple of weeks before. That thought undid me all over again.

"Oh, I know that must have been hard, but I'm so grateful to you, Ellen," Mandy said, coming over to the table and patting my arm. "You did great. Your mom was so happy to see you, and I'm so glad she ate. I was getting really worried."

I blew my nose and tried to pull myself together. "I'm glad too. I wasn't sure what to expect, based on that phone call earlier." I shuddered, partly at the memory and partly at the emotional exhaustion I felt.

Mandy went to the door I'd come in and unlocked it. I picked up my things and followed her. "I'll call you tomorrow and let you know how she's doing," she said. "Hopefully, this will get her back on track, but if not, we may need to do this again."

"I'm happy to come every day if you need me to. And we're just quarantining at the farm, so I'm not coming into contact with anyone else, just so you know. I know I need to wear a mask with her, but she seems really disoriented by it."

"I know, I've noticed the same thing, but I'm already breaking the rules by bringing you here. I can't take a chance on exposing her and everyone else. You definitely need to wear your mask."

I thought about all the staff who came and went every day and the number of people we knew who were scoffing at masks and quarantines and believed COVID was all a political issue. I was pretty sure I was one of the lowest-risk people coming into the facility, but I wasn't going to argue with her. "Of course. I will," I said.

We said goodbye and I drove home, feeling better having seen my mom but worse not knowing when I'd see her again.

Two days later, I was back at Cedarland. My mom's hunger strike had resumed, and Mandy was concerned. This time, I packed up a large bowl of pot roast with carrots and potatoes that I'd made a couple of days earlier. It was one of my mom's favorite dishes, and I was feeling optimistic and confident based on how the first visit had gone.

When I arrived, we went through the same routine to get me in. Once I was in the room waiting for my mom, Mandy said, "She's worse today, just to warn you." I wasn't sure what that meant, but before I could ask, she left to go get my mom.

When my mother walked into the room, my mouth dropped behind my mask. She was mumbling, looking terrible, and had full dementia face. She was wearing multiple layers of clothing, including the same shirt she'd had on two days prior, a sweater over that, and another shirt over that. She was in pants I didn't recognize and that I knew she'd never be caught dead wearing. They were some sort of fleece joggers and definitely weren't hers. One of her feet was clad in only a sock, and her other foot appeared to be sockless inside her shoe. Both of those things were completely out of character for my mother. She detested walking in only socks and never wore regular shoes without them. Her hair, which she never tied or clipped back in any way, was pulled back in sort of a half-ponytail.

I was alarmed but tried to hide it for her sake. "Hey, Mom," I said softly, patting her arm as she sat down at the table. She didn't seem fully aware that I was there. "It's me, Ellen. How are you?"

She looked at me with a frown, so I pulled my mask down to show her my full face and smiled. She just looked away, not returning my smile. I pulled my mask back up, as Mandy was still standing there.

"I brought you pot roast," I said brightly, opening the container for her.

She took the spoon I handed her and took a spoonful, blowing on it.

"It's not hot, but it should still be warm enough for you to eat," I said as I watched her touch it to her lips. Clearly expecting it to be scalding hot, she took a tentative bite. I looked up at Mandy who was standing next to my mom watching, and she looked at me. She shook her head slightly.

"Okay, I'm going to leave you two to visit and eat," she said in a loud voice. "I'll be back in a few minutes to check on you." She turned and walked to the door, glancing back at me as she opened it. "Text me if you need me quickly," she said in a low voice.

I watched my mother eat, disturbed and surprised by the incredible difference in her appearance and state of mind from just two days earlier. I wasn't sure why it shocked me so much. We'd gotten used to extreme and sudden changes by then, but she'd never been dressed like this. My dad had always been there to help her if she got something wrong in that process, and clearly, no one here had done the same.

She talked to me, but I don't remember any of what she said because none of it made any sense. I took a video of her and some pictures but was worried about showing them to my dad. At one point, she stared intently up into the corner of the room over my shoulder. I whipped around to see what she was staring at, but there was nothing there. Goosebumps broke out all over my body. I was totally freaked out by her behavior.

Though she ate every bite again, she never came out of her state of mind. She didn't seem to know who I was, which was a first, but she accepted the food from me, so some part of her must have recognized me.

After a while, Mandy came back and ushered my mom out before returning to chat with me. I broke down as soon as my mom was out of the room.

"Holy shit, Mandy, she's totally out of it today. And whose pants was she wearing? Those are definitely not hers."

"I'm not sure," she chuckled. "But your mom is not someone who takes direction or bossing around, so our collective attempts at getting her clothing properly organized and changing her into her own pants were unsuccessful, as you saw. They are probably her roommate's pants. But it's fine, we'll sort it out when we do the laundry." Her eyes smiled sympathetically at me. "As for her being out of it today, this is a normal part of Lewy body. And the move has caused her to have a decline, which is totally normal."

I nodded, trying to curb my tears and focus. "Yeah, the same thing happened when we moved them up north from their Detroit house. I remember being freaked out and distraught by it. But it wasn't this kind of decline."

"She was much earlier in the progression of the disease then," Mandy reassured. "This is normal for this stage of the disease. She'll likely stabilize and maybe even recover a little bit once she's settled. This lockdown isn't helping any of us. I'm hopeful that we'll be able to open up for visits outdoors in the next few weeks."

"Here's hoping," I said.

She showed me out again and I climbed into my car, my heart much heavier after this visit. I sat for a moment, trying to calm myself down. I was drained, sad, upset, scared, and just wanted to curl up under a blanket and sleep. After a few minutes, I just wanted to be home. I started the car and drove.

Looking Back Now

Even though I felt all the feels in these moments, it's only now that I can recognize what caused their intensity. Role reversal is something we talk about and maybe have some understanding of intellectually, but to experience it and feel the weight of it was something altogether different. I was scared shitless. I didn't want to be in charge. I didn't want the responsibility of making a decision and having it turn out to be the wrong one. But I felt like I didn't have a choice I could live with. If I chose to do nothing, my father would've surely collapsed from a heart attack or something else. The tremendous weight of that responsibility threatened to overpower me.

In hindsight, I recognize that my father and brother could not fully process what was happening in the moment. They were both immobilized by trying to take it all in and sort through it. They weren't capable of responding any differently than they did. But since I'm an external processor, I need to talk, ask questions, and engage verbally. So it was natural for me to take the lead because I was the only one with half a shot at thinking on my feet in the moment. That helps me now upon reflection, but in that moment I was furious, scared, and felt completely alone.

When my mom moved into the care facility, the roller coaster of emotions did not subside as I'd hoped and half-expected they would, nor did they lessen in intensity. If anything, they grew more intense because I didn't have ready access to my mom in either the literal or figurative sense. I felt my heart break over and over during this time and occasionally wondered how much more I could handle. Looking back now, I think it might've helped if someone could've said these things to me:

➢ Feeling guilty or ashamed that you have to make decisions that are different from what your loved one wanted is totally normal. People suffering with dementia in particular lose the ability to accurately assess their own safety and well-being. Making decisions that are in your loved one's best interests must be the priority. Keep their safety and well-being at the forefront, and know that feeling terrible about going against their wishes is completely normal. You're not alone.

➢ I could try to pretty this up with softer words, but that's not my way. Lying to your loved one comes with the territory. Call it "massaging the truth," telling "little harmless lies," or something else if it helps, but it's all the same thing. We cannot afford to be completely honest with our loved ones who are suffering with dementia when it comes to keeping their best interests at heart. What matters most is keeping them calm and helping them feel safe. And that sometimes happens at the expense of our conscience.

➤ There are important differences in the types of care facilities. I am not an expert or knowledgeable enough about those differences to provide guidance. What I do know is that my mother's level of aggression and violence at one point nearly caused Mandy to have to remove her from the Adult Foster Care home that Cedarland is and send her to a skilled nursing facility. Since we were able to control my mom's aggression with medication, that move never became a reality, so I didn't bother to learn the finer points of distinction. But if we'd had to move my mom, it would have been devastating. I encourage you to do your research ahead of time. Talk to your loved one's doctors to learn what they recommend. Talk to facilities to learn about the scope of care they are able to provide and what could cause their ability/willingness to care for your loved one to change.

➤ Be prepared to advocate for your loved one. Be courageous and ask all your questions. Do some research online or through other sources, and learn about options so you know how to make sure your loved one is being best served by their care partners and doctors.

CHAPTER 14

SAYING GOODBYE

As the next two weeks went by, my anxiety level didn't go down to zero as I'd hoped and kind of expected it would. Not having my mom next door definitely brought some relief, but the phone could still ring at any time with Mandy or Amber on the other end. Though it wasn't a daily occurrence, it was often enough to keep me on edge.

In addition to continuing to be the point person Cedarland called for my mom, I was still watching over my dad. He didn't have a chronic illness or mental challenges, but he was living alone for the first time in his life. He'd moved out of his parents' house and into an apartment with my mom when they got married. My mother ran that household, paying all the bills, cooking all the meals, and staying on top of all the logistics. She'd always controlled everything. Now he was a little lost. I think he felt like he was in a holding pattern. There was a huge part of him that really did hope my mom would get better and come back to live with him again. Everything in the house remained as it had been, as if she were on an extended trip somewhere and would be back any day.

My regular calls from Mandy ranged from "Those visits from you with food really worked! Charlotte is back to eating and has stopped saying everything is poisoned" to "Well, we had a little situation today. Charlotte knocked some of our ceramic figurines off their display. She said they were talking to her and mouthing off," "Wow, your mom is a wealth of knowledge about Detroit! She has had quite the life!" and "Your mom seems to be adjusting really well. I think we've finally hit our stride with her."

Then there was this one: "We had a little setback today." Mandy sounded tired. "Charlotte was very agitated this morning and didn't want to get dressed. She was yelling at the aides and threatening them, so they left her in her room to calm down and went to attend to another resident. A few minutes later, she was out in the hallway and had grabbed some fake pussy willows out of a vase."

I gasped, my hand flying up to my mouth as Mandy went on.

"She was whipping them around at the staff and a couple of residents who were nearby, all while yelling at them. We managed to get her calmed down and took them away from her without anyone being hurt. But we need to talk about starting a medication for her that can help stabilize her moods. That's part of hospice care. She's clearly agitated, and we want to help her be as comfortable as possible."

Mandy sounded compassionate but firm. I was shocked. My mother had never in her life behaved in this way. Dr. Wendell's words came back to me: *Imagine the most outlandish things your mother could do but never would have before dementia. Now prepare yourself for those things to happen, because they very likely will.*

"Mandy, I'm so sorry about that," I said, horrified. "This is definitely in the realm of things she never would've done before. I'm glad no one was hurt."

"It's okay, it happens," she said reassuringly. "That's why she's here and not at home anymore. This is the kind of thing we know to expect with the disease. It's not your mom doing these things, it's the disease.

And like I said, it's important that we help her manage the anxiety and frustration that drives behaviors like this. I've spoken with Amber and the hospice team, and they recommend putting her on Haldol, which is an antipsychotic drug that helps with mood stabilization."

"Wait," I said and sat up straighter. "Dr. Wendell told us when she was diagnosed with LBD that she should not be prescribed an antipsychotic because she has a history of depression. He said that's what happened to Robin Williams. He had a history of depression, developed LBD, started taking an antipsychotic, and it made him suicidal." I felt panicky all of a sudden.

"That's true, but how serious was your mother's depression?" Mandy sounded patient and kind, not patronizing. "Was she ever hospitalized for it?"

"No, it wasn't that serious. She took Paxil for more than twenty years to control it. But the first neurologist we saw weaned her off of it because she didn't feel she needed it."

"Okay, that's good to know. It sounds like her depression was mild, so the antipsychotics shouldn't have the effect of suicidal ideations on her, but we'll be monitoring her very closely. We may have to play with the dosage to find the right amount for her, but I can promise you she'll be closely watched."

I hesitated. Another significant decision was in front of me. I wanted to talk to my dad, but I knew he'd just say that whatever I thought was best was fine with him. "How soon are you planning to start this?" I asked.

"We'd like to start tomorrow morning, if you authorize it. We'll start with a low dose and see how it goes."

"Okay, let me just run this past my dad first. I'm pretty sure he'll just go along with whatever the recommendation is, but I feel like I should at least talk to him about it. I'll call you back in a little bit."

I walked over to my dad's house and found him working in the garden. He was weeding around my mother's primroses, tending to them lovingly. Just watching him broke my heart. I couldn't imagine what he must be going through watching his lifelong partner go through this ugly disease.

"Hi Dad," I called as I got close.

He looked up and smiled. "Hello there."

"I just got a call from Mandy. There was another incident today." I paused, watching for his reaction.

He stood looking at me and just said, "Mm-hmm . . ." waiting for me to continue.

"Well, she got a little violent with some pussy willows today," I started, hearing the absurdity of it and smiling in spite of myself. "It seems she didn't want to get dressed, so she grabbed some pussy willows from a vase and started swinging them around at people." We were both chuckling now. "Luckily, no one got hurt. Oh, and did I mention she was in her nightie during this incident?"

"Oh no," my dad laughed, despite himself. I laughed too, but I also felt the deep pain of my mom's distress. I finally understood the expression of not knowing whether to laugh or cry. So I did both. My dad must've felt the same way because tears formed in his eyes as well. It sobered us both.

After a moment, I continued. "Mandy and Amber feel Mom needs to be put on a mood stabilizer to help control her anxiety and even out her moods. They want to put her on a low dose of an antipsychotic."

My dad's eyebrows went up at this.

"I know," I said. "I asked about that with LBD, and she said that because Mom's depression was never serious enough to hospitalize her, and because they will be watching her closely, that it shouldn't be a problem. Their goal is to keep her comfortable."

He nodded, thinking about it and swaying back and forth, arms crossed. I waited. Finally, he said, "I guess if that's what they recommend, we should do it. I don't want her to suffer any more than she already is." His voice broke, and we both teared up again. It was exhausting, this constant state of high emotion.

I nodded. "Okay, I'll let Mandy know," I said, then paused to watch him. "You doing okay?"

His eyes welled up again and he shrugged, smiling weakly. "Just ducky," he said sadly.

I went around the flower bed and gave him a hug, both of us tearing up more. Pulling away, I smiled encouragingly at him, then walked back to my house.

"Hi, Ellen, I have great news! You should be able to have outdoor visits with your mom next week. The restrictions have been changed. Each visit will be forty-five minutes, outdoors, masks required, no touching, six feet of distance. Only two people can come at a time, but at least you'll be able to see her."

"Oh my god, Mandy, that's awesome!" I shouted, then laughed in my glee. "When can we come?"

"I'm contacting all the families, so each resident will get one visit opportunity before I can sign anyone up for multiple visits. But hopefully the restrictions will allow us to do this through the nice weather, so you should get lots of opportunities to see her. Not like you would've had pre-COVID when you could've come and gone from here as you pleased, but better than nothing."

"I'll take it," I said enthusiastically. "It feels like a gift after not being able to see her at all. Well, you know what I mean." I didn't want to bring up how she'd snuck me in. "You just tell us what the schedule options are, and I'll move my work schedule around so me and my dad can come."

We arranged a time, and I ran over to my dad's house eager to share the news.

The following week, we showed up at our appointed time. My mom had been living at Cedarland for just over a month. The last time I'd seen her was three weeks prior when she'd looked so awful. My dad and I were both nervous and excited as we waited for Mandy to bring her out to us.

As my mom came to the door, she was frowning, walking carefully, and saying something to Mandy. We could see Mandy pointing at us and trying to get my mom to look at us, but when my mom did, she couldn't focus on us and kept frowning. We both pulled our masks down so she could see our faces, but that didn't seem to help. Only after opening the door and seeing us in person did her face bloom into a smile of recognition.

Mandy escorted us around the corner and down a short sidewalk along the side of the building to a patio area and gardens. There were two other families visiting their loved ones in that area as well. She parked us at a small table with patio chairs around it and we all sat down. Mandy stayed with us for a few minutes to make sure my mom was doing okay. We'd brought her another Frosty from Wendy's, which she seemed delighted to accept. Given my last visit, we weren't sure what to expect. I was hugely relieved to see that she looked pretty calm and seemed to know exactly who we both were.

My father couldn't help himself and held her hand the whole time, even though we were supposed to be keeping our distance. I took pictures of them and even a short video. While my mom was very calm and happy, she did have a brief hallucination while we were talking with her. She imagined another family sitting in the garden and took great care to stage-whisper to us that the mother had "phony red hair," as though it were a big scandal. There was no conversation of substance. We made small talk, asking her questions and telling her mundane things. We were afraid to talk too much about the farm, for fear she'd start asking when she could come home. But that never happened.

The medication definitely seemed to have calmed her mood, but it also made her a little out of it. I struggled with that. It was hard to accept that the days of having a real conversation with her were really over. I was caught between wanting her to be as calm and comfortable as possible and wanting my familiar combative mom back.

My dad was rejuvenated by visiting with my mom. I think he'd been holding his breath, terrified that she'd unleash her wrath on him for putting her into a care facility. She'd been so adamant and aggressive about extracting commitments from both of us that we'd never do it that it was hard to believe she didn't bring it up. It was a perfect reflection of the fact that we were all still experiencing some level of denial. Logically, I knew we were past that point, but we were conditioned by our lifelong relationships with her and used to her reactions to things, so it was a surprise when things didn't unfold the way they always had in the past.

I began to realize that we hadn't had the space to be in the grieving process while she'd been living at the farm. That experience had been so chaotic that there wasn't any room for reflecting on what we were losing. We were in survival mode. But once my mom wasn't at the farm every day, the grief started to set in.

A few weeks later, Mandy called me. "Ellen, your mom has taken a bit of a turn. As we discussed with you, we increased the dosage on her medication because she's been more agitated these last couple of days. Well, this morning she was really out of it and couldn't walk on her own. We got her to start using a walker."

Surprised, I said, "Oh. Well, that's good that she didn't fight you on it. I'm a little surprised though. Should you cut back on the dosage? See if it's being caused by the medication?"

"Well, remember that our goal is to keep her comfortable," Mandy started, "so we want to give it a few more days before we adjust anything else. These medications are powerful, and it's not a good idea to titrate them up or down too quickly. We need to give it time to work. But I know your dad was planning to come visit today, so I wanted to make sure you had a heads-up about how she's doing, in case you wanted to come with him. It might be a bit of a shock to see her like this. She's not as coherent as she has been lately."

I felt alarmed. Waffling between wanting my mom to be calm and wanting her to be as alert as possible, I wasn't sure what the right balance was. "Okay," I said slowly. "I'll let him know, and I'll try to come with him today. I'll have to see if I can move a couple work things around."

We hung up and I sighed, looking at my calendar. We'd been going to see my mom at least once a week, sometimes twice. My dad would go as often as Mandy would let him, which was sometimes up to three times a week. I was still trying to hang onto my business, so I wasn't able to go as often. And, if I'm being completely honest, I didn't always want to go. I had never had that kind of nurturing relationship with my mom, so it was difficult to figure out how to just sit with her sometimes. But I knew that if she was taking a turn for the worse, I needed to make the effort. My calendar didn't have a lot on it for the day, so I had no excuse to stay home.

I took another deep breath and heaved myself out of my desk chair. I needed some fresh air anyway. I headed out the door and over to my dad's house. My dad was at the sink in the kitchen when I walked in, and he smiled at me. I noticed he was moving with purpose, as he often did when he was going to visit my mom. My heart sank as I watched him for a moment, knowing that my news about her current state would bring him down.

"What time are you heading out to see Mom today?" I asked.

He looked at his watch reflexively. "Well, my visit is scheduled for three fifteen, so probably around two thirty." He looked at me hopefully. "Did you want to come with me?"

I nodded, even though I didn't want to go. "Yeah, I think maybe I should." I paused, deciding how to approach this. "Mandy called."

His shoulders slumped slightly, and he nodded as he finished rinsing off his hands, shut the water off, and reached for a towel before looking at me. "Uh-huh." He waited for me to continue.

I smiled sympathetically. "She took a bit of a turn. Mandy says she's not as coherent today as she has been. She wanted to give you the heads-up before you came today."

He nodded again and said, "Okay, well, she's not always making sense when I see her, so that's no big deal." He sounded optimistic, and I knew he was still holding onto hope that she'd turn some sort of corner and start getting better.

"She started using a walker," I added.

He stared at me, knowing the significance of that change. "Oh" was all he said.

"Yeah."

We were both quiet for a minute.

"So, I think I'll go with you today," I finally said. "See for myself how she's doing and maybe talk to Mandy if she's available."

"Okay, sounds good," he said with another nod. "Do you want to drive my car?" He still deferred driving to me even though my mom wasn't there to insist on it. I think he liked not having to drive.

"Sure, that's fine," I said softly. I didn't love driving his car but knew he was most comfortable sitting in his passenger seat. "I'll meet you out there at two thirty."

We drove the 40 minutes mostly in silence, both of us lost in our own thoughts. I was worried about what sort of state we'd find my mom in, but I was more worried about how it would affect my dad. At one point, I asked him what he was thinking about.

"Your mother. Just wondering how she'll be today," he said.

"Me too."

We drove on in silence.

When we arrived, we went in the entry door to the little vestibule area and rang the bell. I signed the sign-in sheet for both of us, and we checked our temperatures with the forehead thermometer they had there, recording our normal readings on the sheet. As I finished writing them down, one of the aides was guiding my mom down the hallway on the other side of the glass doors toward where we were standing. When I saw her, an involuntary gasp escaped me.

She was hunched over the walker so much that all we could see was the top of her head. She was shuffling along very slowly and sort of leaning toward the aide who was guiding her along. She was dressed properly and her hair was combed, so I knew she'd gotten help with that, but she didn't look up at all while walking. It was disturbing. Mandy was right—it was a significant change from how she'd been just a couple of days before.

We backed away from the door, holding the outer door open so they could get through. It was a very slow process. The aide was encouraging my mom in soothing tones, gently guiding her through the doors. My mom still didn't look up. I heard her croak something out at one point, but she was mumbling so I couldn't make out what she said. The aide responded encouragingly, so I asked her what my mom had said. She looked at me and shrugged, eyes wide, and shook her head in a way that told me she hadn't understood her either.

Once my mom and her walker were completely outside the doors, my dad moved into place next to her to continue guiding her to where we could sit down for our visit. I wasn't sure whether my mom's shocking appearance was due to the new drugs making her this way or something else, but whatever it was, it wasn't good. She croaked something again and my dad leaned in to hear her better.

"What did you say, dear?" He spoke softly in gentle tones. She croaked again, and this time I thought I heard her say "water."

I jumped up, relieved to have a task to attend to. "I'll get her some water. Just a sec." I strode purposefully toward the front of the building, eager to move at a normal pace after the slow crawl behind my mom. I rang the bell again and asked the aide for some ice water.

She indicated she'd bring it out in a minute, so I walked back around the side of the building to where my parents were. My mom was sitting on an outdoor patio couch, still hanging her head way down. But now she was rubbing her fingers on her head, like it was hurting her.

"You okay, Mom?" I spoke loudly, wanting her to be louder too. "Does your head hurt?"

She looked up in the direction of my voice, but her eyes were closed. "What?" She sounded feeble as she croaked out the word.

"I said, does your head hurt? You're rubbing it in a way that makes me think it does." I spoke loudly and slowly. "The aide is bringing you some ice water in a minute."

She mumbled something and lowered her head again. I looked at my dad, my eyes wide in alarm. "Something's not right," I said quietly.

He looked back at her, stroking her arm and shoulder, obviously concerned about her as well. "Do you have a headache?" he asked her. "Do you want me to rub your head?" He moved his hand to her head.

"No," she said feebly but clearly.

He looked at me. I wasn't sure whether she was saying no to having a headache, saying no to him touching her head, or what, but he stopped and moved his hand back to her shoulder.

The aide then came with the water, and I offered it to my mom. "Hey, Mom, I have some ice water here. Do you think you can look up and take a drink?" I moved the straw around in the cup, making some noise with it so she'd hear it.

She looked up again and her lips moved into position to suck from a straw. Her eyes were still closed. As I moved the straw to her lips, she grabbed onto it, drinking deeply but not trying to hold the cup. When she finished, she gave an exaggerated sigh of relief and flashed me a fake smile. Her eyes were closed the entire time, which was oddly disconcerting.

"Mom, can you open your eyes? Can you look at me?"

She squeezed them shut tightly for a second, peeked one open at me, then closed it again after a brief second and lowered her head back down.

"So weird," I breathed to my dad. "Why won't she open her eyes?"

My dad shrugged, continuing to rub her shoulder and arm.

We visited with her like that for the next half an hour, and then it was time to go. There was very little conversation. Mostly we just watched her, and my dad stroked her arm, her hands, and her shoulder. I told him I thought he might rub a rash onto her from repeating the same pathway over and over. I think he was soothing himself as much as her.

It took both of us lifting her to get her up off the couch. She steadied herself with the walker and just stood still for a minute. "Are you ready to head back?" my dad asked her softly, then put his hand on her back to guide her. She began shuffling along slowly, head down and eyes still closed from what I could tell. I followed behind them in slow procession.

According to the aide who came to retrieve my mother from the entry door, Mandy wasn't available, so I asked to have her call me later. We watched as my mother shuffled slowly with the aide guiding her back down the hallway. I heard my dad stifle a sob, which startled me, and I whipped my head around to look at him. He continued to stare after her, openly weeping. I moved closer to him and put my arm around his shoulder, looking back at my mom again too. She was barely recognizable in this form.

"Come on, let's go home," I said softly, pulling gently on his arm. He nodded, still watching the direction she'd gone in, no longer able to see her. The misery and sadness in his eyes overwhelmed me, and I blinked back my own tears. Eventually he turned away, reaching into his pocket for tissues, and we headed back to the car.

It was becoming increasingly evident that the COVID-19 pandemic wasn't going away anytime soon. Because we lived in a rural area where most people seemed to feel it was a political issue rather than a health issue, we were forced to step away from our relationships and involvement with Dani's family for nearly a year. There was a line drawn in the sand at a family gathering we risked attending earlier that year. We were on one side of that line, and most of her family members were on the other. They'd been a big part of our lives since we'd moved back to North Branch, and losing that support system amid everything else was a big blow.

We also noticed Sam behaving in ways that were troubling. A series of conversations and events led me to believe we needed to get him away from North Branch. It was clear to me that he was suffering. Having him stay with us felt like gambling with his safety and mental health. I made one of the hardest decisions I've ever made as a parent when I called my boys' father in suburban Chicago and told him I thought Sam might need to come live with him to finish high school. He was entering his junior year that fall, and I didn't want him to split his junior and senior years. We gave Sam the choice, and he chose to move. The emotional toll this took on me, on Robin who was still with us, on Dani, and on Sam was enormous.

To make matters worse, I came precariously close to losing my business. Dani and I had both been working full-time for my company when COVID hit. The business was thriving and growing, and we were poised to have the biggest revenue year yet. When the shutdown happened in 2020, we figured we'd wait it out, like many other people. By May, I had to lay off Dani and refund tens of thousands of dollars to clients who canceled in-person workshops. I was fortunate to have one client with multiple teams and leaders I was supporting who begged me to figure out how to support them remotely. I did, and it saved the business. By summer, I'd developed a model for delivering the same workshops they'd contracted me to do in person in a day or two into a workshop series that could be delivered over several sessions via Zoom. By fall, I was taking on new clients using this model and the business stabilized, but not enough to support both of us working in it. So Dani managed the farm and the kids and kept all of us going.

The farm was a full-working hobby farm by then. In addition to the horses, donkeys, chickens, and goats we already had, we gained a boar, three pigs, and three cows. Our flock of laying hens plus a rooster numbered somewhere around 40, and we were still raising meat chickens and turkeys. We also had a huge vegetable garden. Feeding and watering the animals twice a day every day was a big enough chore, but there were always projects to be done to improve their quality of life. Dani took care of all of that, and I helped out when I could. Spending time with the animals was so therapeutic for me that I helped with morning and evening chores as often as possible. I'd sometimes take a break and just go pet the mini donkeys, who were my favorites. But I always battled with guilt over not being out there to help more.

My dad was restless and lonely, seeming to be in a holding pattern much of the time. His health had recovered for the most part, and he was sleeping much better. Though the stress of full-time caregiving for my mom was gone, he didn't know what to do with himself. He not only felt her sudden absence deeply but had no senior group to attend, no church to frequent, and nowhere to go. He spent his time putzing around in his workshop, tending his garden, and just being with us, and he visited my mom as often as Mandy was able to give him a visitation slot.

Robin was in the background much of the time. I knew he had mixed feelings about his brother moving to Chicago. The relationship between the boys had deteriorated badly during the time when things were coming to a head with Sam. Robin was somewhat relieved that the house was much quieter without Sam there, but he also missed him terribly. Robin is deeply introverted and has always been very quiet in Sam's shadow. With Sam's departure, Robin began to come out of his shell more. We felt like we were seeing his real personality, sense of humor, and sharp insights into things for the first time.

Meanwhile, my mom was regaining some of her previous mental state and mobility as the medications were adjusted and her body acclimated to them. But the walker didn't go away. When Sam came back from Chicago to pack his things, we all had a couple of good visits with my mom before he left again. She may not have been 100 percent sure who he was, as generational distinctions seemed to be hard for her, but she knew him and that she loved him, and watching them interact did my heart good.

By the end of August, Mandy called to tell me my mom had taken another turn. "She fell out of bed while trying to get up this morning," she told me. "She just sort of collapsed on the floor, we're guessing. She'd been getting up by herself these past couple of weeks, so the aide woke her up and left her for a couple of minutes to go help another resident. When she came back in, your mom was on the floor."

I gasped, imagining the scene. "Is she okay? Did she break anything?" I asked frantically. I had visions of my grandmother falling 25 years earlier and breaking her hip, and I was also recalling Dr. Bowman's words when he'd diagnosed her with Lewy body: *Then you'll fall . . . If you were to survive the fall, which is a big if, you'd break at least one hip. You'd go into the hospital and be dead within a few weeks or months. You'd suffer acute pain during that time.* I shuddered recalling his words and silently reminded myself that she hadn't fallen down the stairs, just out of bed.

"No, nothing seems to be broken," Mandy reassured me. "But she's not talking, she's not able to stand at all, and she's unable to pick her head up." She paused.

"Oh my god," I breathed, trying to process what this meant.

"This is what I call 'falling off a Lewy body cliff,'" Mandy continued sadly. "It's a term I came up with based on what I've noticed about Lewy body patients over the years. It happens suddenly, out of the blue, and involves a dramatic decline like this. Yesterday, your mom was walking with her walker without assistance, she was feeding herself and eating, she was talking and holding her head up. Just last week, you visited and walked around the garden with her. Today, she can't do any of those things. Like she just fell off a cliff."

I was reeling trying to take it all in. "Okay, can we visit her today?" I asked. "I know we're not scheduled, unless my dad had an appointment I didn't know about. But I need to see her." My voice cracked as I teared up.

"Yes. I'm going to just have you come. You tell me what time you can get here. I won't add you to the schedule, I'll just have you come."

That caused me alarm and I sat up straighter. "Wait," I said, "do you think she's . . . you know . . . that this is the end?" I was incredulous and panicked.

"Well, there's no way to know how long she has, but this is why we have her in hospice care. I don't think she's in danger of passing today. Amber should be here to see her in a few minutes, even though she wasn't scheduled for a visit today. I'll know more after she assesses her."

My stomach lurched and I stood up quickly, wanting to get over to my dad's house. "Okay, we will definitely get there today. I'm also going to go over to see my dad right now and we will come whatever time you tell us."

"You can come whenever you're ready. Even if you left home now, you're forty minutes away, so Amber should be done before you get here. Just let me know when you're on your way so I can be watching for you. I'll have you just sit out front with her. The visiting area around back by the garden will be full."

I agreed and ran over to my dad's house while trying to calm my panic. He was in the kitchen washing his breakfast dishes. I watched his eyes fill with tears as I told him what Mandy had said.

"When will you be ready to go?" he asked me, wiping his hands on a towel and looking at me expectantly through his tears. It again broke my heart.

I shrugged, trying to think about what was on my agenda for that day. I pulled my phone out of my back pocket and opened my calendar. "I don't actually have much on my calendar today, so I could go anytime." I looked up at him. "I haven't eaten breakfast yet, so maybe give me a few minutes to grab something and then we can go?"

He nodded and I headed back to my house, fear causing me to shiver in the warm summer morning air. I detoured to the barn, looking for Dani to tell her what was going on. I found her with the goats and brought her up to speed on everything.

"Okay, love," she said. "I'll stay here and make sure the kids are doing what they're supposed to for school." Online classes were underway for Robin, as well as for Chloe, Dani's daughter, who'd come to live with us that summer. My face flushed with guilt as I realized I hadn't even thought about the kids.

"Thanks, honey. I'll keep you posted."

I ran back to the house and headed for the kitchen to grab something to eat. I looked around and realized I had no appetite. I was too nervous and scared about what we were going to find with my mom. So I grabbed a protein bar and some coffee and headed back over to my dad's, texting Mandy that we were heading out. She texted back that I should let her know once we arrived.

We drove in silence, both of us nervous. I played the radio to try to settle my nerves. It worked while I drove, but my stomach started doing flips again as we pulled into the parking lot of Cedarland. I texted Mandy, and we walked to the door, waiting to see whether she wanted us to sign in as an official visit.

A couple of minutes later, she wheeled my mom down the hallway. I inhaled sharply when I saw her. She was completely slumped over in a wheelchair, bent almost in half, and her hair was wild and frizzy. Except for the motion of the wheelchair, she didn't seem to be moving. I heard my dad stifle a sob. My panic returned. She looked terrible.

Mandy brought my mom outside and parked her wheelchair next to the bench that was by the front doors, the whole time talking cheerfully to my mom about who was here to see her for a surprise visit. I marveled at how she could do it. As we sat on the bench and talked to my mom, I rubbed my mom's hands, combed her hair with my fingers, and talked to her in a soothing voice about anything I could think of except for the obvious. My dad was less able to pretend we weren't seeing what we were seeing.

"Darling, can you look at me?" he said softly. "Can you lift up your head and look at me? I want to see your beautiful face." He kept repeating some version of that, patting her leg and her arm like he was trying to get her attention. As his urgency grew, I could see it was being fueled by his own panic.

"Dad," I spoke softly, putting my hand on his knee, "I don't think that's helping. She can't. Just talk to her." He was trying not to cry, and I knew he didn't know what to say to her. Not only because he was panicking at what he saw but because he'd always struggled to communicate with her in any way that was an acknowledgment of her dementia. It's why he'd kept on correcting her long after being told not to by the doctor, by people in our support group, and by me countless times. In his mind, to talk to her about the weather, the farm, or the latest on the pandemic was to acknowledge that she wasn't able to engage in the kind of direct communication they'd always had. So he just stroked one of her hands while I held the other, fighting his tears and staying quiet.

After about 30 minutes, it was too much for me. I became overwhelmed by an ache deep inside. I didn't know whether to scream or cry or run or throw up. But I knew I couldn't sit there any longer. One look at my dad told me he was also struggling but was less inclined to leave her. I think he would've sat there forever.

I looked at him, my tears spilling over as my face crumbled. "I can't stay here," I whispered. "It's too hard. I can't do it. If you want more time, I'll wait in the car. But I can't." My chest hitched as I fought to keep from breaking down uncontrollably.

He nodded, his own tears falling. "We can go," he said gruffly.

I stood up and rang the doorbell for someone to come out. I went back to my mom and stroked her hair again, putting my arms around her in an awkward hug, trying to breathe in the smell of her through my tears. "I love you, Momma," I whispered into her hair. "We'll come back again tomorrow." She made a small sound, the first since we'd gotten there, and I couldn't hold back my sobs.

When I looked up, one of the aides was at the door. I wiped my face and tried to get myself under control, embarrassed at my show of emotion. "Is Mandy around, or is she busy?" I asked, eager to touch base with her again on coming back the next day.

"She's with a resident right now, but I can have her call you if you like," she answered, then walked around my mom's wheelchair and got ready to take her back in. "You ready, Miss Charlotte? We're going to go back inside now."

My mom didn't move or make a sound. My dad and I stood watching her go back in, the aide carefully navigating the doors and the turns so as not to bump my mom into a doorway. We were both fighting for control of our emotions. I felt if I gave in to mine, I might lie down crying and never get back up. I made myself take a few deep breaths, trying to regain enough composure to feel safe driving. Once my mom was out of sight, we turned and headed back to the car, both of us sniffling and wiping our faces.

When we got to the car, I leaned in and grabbed a box of tissues, handing my dad a couple as I grabbed some for myself. After a couple of minutes cleaning ourselves up and regaining control, we both heaved big sighs and then chuckled. We got into the car, and I drove us home.

This roller coaster continued for the next month. My mom recovered some of her strength and consciousness. We would visit, she would smile and laugh and talk to us, sometimes making sense and sometimes not. Some days she was disheveled and in her own world, and other days she smiled at us, a remnant of the person she'd always been. She still teased us and made snarky comments, even though her physical presence was greatly diminished. There were some moments during those visits when her face would cloud over in despair. We'd ask what was wrong, and she'd just shake her head and say, "Nothing, I'm fine."

Though I talked to Mandy by phone several times a week, near the end of September I got a different kind of call from her.

"Ellen, I think we need to organize a care conference for you, your dad, and your brother," she said, then paused.

"What's a 'care conference'?" I asked, feeling leery.

"It's a conference with me and Amber to update all of you on your mom's health status, her current care, and her care plan moving forward. It's just a way to make sure we're all on the same page about her treatment and options." She paused again. I waited this time. "I think we need to do this sooner rather than later."

I stared out the window. "Okay . . . why?" I sounded suspicious, even to myself.

"Well, there are a lot of unknowns. Your mom is still losing weight. At the beginning of this month, she was down to one hundred and twenty-six pounds. We're not sure how this chronic wasting condition will affect her long-term. Also, she's had a couple of Lewy body cliff falls, as you know. And finally, I'm not sure what this fall will bring with the pandemic, but I'm worried we'll get shut down again. If that happens, we won't be able to let you in to see her at all unless she goes into the active dying stage."

I closed my eyes for a moment and took a deep breath. I was exhausted from the roller coaster and constantly battling so many emotions. "Okay." My voice sounded small and tired. "When do you want us to come in?"

"Your dad has a visit scheduled for later this week on Thursday at 3 p.m. Do you think that would be a good time to do it? Can you and your brother make it then?"

"I'm not sure, I'll have to check with him, but I'm free, so we'll try to make that happen. I can confirm with you once I talk to David."

We hung up and I called David. After bringing him up to speed on things, I asked if he could make it.

"Yeah, I'll make it work," he said. "I can always take a half-day or something if I need to. Normally, sneaking out an hour early wouldn't be a problem. But everybody and their fucking brother comes to the park now to walk and whatnot, so it's been stupid busy. But I'll figure it out. I'll be there." David oversees all of the maintenance and grounds at a large county Metropark near his house.

We were so isolated at the farm where we had 22 acres to roam plus a mile-long road through woods and fields that I'd forgotten about how the rest of the world was coping with the pandemic. "Oh yeah. I guess I never think about people needing a place to go to be in nature. We live in it." I laughed half-heartedly.

"Yeah, everybody's a walker now." He laughed too.

We said goodbye, agreeing to meet at Cedarland a few minutes before 3 p.m. on Thursday.

My dad and I rode together from the farm. We were to have the care conference and then stay for a visit with my mom. I was feeling exhausted but also nervous and scared of what we might learn. Having not been allowed to visit Cedarland with more than two people at a time, this was the first time we'd been together as a family of four since our farewell brunch with her in May.

During the conference, I didn't learn anything that was a surprise to me, given that I was in pretty much constant communication with Amber and Mandy. But I'd probably missed some of the details when relaying everything to both my dad and my brother, so it was a relief to have them caught up on everything without me having to be the one to do it. I was beginning to recognize a growing weariness in me that was making regurgitating every detail feel overwhelming.

The bottom-line message was that my mom wasn't doing well. Since moving in four months prior, she'd lost nearly 10 pounds that she could not afford to lose, and she was now permanently wheelchair bound. Without medication, she'd been aggressive, unpredictable, violent, and prone to huge mood swings. With medication, she seemed to be in a daze much of the time. I struggled with that and knew my dad did too. But knowing how much my mother had dreaded being in this state, I tried to take comfort in knowing that if her senses were dulled and she was dazed, maybe it would allow her to exist with less anxiety, fear, and depression. That seemed like the best we could hope for at that point.

My dad and I were both weepy throughout the meeting while my brother looked on stoically, giving nothing away behind his mask. There weren't any recommendations beyond what they were already doing to keep her comfortable. I was afraid to ask where things would go from here, so I didn't. I felt numb.

The meeting ended and Mandy went and got my mom. When we'd all visited her at the beginning, we'd all been nervous and worried that she'd demand to be taken home, yell at us for placing her there, and generally behave how she'd conditioned us to expect her to behave for our whole lives. Now, we weren't sure whether she'd recognize us or not, nor what weird comments she might make.

When Mandy wheeled her in, I was shocked by how my mom looked, even though I'd seen her just the week before. She wasn't wearing a bra, which would've absolutely horrified her in her lucid state, and her hair was a mess. Someone had painted her nails, which she'd always done, but they were green, a color she wouldn't have picked in a million years. It was still hard for her to hold her head upright, but it was much better than it had been just a couple of weeks before when she'd fallen off the most recent LBD cliff. She embodied the expression, "a shadow of her former self."

The hardest part was her reaction to seeing us. She frowned disapprovingly at us but without clear recognition of who we were. It was like she knew us but couldn't place from where. When she spoke, she was very quiet, and we had to strain to hear her. She clearly described a hallucination in great detail, one about a bunch of people being up on top of a pile of boxes, and she readily accepted my brother's reassurances that she was safe and no one got hurt. My dad reached over and took her hand as she talked. She didn't hold his back, but she didn't pull away either as she sometimes did, so I was happy for him.

She kept pushing her hair back from her face. She'd always worn it down, never using clips or hair ties or anything, but now it was longer than she normally kept it. And without being able to hold her head up much, it hung in her face.

"Hey, Mom," I said gently, "can I put your hair back in a clip for you? Maybe get it out of your face? It seems to be bothering you." I got up, took my hair clip out of my bag, and walked over to her.

"Yes, that would be fine," she answered. "I like it when you do my hair."

I chuckled, knowing that she did and basking in the simple, sweet exchange. I combed back her hair with my fingers as she closed her eyes and smiled in her enjoyment. I smiled too, even as tears pricked my eyes. I gathered the front of her hair up and pulled it back into my clip. "There you go," I said, patting her shoulder. She reached up and patted my hand, causing my tears to spill over. I ached with sadness.

I pulled up a nearby chair and sat down, fishing in my purse for another hair tie for myself. My brother chatted with her, as did my dad. I held my mom's hand and added comments every now and then, but mostly I listened to them. Mandy took some pictures of the four of us together, which gave me a terrible sense of foreboding.

I got eight more visits with my mom between September 22 and October 23. I think my dad snuck in a few additional ones. She remained relatively stable, and we all continued to see glimpses of her pre-dementia personality come out when we'd visit, mostly in the form of sarcastic quips, snarky remarks, disapproving facial expressions, and wild gestures.

On October 23, 2020, David and I had planned to meet for a visit with her together. We got to the facility and went through the normal routine. The weather had turned cooler, so the outside visits had all moved to the only room we'd ever been in at Cedarland. David and I sat in that room chatting, having been ushered in by one of the aides. Mandy walked in alone.

"Hey, guys, good to see you." Her tone warned of bad news and I tensed.

"Where's my mom?" I blurted out, suddenly sure something had happened to her.

"I'll bring her in in just a minute, but I wanted to talk to you two first for a second." She was trying to sound reassuring, but I was still worried. "I've just gotten the official word that I have to close the facility to any outside visitors again. There's a resurgence of COVID, as you probably know, and the state has just mandated all facilities be closed to outside visitors."

I sucked in a breath and held it, waiting to see whether she'd make us leave without seeing my mom.

"The awful truth is, guys, that I don't know how long we'll be closed to visitors, and I don't know how much longer your mom has with us. I'm worried that if I don't let you see her today, you won't get another chance if we end up being closed until the weather breaks."

Dr. Wendell's words about my mom having six to twelve months to live came rushing into my mind. That had been on December 18, 2019. If his timeline was correct, she had less than two months left. My heart rate shot up and I started breathing again, feeling panicky.

Mandy said in a low voice, "Plus, you were already here when I got the call, so I feel like I can justify waiting until this last visit ends before closing the doors." She winked at us. "I'm going to go get her now."

Mandy left us and I looked at my brother. He looked back at me and gave a little shrug. "At least we'll get to see her."

I felt tears stinging my eyes. "Yeah, maybe for the last time." My voice broke. I couldn't slow my breathing, so I pulled down my mask and gulped in some air, trying to calm down before my mother came in. True to form, David stared straight ahead, not responding.

A couple of minutes later, Mandy was back, pushing my mom in a wheelchair. My mom had had her hair washed since I'd last seen her, and it looked really nice for a change. The visit went pretty well that day. She seemed to know exactly who we both were the whole time, calling us by our names and mentioning that we were her son and daughter, even while talking about random things that didn't make any sense. We shared a couple of laughs.

There was also a dark moment that will stay with me forever. I'm pretty sure she had a moment of total lucidity, when she knew exactly what was happening even though her heavy dose of medication made it difficult to mentally wade through. She said, "I feel like I'm walking a tightrope between you. David is on one side and you're on the other, and I'm in the middle. No one wants me on either side. I'm just in the in between. And that's why I'm here."

David quickly said, "Oh, that's not true, Mom."

"Oh, I know," she responded. "I know it's not. But that's how I feel." She was sad but didn't cry, which was likely an effect of the medications. They kept her so subdued that she didn't experience strong emotion anymore. My heart sank as I watched her, knowing that she was indeed living in hell, in a purgatory from which she could not escape. It was her worst nightmare to wind up like this. An added cruelty was the way in which the cloud of dementia would occasionally lift and she'd have total awareness of what was happening. I know with certainty that she gave up in those moments.

I held her hands, rubbing lotion onto them, which she loved, while David told her stories of his girls and what they'd been doing. Mandy came in after an hour and a half, having given us double the amount of time we were supposed to have for a visit. As she opened the door, my emotion surged, and I stifled a sob that instantly rose in my throat. I heard David take a deep breath, but we didn't look at each other.

I got up and hugged my mom in her wheelchair, even though we weren't supposed to, telling her I loved her and that we'd see her again soon. I was barely able to keep from breaking down completely, but I didn't want to alarm her, so I made myself hold it together. David hugged her goodbye too, and we watched as Mandy wheeled her back out through the door. The second it closed, I doubled over, physically feeling the emotional pain of that moment, and sobbed. David put his hand on my back, and I heard him stifle a sob too. I stood up and he put his arm around me.

"Come on," he said gruffly. "Mandy will come back any second and we have to walk out of here."

I nodded, doing my best to gulp in air and calm down. I had this terrible feeling in the pit of my stomach that I would never see her again.

When I got home that day, my dad was waiting for me at my house with Dani. They were in the kitchen, my dad sitting at the counter and Dani on the other side making dinner. My dad looked me over as I came in, trying to read on my face how it had gone. They'd both seen her the day before.

"So? How did it go?" my dad asked. He looked concerned, and I assumed the concern was for my mom.

"Well, it might have been the last time we get to see her for a while," I said. I tried to keep my tone light, but the emotion caught up with me again and my tears betrayed me. "Mandy had to shut the facility to outside visitors again. She got word about it just as David and I were waiting for her to bring Mom in. She said she shouldn't let us visit with her, but since we were already there, she did." I left out the part about not being sure how much time my mom had left. "I'm so glad you guys got to go yesterday. Who knows when they'll open up again."

My dad couldn't help but be triggered by my tears, and I noticed he was trying to keep his own at bay. After a moment he said, "Well, I was just telling Dani, I have other news." He sounded serious.

"What's wrong?" I was instantly alarmed.

"Your aunt Monica has COVID." His voice broke on the last word. My aunt Monica was his oldest sister, and she lived in her own apartment at a senior living facility. "It's in her building, and some of those people won't wear masks, so now she's got it along with some other residents."

"Oh no," I breathed, knowing this could be bad. She was diabetic and also had asthma, like me. I was terrified of the virus for that reason. I already knew what it felt like to be gasping for air.

"Your aunt Dolores says she's going to call an ambulance to take her to the hospital if Monica doesn't start improving. She's apparently really sick. I called and talked to her, and she sounds terrible." I now knew that the concern I'd picked up on earlier was for his sister.

Aunt Monica didn't get better. She got worse, and Aunt Dolores did in fact call an ambulance to go get her and take her to the hospital. She was admitted, and after a couple of days, placed on a ventilator. A couple of weeks later, just before the doctors told Dolores it was time to take it out, Monica passed away in the middle of the night.

My dad got the call the next morning and walked over to tell us the news. I don't think he wanted to be alone. As soon as he told us, I looked at my watch to see what the date was and realized it was November 8. My mom's birthday. I quickly looked up at him.

"She died earlier this morning? Today?"

He nodded. "Yes. On your mother's birthday. It was the first thing I thought of too."

"We're supposed to try and FaceTime with her later today," I said, then paused. "We should not tell her this news."

He was already shaking his head. "No, definitely not. She probably wouldn't remember anyway."

"Regardless of that, I don't want to upset her, especially not today."

We reached out to Mandy later that day, when Robin was with us too, letting her know that we were ready to FaceTime with my mom. Mandy had an iPad she could call us on so that my mom would be able to see us better. We gathered around my phone, sang her "Happy Birthday," and were rewarded with big smiles. Though it wasn't even 7 p.m. yet, she was in her pajamas already. She talked with us but didn't seem to know quite who we were. The sounds of our voices seemed to reach her and make her happy, though, and I snapped several screenshots of her face. We knew that it was hard for her to focus on screens by then, so it was a short call.

I'm so glad I got those screenshots. It was the last time we saw her smile.

On Saturday, December 5, 2020, at around 7:30 p.m., while lounging on the couch watching TV, we got the call from Mandy we knew was coming. I looked at Dani as I answered the phone on speaker, knowing she wouldn't call this late or on a weekend unless something had happened.

"Ellen, I know it's dinnertime, but you need to come to Cedarland." Tears came from nowhere and my heart rate shot up. Dani sat up and looked at me with concern. "Your mom has entered what we believe to be the active dying stage, and I'm afraid to wait until tomorrow to have you come see her. Can you get here this evening?"

I was already on my feet and heading to the door to grab my coat and get my dad, with Dani close behind. "Of course. I'll let David know. Can we all see her?" I choked out. I put my coat on with one hand while holding my phone in the other, shoved my feet into boots, and we ran out the door toward my dad's house.

"Yes. You'll have to take turns, but yes, you can all see her tonight. When should I expect you?"

"I'm running to my dad's house now," I sobbed. "We'll leave as soon as I tell him." We hung up as I burst into my dad's kitchen. As soon as he saw my face, he knew, and his own crumpled.

"Dad, we have to go. Mom has entered the active dying phase and Mandy doesn't know how long she has. We have to go now to make sure we can see her before she's gone." I was sobbing uncontrollably as I choked out the words. "I have to call David."

Dani took my phone from me and said she would call him. She walked back into the kitchen, dialing as she went, as I helped my dad get up off his couch. It took him a minute, and I focused on breathing, trying to calm myself enough to drive the 40 minutes to Cedarland. I could hear Dani talking in the kitchen.

We managed to get ourselves together and out the door in record time. Dani drove us, even though she knew she wouldn't be allowed to go in. Only my dad, my brother, and I would be allowed in, and only after a rapid COVID test showed negative. No one talked much as we drove.

David was already there when we arrived, and Lauren was with him in his truck, even though she knew she wouldn't be able to come in either. I felt a surge of love and appreciation for both of our partners supporting us through this hell. We all said hello, our moods subdued. It felt strange to be at Cedarland after dark. I texted Mandy to tell her we were there.

Once our rapid COVID tests showed we were all clear, we met Mandy. She motioned us toward the door and said, "Two of you can come in at a time, so Ron, if you want to come in with either David or Ellen, we'll start there. After thirty minutes, David and Ellen can switch places, so you'll get to stay with her the whole hour, Ron."

David and I looked at each other, and he motioned me in, indicating that I'd go in first with our dad. I was relieved, as I was anxious to see our mom, but I was instantly filled with trepidation as Mandy opened the inner door and we followed her in.

We'd never set foot in the main areas of Cedarland. The lights were dim, as it was nearly 8:30 p.m., and the residents were settled in for the evening. I could faintly hear a TV at the end of the hall and see the backsides of chairs with people in them who were likely watching a movie.

My mom's room was the second door on the right. There was a big sunflower decoration hanging on her door, which my mom would've liked. As we got to her room, I heard our dad saying, "What?" and realized Mandy was talking to us quietly.

She stopped just short of the door and turned to face us. "She's unconscious. We're giving her morphine to keep her calm and pain-free. Her comfort is our only concern now." I felt numb. "Are you ready?" Mandy was watching us both closely. We both nodded.

She led us into the room. My mom was lying in bed, half on her side, tucked in under a blanket, looking like she was sleeping. One hand was curled up by her face, like she was resting her chin on it. Standing at the end of the bed, I heard my dad choke on a sob as we looked at her. Mandy took a chair and sat it next to the bed near my mom's head, then grabbed another one and sat it next to the first one.

"You can sit down and talk to her. She won't likely respond, but many people think they can still hear us when they're unconscious in this state." She indicated for my dad to sit, and he went to the chair closest to my mom.

As soon as he sat down, he took hold of her hand with both of his. "Hi, sweetie pie," he said softly. "I'm here, and so is Ellen."

That broke me. I sat down in the other chair, tears flowing. "Hi, Momma," I said through my tears.

We sat like that for a while, just watching her. She seemed to be dreaming, her face reflecting different expressions but mostly frowning, her eyes staying closed the whole time. She made a couple of soft sounds. As I watched her, she didn't look peaceful, and I wondered whether she was in pain. When Mandy came in to make sure we were okay, I asked her about it.

She looked at my mom for a moment, then said before walking away, "I'll call Amber and see what she thinks. She just ran upstairs to their offices for a minute. She'll be back down soon."

My dad was stroking my mom's hands and I heard him humming softly. I couldn't make out what tune he was humming, but I knew it was something he did when he was soothing others and himself. The whole scene was intensely heartbreaking. I just sat, letting my tears flow.

I felt panicked, angry, sad, and devastated all at the same time. I didn't know what to do with the anxious energy bubbling up in me. I wanted more time. I wanted to be able to go back and resolve some of the shit that existed between me and my mom. I wanted to make sure she knew how much I loved her even though she'd driven me batshit crazy half the time. I wanted to hear her tell me that I wasn't a disappointment to her. I wanted to hear her reassure me that she loved me one more time. All those emotions washed over me in waves as I sat in my anguish.

Amber came in a few minutes later and checked my mom. She had an IV in one arm that I hadn't noticed before, and Amber gave her a shot through the port. She told us it was morphine and that she was administering it because she agreed that my mom's facial expressions indicated some discomfort. I nodded and thanked her, and she left the room again.

Mandy came back a little while later and told me it was time to switch places with David. I nodded and stood up, motioning to my dad to move over so I could say goodbye. I leaned down and kissed my mom's forehead, breathing in her scent and touching my forehead to hers. "I love you, Momma," I whispered as some of my tears fell on her. She wrinkled her eyebrows in reaction to them and I chuckled. "Sorry about that," I said softly as I gently wiped them off. "But it's your fault." I paused, hoping she would suddenly open her eyes and look at me, but she remained the same. "Okay, well, I guess I'll go get your son now. I love you, Mom."

I walked out of the room, looking back to see my dad take her hand again and resume his humming. I turned away, my tears starting again.

Out in the cold night air, I pulled my mask off, grateful to be able to breathe again. Dani and David were standing next to the open window of his truck, talking with Lauren. They all looked at me as I came out. Dani's look melted me. I ran into her arms, sobbing. I was so glad she was there. I pulled away for a moment and said to David, "Your turn. It's rough. Brace yourself." He nodded seriously and headed for the door where Mandy was waiting.

The night air, along with some water, helped me calm down, and Dani, Lauren, and I chatted as we waited for David and my dad to come back out. Dani and Lauren carried the conversation, keeping me focused on anything other than what was happening inside the building next to us. I realized I could see my mom's window from the parking lot, but the blinds were drawn. I turned my back on it, determined to regain some self-control.

After a while, my father and brother emerged from the building, both ripping off their masks. My dad reached into his pocket and pulled out tissues, blowing his nose as he walked. David reached us first and said in a low voice, "Well, that was terrible." I knew he was trying to cope with the awful scene the best way he knew how.

We chatted all together for a few minutes, and David told me that Mandy said she would call me in the morning with an update, sooner if anything happened. I nodded, feeling once again the heavy burden of being the go-to person. We said goodnight and parted ways.

As Dani drove us home, I sent my mom's only brother, Raymond, a text. I wasn't up for a phone call, and he lived in Colorado, two hours behind us, so I knew he'd be up: *Mom has entered the active dying phase. We don't know how long she has. Just wanted to let you know.*

I got a text back a few minutes later: *Well, that's to be expected. Sending our love to everyone there.*

I stared at my phone, then said, "What the hell?"

Dani glanced over at me, concerned. "What's wrong?"

"I just texted Raymond and here's what he said." I read out the exchange to Dani and my dad. From the back seat, my dad scoffed but didn't say anything. I stared at my phone again in disbelief, trying to imagine reacting that way if one of my nieces reached out to tell me similar news about my brother. I shook my head and turned off the screen.

My dad called Dolores to tell her about my mom. His phone was on speaker, as usual, so we could hear the conversation.

"Oh, Ron, I'm so, so sorry," she said softly. "I'll light a candle and pray for her, just as I have been. How are you holding up? How're Ellen and David?"

My dad chuckled his nervous laugh and said, "Ellen is fine. She's a little irritated right now because Charlotte's brother wasn't very compassionate when she told him. But she's alright. David seems okay. Or at least as okay as any of us can be."

I shook my head again, then put Raymond's response out of my mind and thought about my mom. I hoped she wasn't suffering, but also, selfishly, that she would hold on for at least one more day so that we could see her again. I wasn't ready to say goodbye.

The next day, we went again in the late morning. Dani and Lauren stayed at home. I'd adjusted somewhat to the shock of seeing my mom in her current state, and now I just wanted to say my piece to her. I was glad she was holding on and felt eager to get there and see her.

As I drove my dad's car, a thought occurred to me. "Dad, I think we should play some music for her. They say that people who are in comas or unconscious can still hear, and I think she'd enjoy hearing some Matt Watroba. What do you think?" I glanced over at him.

"Mm-hmm," he murmured, turning away from me to look out the window. I wondered whether he was crying. Though I felt less sad this time, more like I was on a mission, I realized as I looked at my dad that this was very different for him. This was his wife he was watching die.

After a moment, I said quietly, "I hope she's not suffering. I don't want her to suffer. And I know she wouldn't want to suffer." I glanced over at him again. He was staring straight ahead now, face firmly set. He nodded but said nothing. "I wonder if we need to give her permission. Like, tell her it's okay to let go."

He stifled a sob and looked out the passenger window again. I left it alone and we rode the rest of the way in silence.

When we got to Cedarland, we went through the same routine of screening and waiting to make sure the results were clear. My brother indicated I should go in first again with my dad. Maybe he sensed that I was on a mission.

Mandy ushered us in, and I looked around now that the lights were all on. It looked like a nice facility, much to my relief. Placing her there blindly had been very stressful, and I was relieved to see for myself that it was at least a nice place.

My mom was in the same condition as the day before, but she was in fresh pajamas so I knew they'd been attending to her. That also gave me comfort. I took my phone out and queued up Matt Watroba, her favorite folk singer, to play softly. We settled into the chairs, my dad taking her hand and humming along with the music.

I looked her over, noting that her face was slacker and less troubled. I wondered whether that meant the end was near. As I looked around her room, I noticed a pile of cards and photos stacked on one shelf. I got up and went over to them, picked them up, and sifted through. I was surprised and delighted to see how many friends and family had sent cards, including a ton of people from the old neighborhood in Detroit. They had sent cards and photos of them with her at various community functions over the years.

"Wow, you've had a lot of people thinking about you, Mom," I said brightly. "I had no idea. That's so nice! I hope someone read you these cards when they came." I sifted through the pile, reading out names of friends as I scanned their cards. I was really moved. There were even a couple of cards from Karen. I was glad to see that her cards were full of love and support for my mom and she could reserve her resentment for me. That was fine.

I found on a shelf the mechanical cat Dani and I had brought my mom over the summer. Being that my mom always loved cats and had at least one at any given time throughout her life, we'd found a mechanical one online. My mom loved it. I think at least some of the time she thought it was a real cat and it delighted her. I put it on the bed next to her now, hoping it might bring her some comfort but knowing it was more for my benefit than for hers at this point.

Amber came by again to check on my mom. When she finished, she said, "She's comfortable. We've increased the morphine a bit because she was restless during the night, but she's comfortable now." Her eyes crinkled in a way that indicated she was smiling behind her mask.

"Is there any way to just, you know, increase the morphine a little more?" I spoke in a low voice, looking at her pointedly, hoping she understood what I was asking.

She nodded and I knew she understood. "We'll do everything we can. I promise." Her tone matched mine, and she squeezed my arm before walking out of the room.

When I knew there were only about five minutes left before I'd have to swap places with David, I asked my dad if I could talk to her for a minute. He got up and switched seats with me. Though I wished I could be alone with her, I couldn't bring myself to ask my dad to leave, so I leaned in as close as I could. I held her hand and stroked her familiar bony fingers, the same ones I'd touched a million times throughout my life. They felt cool and I gently closed my fingers around hers, bringing them warmth.

"Momma," I started, and immediately began to cry. "I'm so sorry for all the things I ever did that hurt you. I know I gave you a hard time, and I disappointed you many times. I'm so sorry for all of it. I'm so sorry for all the ways in which I wasn't enough. For all the times I yelled at you and was ungrateful." I was sobbing now, but I kept going. "I wish so much that we had more time. I wish I could just talk to you one more time without dementia so we could work some of this out. I don't want you to die disappointed in me."

I stopped to try to catch my breath, and my dad put his hand on my back. It only made me cry harder, and I laid my forehead on the bar at the side of her bed. The coolness calmed me a little. "I love you, Mom. I hope you know that in spite of everything else, I love you. And it's okay to let go. You can rest now. We'll be okay. I'll keep an eye on Dad for you. But you don't have to keep fighting. It's okay to go." I was choking on my tears and felt like I was on the verge of hyperventilating, so I pulled away so I could breathe. I raised her hand to my lips and kissed it. "I love you."

When I looked up, Mandy was in the doorway, her eyes conveying deep empathy. She closed them briefly and nodded at me silently, as if to say, *You did good*. I stood up, knowing I needed to let David come in. My dad stood up to let me pass, then sat back down next to my mom. I left my phone for the music, saying he could just bring it back out with him, and walked with Mandy to the door.

It took David a minute to get out of his truck. He'd needed knee replacement surgery and was moving slowly. Mandy waited while he ambled up the sidewalk. I raised my hand as we passed each other and said, "Tag team." He lightly touched my hand as he passed me.

I sat in my dad's car until their time was up and they came back out, my dad carrying my phone. Mandy waved to me as she went back inside. I felt much calmer than I had the night before. I was relieved to get what I wanted to say to my mom off my chest.

My dad got in and we drove in silence for a while. Then he said, "You know, you were always your mother's favorite child. She loved you both, but you were the apple of her eye." My tears started back up again, but I said nothing. He cleared his throat and continued. "You did not disappoint her. She loved you and was so proud of you." We were both sobbing now.

"Stop, you're going to make me go off the road," I laughed through my tears, desperate to stop crying. After a minute, I said softly, "Thank you." We didn't talk again during the rest of the drive.

The following day was Monday, and my dad and I went again to Cedarland. We both felt like we were just sitting at a vigil with my mom the whole time. On the way home, I said to my dad, "I told her yesterday that it was okay for her to let go." I felt tears prickle my eyes when I said it. I was so exhausted from crying and took a deep breath to steady myself. "I wonder if she needs to hear it from you." I glanced over at him.

"I told her, too." He looked miserable.

The next morning, I woke up feeling better. We planned to go see my mom again in the early afternoon. Midmorning, as I was trying to concentrate on some work, Mandy called. My heart was in my mouth as I answered the phone.

"Ellen, your mom is still hanging on, but I have bad news. We had a staff member and a resident test positive for COVID this morning. It means I can't let you into the facility at all today."

My stomach dropped. "Oh no . . . but, what if . . . you know . . ." I couldn't get the words out.

"I'm so very sorry, Ellen, but even then, I can't let you in today. We'd lose our license. Let's hope your mom will hang on for one more day. I'm hopeful we can follow protocols to get this handled today, and you'll be able to come back tomorrow. I'll keep you posted, don't worry."

The combination of intense and uncomfortable emotions came rushing back, making me restless and anxious. I couldn't sit still. I got up from my desk and walked briskly over to my dad's house. He must've seen me coming because, as soon as I walked in the door, he walked into the kitchen, searching my face before I spoke. I could see the trepidation on his face, concerned I had news that my mom had passed.

I told him what Mandy had said and watched his shoulders slump. "I know," I said sadly. "Maybe she'll hang on for another day so we can see her one more time."

The next morning, Wednesday, December 9, 2020, Mandy called to say we were clear to come that afternoon. My mom was declining further, and she said it was just a matter of time. While I'd felt a little better having said my piece to my mom, I hated the waiting game. I just wanted it to be over now, for everyone's sake, but most of all my mom's.

We drove to Cedarland, and David once again was already there when we arrived. We went through our COVID tests, and as he started to head back to his truck, I said, "Hey, why don't you go in first today? I always go in first. Plus, Sam called me as we were pulling in and I wasn't able to talk to him, so I'll just call him back real quick while you guys go in." He shrugged and turned back to go in with my dad.

I walked back to my dad's car and chatted with Sam for about 10 minutes. "Hey, my phone is going to die," I said. "We're in Papa's car and he doesn't have a charger in here, so I'm going to let you go and drive to the gas station real quick so I can grab a charger before it's my turn to go in." We said our goodbyes and I started the car.

I was just starting to back up when Mandy came out the door, waving me down. I looked at the clock. It had only been 15 minutes. My heart dropped into my stomach, and I felt a wave of nausea as she walked toward the car. I pulled back into the spot, turned off the car, and got out. She shook her head and held out her arms.

"NOOOOO!" I screamed, then fell into her. She hugged me hard, holding on tight as I sobbed and continued to moan "Nooooo" over and over again. When I slowed down a tiny bit, she pulled back, took me by the arm, and guided me in. I could see that her eyes were wet.

"She waited for him," she said simply. "She waited for him. And now she's gone." I crumpled into tears again as she led me to the door.

She took me into the room where David and my dad were both crying, my dad still holding onto my mom's hand. David reached for me. I hugged him, unable to control my sobbing. I looked at my mom and could see that she was gone. I wanted to crawl out of my skin. "I thought I was ready," I sobbed. "I thought I was ready! But I'm not." I was hyperventilating again and felt like I was going to lose my mind. "I can't stay in here."

I walked over to my mom's bed, kissed her forehead, and said, "I love you, Mom. Rest in peace." Then I turned to my father and brother and said through sobs, my chest heaving, "I can't stay in here. I'm gonna lose it. I'll be outside."

On my way out the door, I met Amber, whose eyes were also wet. She opened her arms to me and I hugged her hard, sobbing more. I pulled away, feeling that antsy panicky feeling that I knew meant I needed to get out into the air before I threw up. Mandy could see that I was having a panic attack and guided me out into the air.

"Are you okay? Do you need some water?" she asked.

I shook my head, ripping off my mask and gulping in air. I pressed my hands and forehead against the cold brick of the building, willing myself to calm down. "I just couldn't stay in there. I couldn't."

"It's okay, I totally understand," she soothed. "But I want to make sure you're not going to pass out or anything before I go back inside, so I'm just going to stay with you for a moment, if that's alright."

I nodded, pacing around, breathing in through my nose and out through my mouth, slowly starting to calm down. "I'm alright," I said, still pacing.

A few minutes later, my brother and father emerged. "What happens now?" I asked Mandy.

"We'll take care of things here. You'll need to let us know which funeral home you'd like to use, and they will take care of all the arrangements for you. Do you know which funeral home you're planning to use?"

We'd discussed it a few days back when she'd entered the active dying phase, so I had an answer. "Yes. Lynch and Sons in Lapeer."

"Okay, great. We're familiar with them. I'll call them and they'll take care of transporting your mother's body and following her wishes. You'll need to call them tomorrow morning if you haven't heard from them by then."

I nodded numbly, exhausted from my panic attack. Taking one more deep breath as we walked back to our vehicles, I turned to face my dad and brother and saw they were both crying. I hadn't seen my brother cry very many times. I walked over and hugged him for a long time, and we cried together. We stood around awkwardly for a few minutes, trying to pull ourselves together and not wanting to leave each other's company.

"Can you guys come over, maybe this weekend? Or sooner even? I feel like we should all be together." I wished Sam could come home but wasn't sure he'd be able to quite yet. He was planning to come the week of Christmas after classes were done, but he was in live virtual school every day.

"Yeah, probably this weekend," David said, sniffling. "I'll have the girls."

"She waited for me," my dad said quietly through his tears. My mouth went dry. "We walked in the room, sat down, I took her hand and said 'Hello, sweetie pie,' she took a breath, and then she was gone." We were all crying again now.

"She absolutely did," I choked. "She absolutely waited for you." I turned to my brother. "I don't think I could've handled watching it. I'm glad you went in first today. I'm sorry for you having watched it, but I really think I would've lost it even worse than I did. I feel like she knew that and chose her moment."

We all stood there crying for a moment, then slowly began to pull ourselves back together. There was nothing left to do now except go home. And suddenly I very much wanted to be there.

Looking Back Now

It might just be my personality that drove my on-edge reactions to waiting for Mandy and Amber's calls, and I felt and still feel shame around not wanting to go visit my mom every time. But I've heard so many caregivers and family members talk about the immense relief that came from placing their loved one in a facility that I thought you should know that relief is not universal. No one who is caregiving has only that responsibility. We play multiple roles in our lives, and there's shit happening outside of caregiving that makes it that much more stressful to navigate.

Though I was desperate to see my mom and be with her, she was beyond being able to reliably have any conversation of substance by then. I was also the glue trying to hold everything together while often feeling like I was coming unglued myself. Much of the time, I felt like I didn't know what the hell I was doing. I was responsible for the decisions relating to my kids, my dad, and my mom. It seemed like everyone looked to me for guidance, for my opinion, and to lead the family. As much as I was doing all those things, most days it was not with confidence or with grace. I cried during those months more than I've ever cried in my life, except for while writing this book. I struggled to sleep through the night, and I felt like a hot mess most of the time. Dani was my rock. She held me up, sometimes literally. I'm pretty sure I would've cracked under all the pressure without her.

I worried constantly about everything. Had I made the right decision in giving Sam the choice to move? Had I been a neglectful mother to Robin up until then? Had we done enough to try to help Chloe? Had I done enough to try to keep my mom at home? Was I going to visit her often enough? Was I going to be able to make enough money in the business to continue to support our family? Was I supporting Dani enough instead of just taking from her all the time? Was I supporting my dad enough? Was I helping with the farm enough?

You can see the theme. I constantly worried that I wasn't enough. In any way. That I wasn't doing *anything* right. It was grueling. And every time I turned on that Zoom camera, I had to be encouraging and engaging to the leaders and teams I was supporting. I had to be calm, patient, and understanding, and I had to listen carefully, though often I was screaming on the inside.

I needed to continue keeping up on my mom's care, status, and well-being during this time too. In some ways, I felt disconnected from *her* at this point. While she was still having moments of lucidity when we'd see glimpses of her old personality, snarky comments, and other emotions come through, most of the time she didn't make sense. Sometimes she didn't speak at all. I carried so much mixed emotion around my relationship with her too:

- Relief that she wasn't in our full-time care anymore
- Sadness as I watched her decline
- Horror that she was living her absolute worst nightmare
- Helplessness that I hadn't been able to do anything to change it
- Shame because I didn't visit more and didn't want to
- Heartbreak that I hadn't been enough in her eyes for so many years in so many ways
- Anger because we had so much unresolved shit that could now never be resolved between us
- Impatience that there was nothing I could do, no tasks I could accomplish that would make a difference
- Embarrassment for all these feelings

Even though I knew things could not continue as they had been, I still second-guessed my decisions every day. Now, years later, I know they were the right decisions, but it still breaks my heart. She never said, but my theory is that in those moments when my mother would shake her head and say everything was fine, she was fully lucid. She knew what was happening to her, and it destroyed her. In those moments, she lost the will to keep going.

My point in sharing all this context is to recognize that no one is a caregiver in a vacuum. I was not only a daughter caregiver but also a daughter to my father, a spouse, a mother, a sister, a business owner, a farm owner, a friend, a neighbor, and an in-law. All those relationships were deeply affected by my role as a caregiver, and that didn't change when my mom moved into a facility. Coupled with the isolation and stress that everyone was living through during 2020, I'm not sure how I got out of bed some of those days. But I did.

Looking back now, I think it might've helped make things just a tiny bit easier if I'd been able to hear someone say these things to me then:

> ➢ Out of sight does not mean out of mind, nor that your caregiving ends. I assumed I'd feel a lot less weight from caregiving when my mom moved to the facility. I was wrong. In some ways, it was even more stressful because I didn't have constant access to her. Our situation was made more difficult by the pandemic, but even when we were able to visit more regularly, I still worried endlessly.
> ➢ Research medications your doctor prescribes. Get second opinions. Remain an advocate for your loved one.
> ➢ Take photos together if you can. We didn't take any pictures with my mom that day in October, just of her. I have regret about that. I caught my brother on camera in the two short videos I took, but there are no pictures of me with her that day.
> ➢ It's okay to feel however you feel during this journey. There's no "right" way to experience this. The emotions are hard enough to live with. Try not to make it even harder by judging and shaming yourself for experiencing them.
> ➢ You will never feel like you had enough time, no matter what.

CHAPTER 15

"YOUR MOM WOULD HAVE LOVED IT"

The first thing I did before we even got into the car to drive back home was text Dani the news. She asked if I was okay to drive and how my dad was doing, and I told her I just wanted to come home to her. Then I texted Sam and Robin, telling them the news. They both replied with sympathy and virtual hugs.

My dad and I got into his car, me in the driver's seat, and the first thing he said was, "Well, I guess I should call your aunt Dolores." I knew he had relied heavily on his sister through the last couple of years, but it wasn't until he said that that I realized how much. Of all the people he wanted to notify first of my mom's death, he chose his sister. Not my mother's own brother, nor his brothers who'd both lost their wives in the recent past.

I was easing out of the parking lot when she answered. "Hello?" Her voice was loud over the car speaker.

There was a pause, and my dad didn't answer, so I looked over at him as I turned onto the road. His face was crumpled in tears.

"Hi, Aunt Dolores," my own voice breaking. "It's us." I looked at my dad again and he looked away out the window. I knew he wouldn't be able to talk. "Mom's gone." I said simply. My heart was broken for my dad, but there was also a tiny bit of resentment that he was expecting me to speak for him. Again.

"Oh, I'm so sorry to hear that," came my aunt's voice, full of sorrow and compassion. She paused. "Are you driving?" I could hear that she was crying but also alarmed.

"Yes, we're heading home," I answered. "We just left Cedarland."

"You shouldn't be driving. You should pull over. You need to give yourself some time. It's not safe for you to be driving right now." She sounded worried. Though I knew she had the best of intentions, that didn't stop me from feeling a small spark of annoyance ignite in my belly.

"Well, we've cried a lot of tears already, and frankly I'd like to be with my wife right now, so I'm driving. My dad is not in any condition to drive, that's true, but I feel okay." I tried to keep the irritation out of my tone. I have never liked being told what to do.

"I understand, but you should still pull over and wait a while before you drive," she said urgently. She had a lot of fear around driving herself, and it was so clear to me that she was projecting that onto me, which only fueled my resentment and resolve to keep driving. I didn't say anything but kept looking over at my dad. He seemed to be pulling himself together and was reaching for a tissue to blow his nose. I was ready for him to take over this conversation since he'd been the one insisting on calling her right then.

My dad cleared his throat. "She's doing fine. It's me that's struggling." His voice broke again, but I didn't jump back in. I didn't trust myself to say anything else.

My aunt took an audible breath and moved on from chastising me for driving. "Charlotte is at peace now, Ron. Her suffering has ended and she's . . . where she's supposed to be now. Take comfort in that."

She paused. I took note that she stopped short of saying that my mom was with Jesus or in heaven or any of that, which was rare for her. "Have you made arrangements for her with a funeral home?"

My dad cleared his throat again, trying to compose himself. "Yes, with . . ." he paused, not remembering the name and looking to me for help. I felt another spark of irritation and took a breath to try to calm myself, but I kept my eyes on the road and didn't say anything. "It's a funeral home in Lapeer," he continued. "I can't remember the name of it right now." I could feel his eyes on me. "Ellen, what's it called again?" He finally asked, so I felt obligated to answer.

"Lynch and Sons."

"Lynch and Sons in Lapeer," he confirmed to Dolores.

"Oh, so you've already made arrangements?" She sounded surprised.

"Yes," my dad answered. I looked at him, knowing he was confusing giving Mandy permission to call them to transport the body with making actual arrangements for her cremation and remains.

"No," I said, glancing at him. "We just gave Mandy permission to contact them. No arrangements have been made beyond moving her body. I will call them tomorrow for that."

"I'd like to come up and be there, if that's alright," Dolores said with a little hesitation in her voice.

I looked over at my dad and raised my eyebrows, indicating he should answer. "Sure, that would be fine," he said, looking over at me for confirmation. I just shrugged and looked at the road.

They agreed on a time and said goodbye, my aunt offering final words of comfort about my mom being in a better place now where she wasn't suffering. My dad didn't ask any questions when he hung up, and I didn't offer any of my own thoughts.

We drove in silence for a while before I told my dad we should probably let Raymond and Pauline know. I wasn't eager to call Raymond, given the text he'd sent when I'd told him my mom was actively dying, but I still felt obligated to communicate the news. Since his phone was connected to the car, my dad dialed the number. I took a deep breath to brace myself as the phone rang.

Raymond had asked me to stop calling him "Uncle" back in November 2019 when they'd come out for my mom's last birthday party. He'd said that as an adult in my 40s I didn't need to use that title anymore. I'm not really sure why he felt the need to say that, but it had felt very weird to both me and Dani. I think his intention might've been to remove what he felt was a layer of formality, but it instead ended up feeling like he was trying to distance or informalize our relationship.

When he answered, I said, "Hi, Unc—I mean Raymond. This is Ellen. And my dad too." I paused. "We're calling to let you know that my mom passed away this afternoon." My now-guarded feelings toward him protected me from breaking down again.

"Oh, I'm so sorry to hear that," came his reply. His tone was sympathetic. "Even though we knew it was coming, there's nothing that quite prepares you for when it does." I almost laughed at the platitude.

"She's being transported to the funeral home," I continued, "and tomorrow I'll call to make the arrangements. She wanted to be cremated, so we'll just hold her ashes for now. No one is in the frame of mind currently to figure out anything else, so we'll just have to keep you posted." I kept it brief, not wanting to stay on the phone with him.

"Oh, that's fine," he soothed. "Just let us know what you decide when the time is right. We'll let the kids know"—meaning my cousins and their wives—"and I know they would want me to include them when I say we're all thinking of you and sending you our love from Colorado."

I managed to say, "Thank you. We'll talk soon."

We were on our road to the farm by the time I ended the call, so we drove the last couple of minutes in silence. I felt my emotions amping up as we got closer. Dani came out of the house when we pulled into the driveway and met us at the car, which I parked by our house. I didn't think my dad would want to be alone in the carriage house just yet. She hugged him first, both of them crying as they embraced. When it was my turn, I collapsed into her arms, sobbing as the reality of what had just happened hit me again.

After a few minutes, we were all sniffling and messy, so we went into the house in search of tissues and some water to calm down. It was nearing dinner time, and the smell of food hit me as we walked in. Dani had been cooking. I didn't think I was hungry, but my stomach growled at the smells.

Robin came downstairs when he heard us come in and immediately went to my dad and hugged him. My dad started crying all over again, embracing his favorite grandchild. There's something about receiving comfort from your favorite people that really makes you fall to pieces.

Suddenly, I felt like I should call the funeral home. I thought about them transporting my mom, and the raw emotion of losing her started to take over and make me panicky again. "I think I should call today," I said simply. My dad immediately understood.

A kind male voice answered. "Lynch and Sons of Lapeer, how may I help?" He had a practiced, soothing tone that somehow didn't sound at all patronizing.

A lump rose suddenly in my throat and my voice caught as I tried to speak. I cleared my throat, trying to push away the tears, and said, "I think you might have my mom there. Her name is Charlotte Patnaude?" It came out as a question. "Or maybe she's on her way?"

"Just one moment please, let me see . . ." I heard papers moving in the background.

"She just passed away at Cedarland about an hour ago, so maybe she's not there yet?" I felt like I needed to provide more information and spoke in a rush.

"Yes, yes, I have the information in front of me now," he soothed. "We have a team en route now."

The lump in my throat was back. "Okay," I said in a small voice. "I've never done this before, so I don't know what to do next." I couldn't hold back the tears now. "I just felt like I needed to call because I couldn't imagine her lying there without anyone claiming her or making sure you know she has a family." I was choking on my own tears. I felt Dani's arms wrap around me, which did not help my composure but made me feel her strength.

"I completely understand," came the soothing voice again. "It's alright. I'm glad you called." He paused for a beat. "Would you like to come in tomorrow to discuss the arrangements?"

I took a breath to steady myself. "Yes, that would be great. What time?"

"How's 10 a.m.?"

I was grateful for the suggestion. I felt lost. I was sure he knew people in my state couldn't readily make more decisions than necessary. "That sounds fine," I said. "Thank you so much."

"We'll take good care of your mother." The reassurance was unexpected and sent me back into tears.

"Thank you," I whispered again.

I texted David the time for the appointment the next day and was aware of my dad calling Dolores to convey the information as well. We moved through the next couple of hours in a fog. There was something very cathartic about feeding and taking care of the animals, so we all went out together and did chores. Just being around the animals, especially the horses and my beloved mini donkeys, had a noticeable calming effect.

During dinner a bit later, Dani tried to carry the conversation and keep things light, but it didn't really work. We ended up talking about our plans for the next day, which was Chloe's birthday. COVID-19 was surging again, and the vaccines were in their earliest stages of being available, so we were trying to be mindful of how and where we were moving around. We were sure Chloe wouldn't be coming to our house for the weekend, but we wanted to make sure she knew we were thinking about her. We'd gotten her a gift, so we decided we should wrap it and write out her birthday card. I felt numb the whole time, which I'd always heard people talk about but hadn't really understood. Now I did. I felt like I was on autopilot, acting with no intention, just going through the motions.

We headed up to bed and I took a long, hot shower. When I was done, I got myself ready for bed and collapsed into it. I laid there for a moment feeling listless, then suddenly tears overtook me. I cried harder than I ever had, sobs racking my body, snot leaking all over my pillow. My lungs were working hard to keep up with me, and I soon started to feel like I'd hyperventilate if I didn't get myself under control. But I couldn't.

And then Dani's arms were around me, half lifting me up to cradle the upper half of my body in her lap. She rocked me, murmuring soothing things to me as she smoothed my hair and held me tight. I felt like I might not ever be able to stop crying. But after a while, it slowed down. My breathing got back under control, my chest hitching occasionally in the aftermath. We curled up together, holding each other tightly, and I fell asleep. I slept more soundly that night than I had in many, many months.

The next morning, Dani and I got up to the alarm at 5 a.m. like we always did. Even though I'd slept so deeply, I was still exhausted. I got out of bed, surprised at how stiff and sore I felt. Dani and I didn't talk much, but I could see her watching me closely to make sure I was okay to be left on my own. She'd gone back to work just a few weeks earlier and was hesitant to miss more days than necessary. We'd agreed she should go to work, but I could see her second-guessing that decision. She knew I'd have to be the strong one for my dad. I felt the weight of that responsibility pushing my shoulders down, prompting an ache at the back of my neck that started creeping down my spine.

When Dani left for work, heading down the road into the darkness of the early morning in her truck, I bundled up in a warm coat and hat and headed to the back door with my coffee in hand. The air was cold and still, quiet except for the sounds of the predawn hours. I could make out the horses moving in the pasture, their shapes gray in the dim moonlight. I breathed in the cold air deeply, feeling it contract my asthmatic lungs but still enjoying the clean, fresh feeling of it.

I closed my eyes and tried to feel my mom. I felt nothing. After a few minutes, I began to feel self-conscious, silly for trying to sense her presence when I didn't believe in that anyway, and dumb for standing out in the freezing cold when I knew it would trigger my asthma. I headed inside and added wood to the fire in our stove, which Dani had laid and lit before going to work. I usually did it myself, but it was a way she could take care of me, which is her love language, so I'd gratefully accepted her offer to do it.

I wasn't sure what to do with myself. We wouldn't be leaving for the funeral home for a few more hours, and I needed to keep myself busy somehow. I wandered into my office and got lost working on the computer for a while as sunshine slowly came up through my side windows and revealed a beautiful sunrise.

Eventually it was time to make sure Robin was up and starting on his online schoolwork and for me to get myself ready to go. I texted my dad to make sure he was up and doing alright. A moment after I sent the text, my dad called.

"Good morning," I said, my voice sounding tired and subdued even to myself. "How are you?"

"Good morning. I'm just ducky," came the sarcastic reply. "How are you?"

"I'm doing alright. I slept better than I have in a very long time. But I'm still tired." I chuckled. "What about you? How did you sleep?"

"Not too bad. Not too good, but not too bad." It was one of his favorite replies, delivered in a funny, mildly accented voice, mimicking one of his old Polish coworkers from whom the expression had come.

I figured if he was able to make an attempt at being funny and normal, he must be doing okay. I let out a breath I didn't realize I'd been holding. "That's good," I said, then paused for a beat. "You want to take your car or mine today?"

"Oh, it doesn't matter to me, as long as you're driving."

I frowned. "Why? Are you not feeling good?"

"Well, let's just say my feelings are . . . unpredictable right now." I could hear his voice tremble a little and knew exactly what he meant.

"Got it. No problem. I'm happy to drive. Let's take my car for a change. I'll pick you up in about half an hour, okay?"

He agreed and we said goodbye. I wondered whether I was being rude in not offering to make him breakfast, but frankly I wasn't hungry myself and didn't feel like taking care of him right then. Carrying guilt about that, I went upstairs to make sure Robin was up. He was, and he already had his laptop open on his lap and appeared to be engrossed in school. But I saw a guilty look flash across his face before he composed a more innocent one for me. I knew he was looking at something other than school, but I simply lacked the energy that day to even ask about it.

"I'm heading into Lapeer with Papa to go handle Grandma's funeral arrangements," I started. "Then I'm dropping a gift off for Chloe. Today is her birthday if you want to text her. I'll be back in a few hours." I looked at him, trying to muster more energy than I felt. I now knew the real meaning of feeling "listless," another term I'd often heard but hadn't emotionally connected to.

He smiled that innocent smile at me and said, "Okay, Mom. Do you need a hug?"

Tears instantly pricked at my tired eyes. I nodded, not trusting myself to speak. He set his laptop aside and then came over to me, putting his arms around me as he did. I noticed we were the same height at this point. As he hugged me, I closed my eyes, tears spilling down my cheeks even though I wasn't sure how there were any left in me at this point.

"Thank you," I whispered over his shoulder. He hugged me a little harder in response. I took a deep breath and pulled away. "I've gotta go. You'll be fine on your own, doing what you need to do?"

He nodded solemnly. I wanted to believe him but was a little skeptical. I know my child. I raised an eyebrow at him, and he contorted his face to try to mimic me. He pushed one eyebrow up with his finger when it didn't work, which made me smile, then I went to get the car.

I pulled up next to my dad's house and he came out, clearly having been watching for me. We smiled weakly at each other once he got in, but we didn't say much during the drive. After a while, I cleared my throat and said, "Okay, I think we should just make sure we're on the same page before we go in there. About Mom's wishes and what we want to do." I glanced over at him. He was staring out the front window.

He nodded and said softly, "Mm-hmm." He seemed a little dazed.

"You okay?" I asked, mildly concerned.

He nodded again but didn't say anything. I noticed tears in his eyes and thought, *Well* that *was a dumb question.*

"She wanted to be cremated, so we're still doing that," I continued. It was more a statement than a question, as I didn't want to give him the impression that there was an option to disagree.

He nodded, still not saying anything.

"I don't think we should try to organize any sort of memorial service now, with COVID and everything. I think we should wait till warmer weather when we can plant a tree or something. What do you think?" I glanced over at him again.

"Mm-hmm," came the same reply.

I felt a tingle of irritation at his lack of engagement, but I also felt deeply sad for him and knew he was feeling lost. No one, including both of my parents, had ever expected my mom would die before my dad. Longevity on her side of the family and multiple health challenges he'd had over the years made that seem impossible. Thinking about it, I suddenly realized she'd passed away just one month after her 78th birthday. Her father had died at 84 and her mother at 96. It felt like she'd died quite young by comparison.

I also felt resentful of once again being in the driver's seat (literally at that moment as well as figuratively) for all the decisions related to my mom. I hoped David would come ready to give more input.

Aunt Dolores had wanted to come up to support my dad and be there to support all of us as we spoke to the funeral director. I was grateful for the extra support, but I also worried I might have to argue with her about my mom's wishes. I was prepared to do that but wasn't looking forward to mustering the energy. I took a deep breath to steady my nerves as we all converged in the parking lot.

With masks on, we walked into the empty funeral home. There weren't any funerals being publicly held yet, making the place seem even sadder and more depressing. I felt an involuntary chill go down my spine and immediately thought about my mother's saying that getting the chills meant a goose was walking across your grave. Imagining my mom as a goose stomping around on my final resting place, I suppressed a slightly hysterical laugh that bubbled up in my throat.

The funeral director was just as soothing in person as his voice had been over the phone. He ushered us to a conference area to sit down and go over things together. He gently asked questions, was very respectful in his tone and manner, and was quick to reassure me when there was something I wasn't sure about.

"Will you be writing an obituary for us to put in the paper and on our website?" he asked.

I blinked, not having thought about that for some reason. I looked at my brother, father, and aunt, all of whom were looking back at me. David nodded. I turned back to the director and said, "I guess so?"

"You're the best writer," David said quietly. "But I'll help you if you want." I gave him a watery smile of gratitude and nodded.

"And would you like to include a picture of your mother?"

Another unexpected question. I wasn't sure why these questions were catching me off guard since they were a normal and logical thing associated with learning of anyone's death. But for some reason, they hadn't occurred to me as things I'd need to take care of. My mother had been in her midsixties by the time her own mother had passed. At 47, I simply thought I'd be a lot older and in a different phase of life before I had to do all of this.

I looked around the table again. "I think we should, but which photo . . . I'm not sure." I raised my eyebrows in a questioning look at the others.

My dad cleared his throat and pulled out his wallet. Fingers shaking, he carefully extracted a photo from deep in one of the compartments, then laid it on the table gently. It was a photo of my mom I recognized, but I wasn't sure exactly when it had been taken. She was young and it was in black and white. I looked up at my dad, whose eyes were wet. He looked unable to speak and was gently pushing the photo toward the director.

"When is that photo from, Dad?" I asked softly, my voice breaking for the thousandth time that day.

He cleared his throat. "It was a picture they took when she started teaching." That would've been in about 1965 when she was twenty-three years old. "I've always loved that picture of her," he said gruffly.

"And that's how she now looks, for eternity," Aunt Dolores said quietly to my dad. "You can remember her like that because she's in heaven now, and that's what she looks like forever."

I sobered, my sadness quickly turning to dull anger at this very religious view of things that did not reflect my mother and her beliefs or values at all. She'd always been adamant that she not be identified as Christian.

"I think that's a good picture to use," I said quickly, turning my attention to the director and wanting to wrap things up. "I'll work on the obituary and have something over to you in the next day or two. What's my deadline?"

The director was watching all of us, and his careful expression told me he hadn't missed anything, but he was keeping his face as impassive and neutral as possible. He nodded at me and said, "Tomorrow would be perfect. Then we can get it out to the paper and up onto the website on Saturday. Will there be a service?"

I jumped in again quickly, before Aunt Dolores could suggest a Catholic funeral mass. "No, not right now. I was thinking maybe we would wait until next spring or summer when the weather is nicer, and hopefully we can gather more safely with friends and family to have a memorial service for her." I looked at my brother, hopeful he'd back me up. He nodded firmly in agreement. I went on, saying emphatically, "But she was not Catholic or religious and did not want any sort of Christian anything, so let's move forward with the cremation. We'll plan something for next year. I'll include that in the obituary, that a future date will be planned."

To my relief, neither Aunt Dolores nor my father protested or made any comment, and we soon brought the meeting to a close. Outside, I ripped my mask off, gulping in the cold, clean air. We all ambled back to our cars.

"I need to head over to see Chloe and give her a birthday present," I said. "Today is her birthday and we won't see her this weekend."

Aunt Dolores turned to my dad and asked, "Would you like to ride with me back up to the farm?"

He looked at me and I nodded, wanting to be alone for a bit anyway. I thought the solitude of the drive would do me some good.

David cleared his throat. "Well, I'm going to head back home. If you want to talk about the obituary before you send it in, just let me know." He directed the last comment to me, and I nodded my agreement.

"Do you think you and the girls could come up this weekend?" I asked him. "I just feel like we should all be together."

He agreed and said he'd be in touch with specifics once he talked to Lauren about what else they had planned. I felt a flash of annoyance that there could be anything more important than gathering with his family to mourn his mother who had just died, but I bit back any comments. I'm sure my face said enough.

We parted ways, and I drove to Chloe's house just a few minutes away. We awkwardly spent a few minutes together. She wanted to be excited about her birthday and the fact that I was there bringing her a gift, but she was also uncomfortably aware that my mom had just died the day before. I felt bad for her. I didn't want to bring her down on her birthday, so I just smiled and tried to keep things light.

On the drive home, I queued up an old favorite Indigo Girls album on my phone and cranked up the volume, cathartically singing my heart out and crying when the words struck me.

The death certificate took six weeks to arrive. The backlog that COVID deaths had created, even in our rural area, was overwhelming the few employees who processed the certificates. When it arrived, a fresh flood of tears and grief hit me. I opened it up and looked it over, my face crumpling as I read the dates of birth and death attached to my mother's name. When I got to the cause of death, I froze.

Dementia was listed as the first cause of death, which I expected. But listed as the "immediate" cause of death was anxiety. So . . . my mother had literally worried herself to death? I stared at the paper for a long time, my heart breaking all over again.

Within a week of receiving the death certificate, my father received a letter from the company that held my parents' former time-share. Back in 2016, one of the ways I'd come to realize my mom was becoming confused about things was that she confessed to being in over their heads with a large time-share company. My brother and I had been warning and telling them for years that these "owners' weekends" that were regularly offered were just ploys to get more money out of them. My mother had been adamant that this wasn't the case, that the kind, young salespeople were genuinely nice to them and interested in doing what was best for them. My parents were wined and dined and always ended up coming back with some sort of upgrade. My brother and I would scold them and shake our heads knowing it was their money to waste how they pleased.

By 2016, my mother had been robbing Peter to pay Paul, as she was fond of saying. She told me she needed to talk with me about how to get out of the time-share and asked me not to get mad at her. I recognized in that moment that she was scared and asking for help, so I kept my normal impatient response under control. Working with three attorneys over a period of three years, we pursued every avenue we could think of to get them released. I had a lot of work to do on my side as my mother's memory and coherence levels fluctuated dramatically. The back and forth had gone on and on, but we finally got a letter releasing them from their obligation in 2019.

So when the new letter came just a few days after the death certificate arrived, I felt like shackles had been slapped back on—on my dad's wrists for the financial obligation and on mine for having to be in the driver's seat, yet again, to take care of it. I wailed in frustration when he brought the letter over, screaming out my anguish.

Creditors come out of the woodwork when someone passes away. Having had no direct involvement in handling anyone's estate, this was something I'd never experienced. I kept copies of my mother's death certificate handy, both in print and digitally, so I could send one out to any bank or company that needed it. But the death certificate had not been dated when the clerk had signed it, so the time-share company rejected it as invalid.

I reached out to the county clerk's office to request it be fixed, and though it took a few more weeks to arrive, it did get corrected. The dates of her birth and death are correct, but the date my mother's death certificate was signed is April 5, 2021, even though my mom passed away on December 9, 2020. (I imagine there are many, many families with similar experiences during that first year or so of COVID.) What struck me was the compassion I received not only from the staff at the county clerk's office but from the customer service agents I spoke with at a number of companies I called to remove my mom from their accounts. Maybe people working in "bereavement services," as they're often called, receive different training, and I found myself tearing up unexpectedly at their kindness. With only one or two exceptions, they were very thoughtful and helpful.

Within a few weeks, everything regarding my mom's estate was handled, so my brother and I figured out a date that would work for holding a memorial gathering for my mom. It was to be held at the county park where David managed the grounds. There's a spot there my mother always loved where a gazebo overlooks a lake. It's a beautiful place with an extensive garden outside the gazebo. David got permission to plant a tree there in memory of our mom and would be able to tend to it himself every day. It was the perfect spot, and she would have loved it. We decided we would gather to plant the tree when the frost broke in the spring and hold the memorial gathering for her in July of 2021.

In the meantime, my dad didn't want to stay at the farm. He didn't like the very conservative politics in the area, and Dani and I had begun to feel like we didn't want to be there anymore either. But with our full farm, uprooting for us was much more complicated. With my help, my dad ended up finding a senior living apartment in Lapeer and moved there in February of 2021. When Dani and I were ready to sell the farm, we decided to sell the carriage house and parcel as well because we wanted to give a buyer first dibs on buying both. My dad's move to Lapeer was something of a relief, as we felt like we were slowly reclaiming some space for ourselves. Everything seemed like it was settling.

On April 28, 2021, we gathered to plant the tree. The funeral home had divided my mom's ashes into three containers for us, one for my dad, one for me, and one for David. We all brought our containers with us, and David bought a beautiful flowering peach tree. It was the day before what would've been my parents' 54th wedding anniversary.

As we sat in the pavilion eating pizza before we got down to business, my dad's phone rang. He answered and put it on speaker as he always did.

"Hi, Ron, this is Missy." Missy was the closest person my parents' dear friend and neighbor Bonnie had to a daughter. Bonnie had developed Alzheimer's about five years before my mom started showing signs of memory loss, and she'd been living in a care facility for the past several years. "Ron, I wanted to let you know that Bonnie passed away this morning. She died peacefully."

We collectively gasped in sadness. By Alzheimer's standards, Bonnie's struggle with the disease had been relatively short. She was just a few months older than my mom, a fact my mother had affectionately teased her about for years by referring to her as a "much older friend." She, too, passed away at the age of 78.

After the call ended, we sat quietly, reflecting on yet another loss of the matriarchs in our circle. The coincidence of Bonnie passing on the same day we were planting the tree to memorialize my mom was not lost on any of us. We joked quietly that they'd be together "up there," bickering fondly like they always had and telling each other how we were doing it wrong as we planted the tree. Tears mixed with our laughter as we reflected on the two strong women who'd been such a central part of my and David's upbringing.

When it came time to get on with planting the tree, the sadness threatened to consume us. David and I were to carry the tree to the hole he'd dug earlier that day. It was heavy, and we gripped the pot on either side. As David and I struggled with this massive pot and I fought off tears, music suddenly started playing behind us. David and I whipped our heads around and saw my beautiful wife holding her phone up like she was at a concert. The song playing was "My Heart Will Go On" by Celine Dion, but not the version performed by her. It was the Shittyflute version in which someone plays hilariously obnoxious versions of well-known songs on a recorder very, VERY badly on purpose.[5]

With Dani's face serious, concentrating on this horrible song like it was the real version, David and I lost it. We both started laughing through our tears and dropped the tree, stumbling on the path and nearly toppling the whole thing over. After a few attempts, the obnoxious song playing the whole time, we finally made it down to the hole.

My dad, David, and I took out our containers of my mom's ashes and sprinkled a little bit into the hole. Then we placed the tree in the hole and David grabbed the shovel. We all took turns putting some dirt into the hole, just like we were at a funeral where they have family members place some dirt on the lowered coffin. My dad was a wreck, and we all took turns comforting each other. David's two daughters were there, but Robin was the only one of our three kids who was with us, and he kept a close eye on me, folding me into his embrace whenever he sensed I needed it. It was such a sweet gesture, and I found myself gladly accepting his hugs.

We took some pictures all together, holding hands in a semicircle around the tree and taking advantage of a willing passerby to snap the photos. After we'd stood around for a while, we decided the best way we could celebrate and honor my mom was to go get ice cream. She loved ice cream, and there's a dairy farm that makes their own just a few miles from the park. We piled into cars and headed up there. It was a great way to end the emotional day.

On July 18, 2021, we returned to the park to hold a memorial gathering for my mom. We'd sent out invitations to everyone we could think of who might want to come, and I was overwhelmed by the turnout of over one hundred people over the course of the afternoon. People came from the old neighborhood in Detroit, as did some members of Dani's family, my dad's family, my mom's brother and his family, our friends, members of Seniors, people from our support group, and other friends from over the years. I'd created photo boards with pictures of my mom with friends and family, from her childhood on up to the last gathering we'd had at the farm pre-COVID to celebrate her 77th birthday. Small groups of people took turns looking at all the pictures, exclaiming in delight as they spotted themselves or other people they knew with my mom.

We didn't plan a program or speeches, just a gathering to eat, visit her memorial tree, and be in community with one another. Several people asked me if I was going to speak. I said no firmly each time. I was very emotional and really didn't want to sob my way through some sort of speech. My brother had anticipated the possibility that someone would want to say a few words, and he figured we at least needed to thank everyone for coming, so he'd had his crew set up the sound system in the pavilion. He absolutely hates speaking in front of people, so he tried to get me to do it, but I refused. To my surprise and to his credit, he took the microphone and asked for everyone's attention.

"Thank you all so much for coming out today," he began. I could hear the effort in his voice to remain calm and unemotional. "It is truly impressive to see how many people came to join us here. Mom would have loved it." His voice broke a little and he cleared his throat. "Is there anyone who would like to share a memory of her?"

One by one, people stood, took the microphone, and shared memories of my mom. People from every walk of her life shared, from the next-door neighbors they'd had in Detroit for 40 years to other friends from the old neighborhood and extended family members. As people shared, there were a few tears, but mostly there was laughter. Once everyone who wanted to speak had, my brother took the microphone back. He raised his eyebrows, looking at me standing next to him and extending it out. I shook my head yet again. One longtime friend of my parents standing nearby said quietly, "Oh, Ellen, you have to. You know your mother would have wanted you to."

I looked at her tearfully and shook my head. She smiled encouragingly. I took a deep breath and reached out my hand, took the mic from my brother, and smiled at the room. "I didn't want to do this today," I started, not able to hold back my tears, "because I knew this would happen." I laughed, and many others did too. There were supportive words from several directions, so I took another deep breath, trying to collect myself.

"My mom and I had a pretty difficult relationship," I continued. "Any of you who knew us together knew that. And even those who never met her but have supported me and my family on this terrible journey know that too." A few more chuckles spread around the room. "I honestly did not plan to speak today, so I don't have a favorite specific story to share with you. What I want to share are the big pieces my mother has left me with."

I paused, the tears coming again. I tried to regain my composure, but it didn't work. I stomped my foot in frustration and said, "I did not want to cry!" Encouraging chuckles and sympathetic noises came from around the room. I took one more deep breath before going on.

"My mom and I loved each other fiercely, and we were also each other's biggest critics. She had the unique ability to make me feel like I was failing at everything while also speaking incredibly highly of me to those around her in the next breath. Our relationship was a living, breathing contradiction. When her memory and mind started to be affected by dementia, I lost my sparring partner. I tried to learn new ways to communicate with her, but I know I failed. All the time. It was nearly impossible to break those well-worn pathways of how we communicated with one another." I was openly sobbing now.

"I guess what I want you to know is that in spite of all the battling we did, we loved each other so much. And I miss her and her damned feistiness every day." Another shaky breath came through choked sobs, then a laugh. "She won in the end. She would've been heartbroken if I hadn't spoken, so I spoke." I looked up at the ceiling and waved my hand up. "You're welcome, Mom! You got your final wish!" Sympathetic laughs and some sniffles traveled around the room.

"Thank you all so much for coming today. In all seriousness, I know she's beaming at all of us, wherever she is. She loved all of you and would be so incredibly happy that you all came to see us today. So thank you."

Thunderous applause erupted as I stood sobbing, and my brother came and took the microphone, hugging me.

Everything after that is a blur. There were loads more hugs, kind words, my cousin handing me a flask to take a drink, more hugs, and cleanup. After everything was done and the cars were loaded, I sank into the passenger seat of Dani's truck and finally took a genuine deep breath. She looked over at me and smiled. "You did great, babes. Your mom would have loved it." And the tears flowed again.

Looking Back Now

During my mom's final weeks and days, I could not think about what would happen once she was gone. Call it one more final example of denial. I know some people who are able to put these sorts of plans in place beforehand, but I was definitely not one of them. So I didn't. Instead, I did what felt most natural to me, which was to be in the moment with my mother and wait until she passed away before making any arrangements.

Grief is a deeply personal experience. There's no right or wrong way to experience it, respond to it, move through it, or heal from it. I had a clear track record at this point of carrying the weight of everyone else's expectations and feeling like I wasn't doing things right. Even in the aftermath of her death, I didn't want to let my mom down. Looking back now, I realize that I should've cut myself some slack. I dearly wish someone could've said these things to me then:

> ➤ Try to let go of believing that there's a right way to grieve. Give yourself some grace and room to exist in the way you need to, and be fiercely protective of your right to do so. You've probably spent a long time caring for your loved one. Now's the time to care for yourself without apology.
>
> ➤ Don't assume all family members will respond the same way to the news of your loved one's death. In fact, don't take any ownership of anyone else's response. Turn your attention to yourself, and grieve how you need to grieve. It's not only okay to do this but essential to your well-being. Since grief is a deeply personal journey, it means that everyone is allowed to experience and navigate it in their own way. Let them.

➤ There are excellent manuals and guidebooks on how to navigate settling someone's estate. I didn't get one, nor did I think about trying to find one. But I met another author while writing this book who has created a series worth checking out. The titles and information are listed in the Reader Resources section at the back of this book. If you're at a loss on where to start or how to navigate the process, I highly recommend looking into it.

➤ Because I didn't use a guidebook, I stumbled my way through the process. I simply tried to make a list of every account my parents had that had my mother's name on it. I found phone numbers for each company and just started calling. The process went on for several weeks and often left me feeling paranoid and anxious that something was falling through the cracks. This period of time is hard enough. Don't make it harder on yourself. Use the resources at the back of this book or some sort of guide to help you.

HOW IT'S GOING NOW

I sit in the dark in Dani's truck, waiting for the train to pull into the Lapeer station. I open the Amtrak app on my phone, refreshing the status information on the train arriving from Chicago. It's early for a change. A whistle sounds in the distance. I look up, a smile starting in anticipation. As the gates come down at the crossing near the station, I get out and head to the platform.

"Mom!" Sam calls to me as he climbs down, carefully balancing his bags and beaming.

A smile lights up my face as I hold out my arms to him and reply, "Baby!"

"Mom!" Robin's voice chimes in as I hug Sam hard, closing my eyes to breathe in his scent. I open them, smiling at my youngest child approaching over Sam's shoulder. Sam hugs me harder, not letting me go, and Robin encircles both of us in their long arms, towering over us by about three inches.

"Other baby!" I exclaim, chuckling as Sam starts to laugh and struggle to get out of his sibling's tight embrace. We're all giggling now, Robin playfully holding onto both of us.

"Come on, you two," I say. "Let's go home. It's cold out here!" We split apart and I gaze at my kids adoringly. "Dani and Chloe are waiting for us at home."

"Am I still driving?" Robin asks, looking at me hopefully. They love to drive, especially Dani's big truck. I chuckle again. "Yes, dear," I intone in a mocking drone. I don't have great night vision anymore, so I'm more than happy to have them drive.

We pile in and I sit back quietly, enjoying listening to the kids banter playfully back and forth. I think back to 2020 when Sam left for Chicago and how they could hardly stand to be in the same room. Sam has lived in Chicago with their dad since then and I marvel again at how close the two siblings have become.

The drive takes just 15 minutes to get to our home in Lapeer. As we pull into the driveway, Robin nestles the truck between my small car and their own. We can see Dani and Chloe through the window in the kitchen. I sigh softly, happy to be home and elated to have all three kids with us for at least a few days, yet I mildly brace myself for the effect the close quarters of our smaller house will have on all of us after a day or two.

I still miss our farm with its rambling big house, large common areas, and ample space for us to all spread out. Dani and I still can't bring ourselves to hang pictures of our beautiful farm in our house. Leaving it logically made sense, but we both still carry the emotional wounds of making that decision under difficult circumstances.

Taking a deep breath of cold night air, I climb out of the truck and shake away those thoughts. My little family is all together for the first time since Sam was here for Thanksgiving more than a month ago. *Focus on the presence*, I tell myself, smirking at my own little joke in my head. Having the kids here makes it finally feel like Christmas, though it's nearly New Year's Eve.

The next morning, Dani and I get up earlier than the kids. At 17, 19, and 20, they aren't going to be seen until noon unless we wake them up sooner.

"Shall I start the bacon cooking?" Dani asks with an innocent smile, knowing the smell might attract them. I nod, smiling back.

Soon we're all gathered in the kitchen, catching up, talking over each other, and eating. I participate in the banter while trying to soak in the moment with every fiber of my being. I look around at each of the kids, glowing with pride as I do.

Robin still lives with us. Though they're a senior in high school, they're participating in an early college program, which means they don't go to the high school for classes but to the local community college. After a "13th year" as it's known, they'll graduate with their high school diploma and an associate degree in applied automotive technology. Robin wants to be a mechanic. I marvel to myself at how responsible they've become. They balance taking college classes, being a captain of the color guard in marching band, working 20 hours a week, and maintaining a small but tight group of friends. I feel my chest swell with pride as I watch them respond with quick wit to a jab from Sam. Still introverted but much more vocal and confident than before, Robin is still the one who worries about me. I get hugs from them multiple times a day. I can see so much of my dad in their gentle, patient, and calm nature.

Sam throws a napkin playfully at Robin, and I shift my gaze to my eldest. I miss this kid every day, but I know with certainty that we collectively made the right decision to do what was best for him at the time he moved to Chicago. Tears prick my eyes at the hurt it still causes me, and I take a quiet deep breath to steady myself. Sam is in his second year of community college, working 20–30 hours a week in an early childhood center while also studying to earn his degree in early childhood education. My boy wants to be a kindergarten teacher, following in the footsteps of his grandmother who taught third grade for a few years before staying home to raise us. He's back to being so much more comfortable in his own skin, and he's wise beyond his years and happy-go-lucky. I'm equally proud of him in the way he balances his classes, a job, and a full social life while paying his own way through school.

Sam makes a face at Robin, and I see my mother there, causing me to blink away more tears. He was the first grandchild and the apple of her eye.

"Stop, you two!" Chloe exclaims, laughing as the napkin intended to hit Robin narrowly misses her head.

At 19, Chloe is the child over whose life we've had the least influence. We've strongly suspected for years that she's mildly autistic, and when I look at her I can't help but feel regret, sadness, and those old familiar feelings of not doing enough. She graduated from high school last spring and is enrolled in a program to study marketing and customer service at a career and technical institute for individuals with disabilities in western Michigan. However, her start date has been pushed back a couple of times. We don't get a lot of information from her mom, and Chloe doesn't have the information herself, so I work a lot on practicing living in the moment with her. I can't let myself worry about what comes next for her. All I can focus on is what sort of experience of love and family she has when she's with us. She catches me looking at her and gives me a smile. I smile back, full of mixed emotions about our relationship.

Dani notices that I've been quiet and smiles tentatively at me when I look at her, her expression full of question about whether I'm alright. I nod once, closing my eyes for a long blink at her. She guesses that I'm feeling nostalgic.

After exchanging gifts together, the kids all retreat to various spaces while Dani and I make preparations for my dad and his companion, Sue, to come over for a visit. I would've invited David, Lauren, and their girls to join us, but they'd left on a cruise the day before with Lauren's parents. We'd seen them on Christmas Eve, which Dani and I hosted.

My dad and Sue arrive exactly at the time I gave, making me chuckle. My dad's new habit is to always be early, as if he's making up for more than 50 years of chronically running a few minutes late when my mother was alive. I've grumbled at him a few times over the three years since my mom passed away because his early arrivals have caused me stress. Those feelings of being not enough or not doing anything right show up when he's early, making me feel like I should already be ready.

He looks at me and smiles nervously as he and Sue come inside. I smile back, trying to reassure him that I'll be on my best behavior today. He knows my feelings about Sue are complicated.

Dani greets them warmly, ever the hostess and never wanting anyone to feel anything less than wanted and welcome. I chuckle again, recognizing that this is why she's the favorite of so many of our family members.

"Welcome, welcome," I say, trying to follow her example. Then I yell, "Kids! Papa and Sue are here!" over my shoulder. We hear Robin and Sam racing each other down the stairs from Robin's room as Chloe emerges more quietly from hers. They all come greet my dad and Sue, and we sit down around the dining room table to visit and snack.

After a little while, I get up and ask my dad if we can give him our Christmas gifts. I'm eager for him to open the calendar I've made him. For years, I handmade a scrapbook calendar for my parents. It was an enormous amount of work, but I enjoyed doing it and basking in my mother's high praise and delight every year. Once she passed away, I didn't see the point in going to so much trouble anymore. Since then, I've taken the easy route and ordered calendars online using pictures of us from each year.

As soon as I hand my dad the flat package, his eyes twinkle. "I know what this is," he says softly, delight clear in his voice.

"What is it?" asks Sue, who's sitting next to him with her hand on his arm.

He carefully removes the paper and turns the calendar over. "It's a calendar!" he says with mock surprise and genuine delight in his tone.

"Oh, those are so nice," Sue says, smiling approvingly at me. "I just love it when people make these."

"Ellen makes me one every year," my dad says. "Remember seeing the one she made me last year? You were with me when I opened it. Remember? She put pictures in it of us together." His tone reminds me of the days when he talked to my mom like that, trying to get her to remember something without pointing out that she'd forgotten. I sigh quietly.

My dad starts slowly flipping through the pages, carefully examining the pictures on every page as he goes, chuckling, pointing, and commenting on them. Sue leans on his arm, looking at the pages with him. "These are so nice. I just love it when people make these," she says again with a smile, an exact reproduction of her expression and comments just five minutes ago. I nod, smiling back.

My dad gets to May, which is Robin's birthday month, so the page has several pictures of Robin on it. Never good at hiding that Robin is his favorite grandchild, my dad oohs and ahhs openly. I smile at Sam, shaking my head as he gives Robin a look of mock annoyance.

"These are so nice. I just love it when people make these," says Sue once again.

My smile is tighter this time. "Mm-hmm," I manage.

My dad first met Sue in the summer of 2021 when she moved into the senior living apartments at Daleview where he spent six months after my mom died. He hadn't wanted to stay there beyond those six months because he felt like his level of mobility and energy was significantly higher than everyone else there. "I'll die prematurely if I stay here" had become his common refrain. I helped him buy a mobile home in a nice community in Lapeer, where he's lived since. But always a charmer, he made many friends at Daleview, and Cathy, the director who'd so lovingly told us my mom couldn't live there with LBD, adores him. She makes sure he feels welcome to continue coming to Daleview for activities and visits with his friends.

My dad wasn't interested in Sue or anyone else for a long time. He'd tell Dani and I about the many women who openly hit on him, some even asking him out on dates and making their intentions clear. He'd blush with embarrassment and stammer to us that he just wasn't ready yet while making polite excuses to the ladies.

In the fall of 2022, Sue's persistence paid off and they started dating. I made it clear that I had no problem at all with him finding a new partner and companion. His health had been so compromised from caregiving and grief that for the first 18 months after my mom died we weren't sure whether he'd beat the odds and survive more than a year or two beyond her. When he started dating Sue, that changed. Within a couple of months, his health issues dramatically subsided.

When they first started dating, we invited them to dinner at our house to meet everyone. Over the course of a couple of hours, I noticed Sue repeating herself and returning to the same story several times of how she and my dad had met. Having become certified as a volunteer community educator with the ALZ in 2021 and having given workshops on how to spot the early signs of dementia, I was immediately suspicious. When I shared my suspicions with my dad, he brushed them off at first, but he confessed later that he could see them too. Despite the signs, Sue makes my dad happy. He's enjoying life for the first time again since we lost my mom. I have no intention of trying to take that away from him.

My dad and Sue remain living in their own residences, but they spend most of their time together. They go out dancing with friends at local bars when there's live music, and they laugh a lot together. They come from similar backgrounds and seem very happy.

Once it was clear to me that Sue may have dementia, however, I decided I needed to back away. While I fully respect my dad's autonomy and right to date whomever he chooses, I'm now also respecting my own right to not travel down this road again with someone I've come to know only recently. Dani and I spend limited time with the two of them, and I make it a point to talk to my dad multiple times a week and spend time with him on his own on a regular basis.

This fall, Dani and I celebrated 15 years together. Our relationship has never been stronger. She's the only person with whom I can imagine navigating life. When we decided to sell our farm and move down to Lapeer, we sold off all our animals except for Duke, the first horse we bought together. Our need to find somewhere for him to live opened a door for us to try again at building a relationship with her family. He's been living with Dani's sister and her two horses since May 2021 when we moved to Lapeer.

Dani's career has advanced, and my business is doing well. Our lives are much calmer than they were during those years of caregiving. We remember my mom to one another often, laughing at how she would've reacted to a particular situation. She's with us, but her presence doesn't dominate our lives anymore.

Writing this book has helped me tremendously with processing my grief. I visit my mom's tree periodically, but not as often as I'd like. Life gets in the way too easily. But I don't beat myself up about it anymore. I talk to her often, sometimes out loud while I'm taking a walk with our dog and sometimes through the pages of my journal. Giving myself permission to do that has helped me make peace with our relationship.

I'm learning to live with more self-compassion, and while I certainly make no claim to be perfect (nor would I want to be; how boring!), I feel like for the most part, I'm doing it right.

Someday, we'll have another farm. We'll welcome our kids, our families, our friends, and others to visit. But this time, it will be just ours.

Dani, Sam, Ellen, Robin, and
Chloe in the fall of 2023

Ellen and Ron, December 2023

WHAT NOW?

If you've come this far, I'd like to invite you to join me outside of the book, in real life. There are a number of ways you can do that:

- ➤ One of the top ways people find their next book to read is by looking at book reviews. This book is available on several online platforms, but the one with the biggest readership is Amazon. I'd love for you to leave a review with your thoughts about this book. To find the direct link, please visit the website or scan the QR code below.
- ➤ Many people asked to see photos of our journey, our farm, and some of the moments or scenes I describe in the book. I've created an online photo album that you can access by visiting the website or scanning the QR code below.
- ➤ After this section, there's a page of my recommendations for books, websites, and podcasts you might find useful. Please check them out.
- ➤ Twice a month, I send out a letter to my readers with thoughts, tips, and updates on resources available to support them. If you'd like to receive that letter, please visit the website or scan the QR code below. I never sell anyone's information, and I don't spam anyone. You can unsubscribe at any time.

What else would you find useful to support you on your journey? I'd love to know, genuinely. Connect with me on social media and drop me a private message to let me know if there are other resources you'd find valuable. If I can provide them, I will. If I can connect you to someone else who can provide them, I will.

People who are truly doing it wrong don't read books like this. They don't worry that they're doing it wrong. You're doing it right. And you're not alone.

Website: NotDoingItRight.com

READER RESOURCES

Books

> - *I'll Be Right There: A Guidebook for Adults Caring for their Aging Parents* by Fern Pessin
> - *When Can We Talk? A Caregiver Guidebook for Holding Discussions Around Difficult Topics* by Fern Pessin
> - *The Spectrum of Hope: An Optimistic and New Approach to Alzheimer's Disease and Other Dementias* by Gayatri Devi, MD

Podcasts

> - *The Whole Caregiver* by the Caregiver Revolution: https://podcasts.apple.com/us/podcast/ the-whole-caregiver-podcast/id1716289788
> - *Twenty-Four Seven: A Podcast about Caregiving* by Texas Public Radio: https://www.npr.org/podcasts/1045670834/ twenty-four-seven-a-podcast-about-caregiving

Organizations

- ➢ Alzheimer's Association: https://www.alz.org/
- ➢ Lewy Body Dementia Association: https://www.lbda.org/
- ➢ Eldercare Locator (government agency for information): https://eldercare.acl.gov/Public/About/Aging_Network/AAA.aspx
- ➢ Cariloop: https://cariloop.com/

ACKNOWLEDGMENTS

This is a book I never longed to be in a position to write. Instead, I felt *compelled* to write it. What we lived through as a family took a toll on all of us, with my mom paying the ultimate price.

Two years after her death, I found myself still grieving the loss of my mother in a way that felt very unresolved. Thinking I just needed to take a few days to myself to "get over it," I went away alone to reflect, grieve, and try to find my way forward. What I realized was that I'd simply moved on with life after her death. I went right back to raising kids, running a business, helping my dad manage himself without her, and staying busy with the tasks of life. I didn't take any time to process my own loss nor the very complicated nature of my grief due to the even more complicated nature of our relationship.

Having published another book with PYP in 2022, I was familiar with their six-month writing program "Getting Started for Authors," and I decided to join the next cohort. Still undecided when the program began, I shared my two book ideas with the cohort members. As I described my frustration with not finding many (any, at the time) stories like mine in print, I realized this was the book I needed to write. Once I started, it poured out of me.

But I would not have had the courage to face the emotional toll that writing this book took on me without the support of that cohort. Thank you, Steve Clarke, Dan Kagan, Barb Nangle, and Veena Harbaugh (my accountability partner!) for your encouragement, your feedback, and all the support. A special thank you to Brandi Lai for holding my hand and kicking my ass (lovingly) from start to finish. I simply could not have done it without you.

Thank you, Jenn T. Grace, for your friendship and encouragement and all the reality checks along the way. Thank you, Nancy Graham-Tillman, for being exactly the editor and partner in this process I needed you to be, every single step of the way. You are simply the best, my friend. Thank you to everyone at PYP who works behind the scenes, including Niki Gallagher-Garcia and Alexander Loutsenko. You all help us turn our caterpillars into butterflies.

Thank you to all my early readers, all of whom are former or current caregivers. Without your input, feedback, encouragement, and validation, I would not have had the courage to publish.

Thank you, Dad and David, for your willingness and trust in me to write our story.

Thank you, Dani, for living through hell with me and continuing to walk through life with me, holding my hand. I simply would not have made it without you.

ABOUT THE AUTHOR

Photo credit to
Anavista Photography

Ellen Patnaude is a native of Detroit, Michigan. She grew up in the house she later moved her parents out of in 2017 when they relocated to the farm. She's a graduate of Alma College with a Bachelor of Arts degree in biology and French. She thought she wanted to be Jacques Cousteau, but her first few science-based jobs clearly pointed toward working with people as a better fit, and she's spent the last 25 years doing just that.

Ellen is now a professional certified coach (PCC), helping teams and leaders from companies around the world with communication challenges. She's also the author of *"I Thought You Knew . . .": Confessions of a Chronic Assumer* (2022). She volunteers as a community educator with the Alzheimer's Association of Michigan and is active with several Chambers of Commerce throughout southeastern and mid-Michigan. Ellen now lives with her family in Lapeer, Michigan.

ENDNOTES

1   Alzheimer's Association, "2023 Alzheimer's Disease Facts and Figures," Alzheimer's & Dementia 19, no. 4 (2023), https://doi.org/10.1002/alz.13016; Amanda N. Leggett, Amanda J. Sonnega, and Matthew C. Lohman, "Till Death Do Us Part: Intersecting Health and Spousal Dementia Caregiving on Caregiver Mortality," Journal of Aging and Health 32, no. 7–8: 871–879, https://doi.org/10.1177/0898264319860975; Joseph E. Gaugler et al., "Caregivers Dying before Care Recipients with Dementia," Alzheimers Dement (N.Y.) 4, no. 1 (2018): 688–693, https://alz-journals.onlinelibrary.wiley.com/doi/10.1016/j.trci.2018.08.010.

2   "What Is Dementia?," Alzheimer's Association, accessed January 12, 2024, https://www.alz.org/alzheimers-dementia/what-is-dementia.

3   Joseph Grenny et al., Crucial Conversations: Tools for Talking When Stakes are High, 3rd ed. (New York: McGraw Hill. 2021).

4   "About LBD," Lewy Body Dementia Association, accessed January 12, 2024, https://www.lbda.org/about-lbd/.

5   Paulbros, "My Heart Will Go On - Shittyflute (Original by Celine Dion)," YouTube, January 2, 2019, video, 4:44, https://www.youtube.com/watch?v=5jvOBbP6u2o.

The B Corp Movement

Dear reader,

Thank you for reading this book and joining the Publish Your Purpose community! You are joining a special group of people who aim to make the world a better place.

What's Publish Your Purpose About?

Our mission is to elevate the voices o en excluded from traditional publishing. We intentionally seek out authors and storytellers with diverse backgrounds, life experiences, and unique perspectives to publish books that will make an impact in the world.

Certified

Corporation

Beyond our books, we are focused on tangible, action-based change. As a woman- and LGBTQ+-owned company, we are com- mitted to reducing inequality, lowering levels of poverty, creat- ing a healthier environment, building stronger communities, and creating high-quality jobs with dignity and purpose.

As a Certified B Corporation, we use business as a force for good. We join a com- munity of mission-driven companies building a more equitable, inclusive, and sustainable global economy. B Corporations must meet high standards of trans- parency, social and environmental performance, and accountability as determined by the nonprofit B Lab. The certification process is rigorous and ongoing (with a recertification requirement every three years).

How Do We Do This?

We intentionally partner with socially and economically disadvantaged businesses that meet our sustainability goals. We embrace and encourage our authors and employee's differences in race, age, color, disability, ethnicity, family or marital status, gender identity or expression, language, national origin, physical and men- tal ability, political affiliation, religion, sexual orientation, socio-economic status, veteran status, and other characteristics that make them unique.

Community is at the heart of everything we do—from our writing and publishing programs to contributing to social enterprise nonprofits like reSET (https://www.resetco.org/) and our work in founding B Local Connecticut.

We are endlessly grateful to our authors, readers, and local community for being the driving force behind the equitable and sustainable world we are building together.

To connect with us online, or publish with us,
visit us at www.publishyourpurpose.com.

Elevating Your Voice,

Jenn T. Grace
Founder, Publish Your Purpose

www.ingramcontent.com/pod-product-compliance
Lightning Source LLC
Chambersburg PA
CBHW051131120626
46547CB00012B/753